The Power to Name

NEW AFRICAN HISTORIES

SERIES EDITORS: JEAN ALLMAN AND ALLEN ISAACMAN

Books in this series are published with support from the Ohio University National Resource Center for African Studies.

David William Cohen and E. S. Atieno Odhiambo, *The Risks of Knowledge: Investigations into the Death of the Hon. Minister John Robert Ouko in Kenya, 1990*

Belinda Bozzoli, *Theatres of Struggle and the End of Apartheid*

Gary Kynoch, *We Are Fighting the World: A History of Marashea Gangs in South Africa, 1947–1999*

Stephanie Newell, *The Forger's Tale: The Search for Odeziaku*

Jacob A. Tropp, *Natures of Colonial Change: Environmental Relations in the Making of the Transkei*

Jan Bender Shetler, *Imagining Serengeti: A History of Landscape Memory in Tanzania from Earliest Times to the Present*

Cheikh Anta Babou, *Fighting the Greater Jihad: Amadu Bamba and the Founding of the Muridiyya in Senegal, 1853–1913*

Marc Epprecht, *Heterosexual Africa? The History of an Idea from the Age of Exploration to the Age of AIDS*

Marissa J. Moorman, *Intonations: A Social History of Music and Nation in Luanda, Angola, from 1945 to Recent Times*

Karen E. Flint, *Healing Traditions: African Medicine, Cultural Exchange, and Competition in South Africa, 1820–1948*

Derek R. Peterson and Giacomo Macola, editors, *Recasting the Past: History Writing and Political Work in Modern Africa*

Moses Ochonu, *Colonial Meltdown: Northern Nigeria in the Great Depression*

Emily Burrill, Richard Roberts, and Elizabeth Thornberry, editors, *Domestic Violence and the Law in Colonial and Postcolonial Africa*

Daniel R. Magaziner, *The Law and the Prophets: Black Consciousness in South Africa, 1968–1977*

Emily Lynn Osborn, *Our New Husbands Are Here: Households, Gender, and Politics in a West African State from the Slave Trade to Colonial Rule*

Robert Trent Vinson, *The Americans Are Coming! Dreams of African American Liberation in Segregationist South Africa*

James R. Brennan, *Taifa: Making Nation and Race in Urban Tanzania*

Benjamin N. Lawrance and Richard L. Roberts, editors, *Trafficking in Slavery's Wake: Law and the Experience of Women and Children*

David M. Gordon, *Invisible Agents: Spirits in a Central African History*

Allen Isaacman and Barbara Isaacman, *Dams, Displacement, and the Delusion of Development: Cahora Bassa and Its Legacies in Mozambique, 1965–2007*

Stephanie Newell, *The Power to Name: A History of Anonymity in Colonial West Africa*

The Power to Name

*A History of Anonymity in
Colonial West Africa*

Stephanie Newell

OHIO UNIVERSITY PRESS ATHENS

Ohio University Press, Athens, Ohio 45701
ohioswallow.com
© 2013 by Ohio University Press
All rights reserved

To obtain permission to quote, reprint, or otherwise reproduce or distribute material from Ohio University Press publications, please contact our rights and permissions department at (740) 593-1154 or (740) 593-4536 (fax).

Printed in the United States of America
Ohio University Press books are printed on acid-free paper ∞ ™

23 22 21 20 19 18 17 16 15 14 13   5 4 3 2 1

Library of Congress Cataloging-in-Publication Data
Newell, Stephanie, [date]
 The power to name : a history of anonymity in colonial West Africa / Stephanie Newell.
  pages cm. — (New African histories)
 ISBN 978-0-8214-2032-4 (pb : alk. paper) — ISBN 978-0-8214-4449-8 (electronic)
 1. African newspapers—Africa, West—History—19th century. 2. African newspapers—Africa, West—History—20th century. 3. Anonymous writings—History—19th century. 4. Anonymous writings—History—20th century. 5. Literary forgeries and mystifications. 6. Africa, West—Intellectual life—19th century. 7. Africa, West—Intellectual life—20th century. 8. Books and reading—Africa, West—History—19th century. 9. Books and reading—Africa, West—History—20th century. I. Title. II. Series: New African histories series.
 PN5450.5.W34N49 2013
 079.6609—dc23
                    2013020423

Contents

List of Illustrations		vii
Acknowledgments		ix

Introduction Anonymity, Pseudonymity, and the Question of Agency in Colonial West African Newspapers — 1

PART ONE NEWSPAPERS IN COLONIAL WEST AFRICA

Chapter 1 The "Fourth and Only Estate"
Defining a Public Sphere in Colonial West Africa — 29

Chapter 2 Articulating Empire
Newspaper Networks in Colonial West Africa — 44

PART TWO CASE STUDIES FROM THE COLONIAL OFFICE

Chapter 3 The View from Afar: The Colonial Office, Imperial Government, and Pseudonymous African Journalism — 65

PART THREE CASE STUDIES FROM WEST AFRICAN NEWSPAPERS

Chapter 4 Trickster Tactics and the Question of Authorship in Newspaper Folktales — 101

Chapter 5 Printing Women
The Gendering of Literacy — 122

Chapter 6 Nominal Ladies and "Real" Women Writers
Female Pseudonyms and the Problem of Authorial Identity in the Cases of "Rosa" and "Marjorie Mensah" — 159

Conclusion	"New Visibilities" *African Print Subjects and the Birth of the (Postcolonial) Author*	170
	Appendix I. T. A. *Wallace-Johnson in Court*	183
Notes		193
Bibliography		231
Index		249

Illustrations

1. "Change of Name: 'Torto' for Morgan," from the *Gold Coast Leader*, 10 January 1914 — 18
2. "Change of Name," from the *Sierra Leone Weekly News*, 29 February 1908 — 19
3. "Change of Name," from the *Lagos Standard*, 29 December 1915 — 19
4. "In Memoriam," from the *Gold Coast Leader*, 17 July 1915 — 20
5. "Fabulous Origin of a Chama Family," from the *Gold Coast Leader*, 11 March 1905 — 117
6. "Lady Clifford's Prize Competitions in Aid of the Red Cross, 1918," from the *Gold Coast Leader*, 29 June 1918 — 123
7. "House Keeping on the Gold Coast," from the *Gold Coast Leader*, 16 May 1914 — 125
8. "Up and Doing": illustration by Elise Lindsley-Sims — 165
9. "We Squeeze and Squeeze Our Men": illustration by Elise Lindsley-Sims — 165

Acknowledgments

In the six years it has taken me to research and write this book, I have benefited from the ideas and feedback of numerous scholars. Above all, I am indebted to Karin Barber, David Pratten, and Derek Peterson, not only for sharing their treasure troves of archival discoveries but also for the sheer intellectual force of their engagement with colonial African newspapers. The ideas in the chapters that follow have been inspired by workshops, discussions, seminars, and dinners with these scholars.

Other people who generously shared ideas and work, often ahead of publication, include Jesse Shipley, Kate Skinner, Bianca Murillo, Tunde Awosanmi, and David Kerr. Lively environments for discussion of my ideas about folktales were provided by Chris Warnes and the visiting fellows of 2010 at the African Studies Centre in Cambridge: Eiman el-Nour, Kenneth Simala, James Tsaaior, Tunde Awosanmi, and Oyeniyi Okunoye.

Research for this book would not have been possible without a generous British Academy Research Development Award (BARDA) in 2010–11. Two chapters had previous incarnations as scholarly articles: a short version of the introduction was first published as "Something to Hide? Anonymity and Pseudonyms in the Colonial West African Press," *Journal of Commonwealth Literature* 45, no. 1 (2010): 9–22, and chapter 2, "Articulating Empire: Newspaper Networks in Colonial West Africa," was first published as "Articulating Empire: Newspaper Readerships in Colonial West Africa," *New Formations* 73, no. 2 (2011): 22–38. I am grateful to the publishers for permission to reprint material from these articles.

Above all, I am indebted to Bart Cammaerts for his suggestions, ideas, humor, brilliance, and delicious dinners, and I dedicate this book to him with love.

INTRODUCTION

Anonymity, Pseudonymity, and the Question of Agency in Colonial West African Newspapers

> What cannot one say behind the screen of a *nom-de-plume?*
> —Charles E. Graves[1]

SCHOLARS OF the imperial encounter are generally keen to emphasize the agency of colonized subjects in questions of political resistance, personal testimony, and anticolonial activism.[2] In a study of the techniques employed by Jomo Kenyatta between 1909 and 1952 to fashion his subjectivity, for example, Simon Gikandi asks how colonial subjects participated in the production of their own conflicted identities through the simultaneous endorsement and critical reformulation of colonial modernity.[3] He locates the African subject "at the intersection between colonial governmentality (the semantic and material conditions of colonial politics) and the realm of subjective desires (the colonial subject's cultivation of their selfhood through the mastery of the trappings of colonial modernity)."[4] Gikandi focuses on an East African educated elite whose relationship with colonial authority was contradictory, vexed, and elaborately performed but whose agency he nevertheless describes using terms that indicate intentionality, including *self-making, mastery,* and *sincerity.* Always situated in the wake of empire, African elites were not its passive products, he insists, but "active agents in the making and remaking of their colonial worlds."[5] As with many social and cultural histories of colonial Africa, one gets the impression that the African subjects he describes took themselves very seriously in their vocalizations of identity as they sought a mode of self-expression for their self-made subjectivity in colonial settings.

Across the continent from Gikandi's colonial subjects, in British West Africa the concepts of identity and agency need to be reconsidered in order to understand the ways in which colonial elites articulated their "selves" in print, for if the ability to read and write conferred on Africans an array of new opportunities for social advancement and genres for self-expression, their uses of anonymity and pseudonymity dramatically complicated the selves that were expressed.

Between the 1880s and the 1940s, the region known as British West Africa became a dynamic zone of literary creativity and textual experimentation. African-owned newspapers offered local writers numerous opportunities to contribute material for publication, and editors repeatedly defined the press as a vehicle to host public debates rather than simply as an organ for the communication of news or editorial ideology. Literate locals responded with great zeal, and in increasing numbers as the twentieth century progressed, they sent in letters, articles, fiction, and poetry for publication in English- and African-language newspapers. But if African writers' self-actualizations were part of a public process, occurring in print and intended for the consumption of reading publics, the selves that were articulated were often pseudonymous and playful rather than reliable sources of opinion. For much of the colonial period, English- and African-language West African newspapers were filled with the writings of untraceable authors using invented personae.[6] Contributors carefully concealed their identities behind the "screen" of print.

Robert J. Griffin points out that writers have many different reasons for withholding their names. In eighteenth- and nineteenth-century Europe, these included "an aristocratic or a gendered reticence, religious self-effacement, anxiety over public exposure, fear of prosecution, hope of an unprejudiced reception, and the desire to deceive."[7] With these categories in view, this book seeks to define the shape of a history of anonymity in colonial West Africa and to ask about the ways in which it shadows or diverges from the explanations offered by scholars of pseudonymous writing practices in Europe. This is a paradoxical task if one agrees with John Mullan that anonymity, by definition, "does not exactly have a history."[8] Given the manner in which anonymous and pseudonymous contributors to the West African newspapers drew power from print and playfully engaged with colonial identity, however, this book will argue that anonymity *does* have a history in the region, distinct from its history in European countries, and that the study of anonymity and pseudonymity in African newspapers can reveal a great deal about the cultural histories of colonial societies.

The chapters that follow bring together two fields of study, broadly defined as book history and imperial cultural history, in order to fill some of the gaps in current studies of the history of anonymity, which remain exclusively European in focus.[9] Through a series of African case studies, the book will examine a wide range of anonymous and pseudonymous writing practices in anglophone West African newspapers between the 1880s and the period after World War II, arguing that new forms of subjectivity and new political possibilities emerged in relation to the newspaper in colonial West Africa as a direct consequence or by-product of print. Yet the print subjectivities described in this book were not exclusive to English-language presses, as demonstrated by the Yoruba-language material discussed in chapter 5 and by Karin Barber's groundbreaking work on the Yoruba press in 1920s Lagos.[10]

In Europe, the study of authorial masking frequently involves a biographical turn, or the discovery and disclosure of authors' "real" identities and secret intentions. Carmela Ciuraru's recent book, *Nom de Plume: A (Secret) History of Pseudonyms*, is entirely motivated by the quest to uncover the (secret) identities of masked writers.[11] Similarly, Mullan's *Anonymity: A Secret History of English Literature* is preoccupied with the identities and motivations of self-concealing authors, particularly when their gender-crossing writings hid "women being men" and "men being women."[12] Methodologically, therefore, Ciuraru's and Mullan's histories of anonymity paradoxically morph into their opposite: with indexes packed with "proper" names, they yield a plethora of historically situated, intentional bodies, albeit bodies full of mischief and mockery.

Surprisingly, given their deployment of sociological categories of identity to understand pseudonymity, race is ignored in both Ciuraru's and Mullan's studies. Ciuraru writes an entire chapter on Isak Dinesen without mentioning Africans or colonial rule,[13] and the sole reference to the history of race in Mullan's book is a passing comment on Aphra Behn's refusal to write pseudonymously in the slave narrative *Oroonoko*. Mullan argues that Behn contravened seventeenth-century feminine modesty conventions by using her real name to make herself "public property."[14] He does not, however, discuss Behn's own use of multiple pseudonyms in her writing;[15] nor does he address the politics of naming and renaming in slave history, famously exposed by Malcolm X in his Afrocentric "Who are you?" speech, which demands: "What was your name? . . . And why don't you now know what your name was then? Where did it go? Where did you lose it? Who took it? And how did he take it? What tongue did you speak? How did the man take your tongue? Where is your history? How did the man wipe out your history?"[16]

Malcolm X's vehement exposure of the racially violent politics of naming and his particular mode of resistance to imperialist interpellation help to explain why the study of pseudonymity and anonymity in African, Caribbean, and African American print cultures should be regarded as more historically complex and politically charged than in the European literary histories presented by Mullan, Griffin, Ciuraru, and others. In the diverse cultures of the black Atlantic, as Malcolm X makes clear, many given names carry the violence of a brand. To write under one's given name is thus to sign into a particularly conflicted strand of black history.[17]

This immersion of personal identity in the dynamics of violent cross-cultural encounters was palpable in colonial West African societies in the late nineteenth and early twentieth centuries, particularly among the Creoles of Sierra Leone and the Saro of Nigeria, where slave crossings and displacements could be mapped onto the recent past of most families. The transcripts of the Reverend R. A. Coker's testimony at a court case brought in 1911 by his daughter, Adel, against the "ordinance" marriage of Sarah E. Olaore Green to Dr. Oguntola O. Sapara—to whom both women were already allegedly married by custom[18]—exemplify the slave geographies behind many anglicized West African names:

> My father's name is John Coker born in Egbaland he was carried off as a slave and rescued to Sierra Leone. He died at Abeokuta.... My mother's name is Sarah, an Egba woman was carried off to the same place and returned with him. They were married at Sierra Leone. I was born at Abeokuta at the beginning of 1844, I never went to Sierra Leone with my parents.... [My wife] came from the West Indies, was born in Jamaica, of West African parents, who went from Sierra Leone to the West Indies and her parents returned with her to Sierra Leone and then she came to Lagos.[19]

Coker's self-identification in court illustrates the striking proximity and pervasiveness of slave histories but also the migratory networks through which ex-slaves moved.

In the colonial societies that supplanted West African slavery, African bodies such as Coker's were subjected to a further layer of inscription through government processes of naming and legal identification, ranging from baptism to school rolls and census records. Indeed, the colonial court's demand for Coker's family history at the start of the testimony as well as the transcription and preservation of his words in the official records exemplify the British colonial preoccupation with the minutiae of naming, a preoccupation that was devastatingly exposed by one prominent anticolonial activist, I. T. A. Wallace-Johnson, whose tricksterlike behavior is discussed in part 2 of this book.

As a consequence of these distinctively West African historical currents, although *The Power to Name* will tread a forked path similar to that followed by Ciuraru and Mullan, moving between the activity of biographizing and respect for pseudonymity, several major differences will emerge. The book seeks, first, to complicate the biographical methods that are frequently used by Western scholars in the study of pseudonymous literary material and, second, to debate the ways in which African pseudonymity and anonymity relate to or challenge existing theorizations of African agency in the British Empire. In this, the book offers a cultural history of newspaper production and consumption that experiments with reading beyond or reading outside the anticolonial nationalist perspective that generally prevails over historical studies of the press in the colonial and immediate postcolonial periods.[20]

The reason for this choice of orientation is that both anonymity (the voluntary condition of nonbeing) and pseudonymity (the voluntary condition of being other) call into question many of our assumptions about agency, subjectivity, biography, naming, authorship, and (post)colonial identity in the British Empire. Several chapters of the book will demonstrate that a striking feature of West African pseudonyms in the colonial period is the manner in which they allowed writers to experiment with voices, genders, genres, and opinions; to vocalize across identities; and to play *against* biographical methods and desires.

Newspapers provide a substantial and unique resource for research into reader reception, cultural production, and political agency in Africa. Far more than an archive to be mined for information, the newspapers studied in this book are productive literary forms with the power to generate (and to be modified by) particular types of discourse.[21] They form a vital part of the continent's literary heritage, and they represent a literary field in which readers participated in debates about moral, cultural, economic, aesthetic, historical, and political issues. When West African literatures emerged in their own right after the 1940s, in the form of pamphlets and short novels, the influence of newspapers could clearly be seen in the "fluent, everyday" quality of language, as well as in "the social realism of the fiction" by local authors.[22] The newspaper thus deserves detailed scholarly attention for the way in which it contributed to the emergence of African reading cultures.

Roger Chartier argues that readers read differently in different social, material, and historical contexts and that debates about print cultures demand contextualization.[23] Given the late appearance of African-owned newspapers in French West Africa, where the first locally managed newspapers were not established until the 1940s and 1950s,[24] and given the stark differences in French and British colonial policies toward education, citizenship, and language, French colonial West Africa is not included in this study.[25] Newspapers in French and German colonies merit a study in their own right for their complex positioning in relation to the power structures of the colonial state. In the wake of missionary publishing activity in the early twentieth century, for instance, many local Cameroonian newspapers were published in African languages in the 1930s, lasting at least until the anticolonial French-language press rose to prominence after World War II; meanwhile, in Togo a distinctive "Ewe print sphere" emerged from early twentieth-century mission stations in direct opposition to German colonialism.[26] By contrast, the African-owned newspapers at the heart of this study started to be published several decades earlier, in the 1880s, largely in English, and they remained dominated by the colonial language until the 1940s and 1950s.

A methodology for addressing the broad postcolonial relevance of localized histories of reading is therefore required, one that avoids meaningless generalizations about "the reader's" relationship to colonial history. Empirical inquiries into situated texts and readerships can help scholars to comprehend the variety of relationships between readers and printed texts in different global locations. Through such situated histories of reading and literary production, we can start to build comparisons between print cultures in different regions of the world and to understand the historical contexts that inform contemporary understandings of literacy.

Full of bias and hope, the West African writers and readers at the center of this study were articulate and playful, often relishing the invisibility and ambiguous subjectivity conferred on them by print. Slippery, pseudonymous, and ventriloquistic, their articulations reveal the necessity for scholars to think beyond homogeneous or binary categories for textual consumption and colonial identity. Local readers were and remain pivotal to the generation of "public" cultures in West Africa, and though literacy meant different things to different social groups in colonial West Africa, it also created a meaningful, shared reference point for readers as print subjects. In focusing upon newspapers as vehicles for specifically print-mediated forms of subjectivity, this study tries to avoid treating texts simply as mirrors of the intentions of individual authors, pseudonymous or otherwise. Instead, writers' printed "identities" are regarded as rhetorical positions mediated by local ideologies, beliefs, and power structures but different in fundamental ways from other types of "publicness." Ultimately, this book seeks a method for conducting African cultural history that is capable of including—and respecting the integrity of—the pen lives of pseudonymous writers without reimposing the very social and ethnic categories with which these writers dispensed.

The blanket application of identity markers can introduce misunderstandings and reductive generalizations, but the near impossibility of avoiding categories such as race, gender, and class in scholarly investigations of colonial print cultures illuminates an important feature of colonial societies that cannot be ignored. In the most concrete sense, identities *mattered* in colonial settings: people's access to resources was mediated by factors such as race and gender. The social and political systems produced by British colonial rule therefore necessitate an inquiry into names, agency, and intentionality in colonial contexts. In other words, the interpretation of a text *should* be markedly different if we visualize the author as a white colonial administrator rather than an African clerk or as a female ex-prostitute rather than a Lagosian male editor with a passion for Yoruba newsprint (see chapter 5).

Pseudonyms took many different forms in the African-owned newspapers. Some correspondents buried themselves beneath generic names such as "A Youngman," "Tired," "Overworked," "Bashful," "A Man about Town," "A Banker," "A Reader," or the ironically misnamed "Proud of Name." Some chose comic or exotic names such as "Bored," "Dick Carnis," or "The Man in the Moon" or aestheticized names such as "Parasite de Sycophant." These pseudonyms were a form of "being away," and they were often vehicles for burlesque or parody, making possible ventriloquism and experimentation with English literary forms.

Other writers chose politically charged generic names such as "Jim Crow," "A Negro," and "Old Black Joe," through which they declared essential(ist) identities. Common pseudonyms such as these reveal the ways in which correspondents selected identities that revealed their cultural or racial affiliations and political interests, as well as a powerful sense of their place in the world. Between April and October 1916, for example, Jim Crow wrote a regular open letter, published in the *Gold Coast Nation*, addressed to various individuals in West African journalism and public life. His name alone commented on and parodied racist labels for people of African descent, and his open letters were polemical and often ardently Afrocentric, criticizing any African who appeared to support "these children of the 'barren north' who are thrusting on us ideas, customs, manners and what not, which are absolutely inappropriate to us in so far as we are a nation having our own history, social ethics, language, customs and usages, religion and feasts."[27]

Used in an imperial setting, Jim Crow articulated British imperial rule through the framework of North American segregationism: the name thus functioned to comment negatively on the racial identities imposed on Africans by colonial regimes in Africa. The name also served to assert the writer's sense of being part of a pan-African network of articulations of African identity, albeit in the form of negative caricatures, adopted in order to comment on the colonial regime. Amusingly, in October 1916 Jim Crow announced a formal change of pseudonym in his final open letter, signed "Jim Crow (to be hereafter known as Rambler)."[28] True to the new name, toward the end of 1919 "Rambler" produced a series of travel articles describing rambles around the Gold Coast countryside in an epic, rambling tone: "Pale, but hale, up he [the traveler] rises with the day's first beam, Aurora bright-enthroned shedding forth his rays."[29] In this, he illustrated a disinvestment in a singular name or identity, and in common with naming practices in numerous other African societies, he demonstrated how "Africans were and are not the passive recipients of names imposed on them by a dominant system or by any other person."[30]

The space occupied by all of these pseudonymous writers can be regarded as an "elsewhere," commenting on the present or the past and often containing political wishes for the future. This is not to suggest a postmodern lack of authorial intentionality or a lack of political resistance. Rather, as several chapters will show in detail, writers' practices of self-naming and renaming can be regarded in large part as strategies to thwart imperialist modes of labeling and containing Africans.

As demonstrated by the example of Rambler, the pseudonyms chosen by correspondents often related to and emphasized the content of contributions. Thus, "A Gold Coast Native" wrote an article entitled "Are We Ashamed of Being Africans?";[31] Rambler wrote on "Life in the Lake District";[32] and the regular column "Home Chat" was composed by "The Man in the Street."[33] Rather than preceding the text, these names often supplemented the content of articles and letters. Through their choice of pseudonyms, contributors therefore tacitly asserted that the message was more important than the messenger and that print could easily hide a person's identity.[34] To this extent, they helped to endorse and sustain the mediated print subjectivities that will be discussed in the pages that follow.

Some pseudonyms were nicknames as well as literary masks: everybody knew, for instance, that the writer named "Zik" was the anticolonial nationalist and newspaper entrepreneur Nnamdi Azikiwe (1904–96), although Zik's lawyer, Frans Dove, exploited the difference to great effect during the prosecution of his client for sedition in the late 1930s (see chapter 3). Less famous internationally, the regular Igbo contributor "Odeziaku"[35]—also "O. Dazi Aku"—was in fact the British palm-oil trader John Moray Stuart Young (1881–1939), who lived in Onitsha and wrote poems and articles for numerous African-owned newspapers between the 1910s and his death in 1939.[36] Similarly, H. B. Herman-Hodge of Nigeria, known locally as "Langa Langa" during his period of service in northern Nigeria, affectionately adopted his African nickname for the authorship of his memoirs, *Up against It in Nigeria* (1922).[37] Both Odeziaku and Langa Langa exemplify what Osumaka Likaka describes as the European appropriation of African nicknames to proudly display their acceptance by local communities, even though such names were often ambiguous, conveying "a subtle counter-hegemonic discourse" and implicit political protests against colonialism, of which their recipients were unaware.[38]

In the West African press, other pseudonymous authors barely concealed their identities, as in letters and articles signed by "J. A. G. of Saltpond," "K. A. S.," or "J. C." Chapter 4 examines the political parables produced by some of these semihidden authors through the medium of the publicly shared discourse of folktales, and chapter 6 analyzes the gender perspective of J. C. in the *Sierra Leone Weekly News*. Such initialized contributions were ways to float writers' "proper" names close to the surface of texts. As with nicknames, these forms of anonymity were not always or necessarily designed to hide a writer's identity. Given the limited size of the literate community in West Africa until the 1930s,[39] together with the fact that African-owned newspapers recruited the majority of their readers from the towns in which printing presses were located, the person behind a pseudonym or abbreviation may well have been known to the reading public. Initials and ordinary names were not necessarily signs of a correspondent's "real" identity, but unlike obvious pseudonyms such as Tired or Overworked, they gave the impression of a writer's authenticity and physical presence behind the text, especially when, as so often occurred, a place-name appeared alongside the abbreviation. If correspondents were known in the world, however, they were protected by their cloak of newsprint.

Only rarely did editors threaten to name and shame pseudonymous correspondents. When faced with "spies and informants" in Cape Coast who had published "fibs" about his staff, the editor of the *Gold Coast Leader* published this irate response: "They seem to think we do not know them—we know them and after getting all the information we want, we shall publish their names to the public, and ask them to shun them as they would a venomous snake."[40] Although the editor of the *Leader* was keen to disclose these antagonists' names, he vigorously protected his own contributors' identities at all times and promised to guarantee their anonymity. Proof of identity was required with all correspondence to the *Leader* "as a guarantee of good faith,"[41] but staff were willing to risk imprisonment rather than disclose the names of allegedly libelous contributors. Thus, the editor twice found himself in court between June 1902 and April 1903, accused—and excused—both times of printing libelous material by anonymous contributors.[42]

Except for the court cases involving the notorious political agitators Wallace-Johnson and Azikiwe, discussed in chapter 3, these principles of nondisclosure were generally also respected by officials at the Colonial Office (CO) in London. "I don't suppose a West African editor . . . is obedient to the best Fleet Street standards," wrote one legal expert at the Colonial Office, Sir Sydney S. Abrahams, in a memo to another, Sir Kenneth Poyser, when the governor of Nigeria attempted to tighten press censorship laws in January 1942: "But at the least he has the sense to know that if he throws his contributors or informants to the wolves he is likely to lose not only these people but his readers into the bargain. . . . Contributors or newsgetters would naturally object to sending in matter which the Governor has the power to deem objectionable."[43]

The case studies presented in part 2 elaborate upon the ideological problems and contradictions generated by London's adherence to such liberal notions of the freedom of the press in Britain's West African colonies, for in tension with London, colonial governors sometimes attempted to flush out and penalize anonymous and pseudonymous contributors of material they deemed to be "seditious" or offensive. In 1942, for example, when the governor of Nigeria, Sir Bernard Bourdillon, attempted to introduce legislation aimed at compelling local editors to disclose the names of pseudonymous and anonymous sources of allegedly seditious articles, officials in London were dismissive of his plans. As the case studies indicate, their resistance reveals ideological disparities between Whitehall and the colonies and between British traditions of press liberalism and the censorious practices of colonial regimes toward African readerships. "Sir Bernard wishes to discover the identity of persons who contribute to the local press matter of a mischievous nature," wrote Sir S. S. Abrahams in a disapproving Colonial Office memo, adding, however, "I understand that it is a fixed canon of editorial etiquette not to disclose the name of an anonymous or pseudonymous contributor or the source of any information used in the paper."[44]

Staff at the Colonial Office frequently had to smooth over—literally, to paper over with memos and diplomatic letters—the tensions that arose within the colonies and between Britain and the colonies when individual governors attempted to introduce legislation to control the press without adequate consultation and guidance from the center or when governors appeared to discriminate more against particular editors than others.[45] Thus, Governor Bourdillon's amendments to existing censorship legislation and his efforts to discover the identities of pseudonymous informers caused Colonial Office staff to undertake a damage-limitation exercise in an effort to maintain liberal ideals of British imperialism, particularly the principle of freedom of expression. Moreover, they did so even as they recognized the politically destabilizing impact of anticolonial African editors such as Azikiwe and the need "not to do anything to hamper the Governor in maintaining good order."[46]

These tensions were compounded by the fact that British officials in the colonies often believed that "native" readers required more stringent press laws and greater general censorship than people in the supposedly mature civilizations of Europe. "A greater measure of control is now necessary," the Gold Coast governor insisted in 1934, during the crisis covered in the first case study in part 2, "in view of the irresponsible and misleading matter which is continually appearing in the local papers and which is readily believed by the half-educated classes."[47] The governor's inspector general of police agreed wholeheartedly, adding, "There is not a single editor of repute or sense of responsibility on any one of the local newspapers."[48] In taking these positions, colonial officials on the ground demonstrated greater conservatism than officials in London, who believed that, "save in exceptional cases, the less banning of literature there is, the better."[49] Indeed, for all their familiarity with established principles of press freedom, critical speech, and the formation of public opinion in Britain, large numbers of Europeans on the ground—including magistrates, educators, and police chiefs—perceived the so-called native newspapers to be alarmingly outspoken in British West Africa, wholly unsuitable for dissemination among uneducated and "semieducated" people.

London's attitude of tolerant liberalism toward West African newspapers stemmed in part from a perception of the region's lack of global strategic relevance until the early 1930s. The metropolitan perspective was also a consequence of the lack of widespread, globally coordinated anticolonial agitation in the region. This situation changed in the "stormy 1930s" and 1940s, as the third case study in part 2 will suggest, when Colonial Office support for the idea that newspapers were vehicles for public opinion started to be tempered by the realization that educated Africans—emergent political leaders—were making use of their literacy to read and write and to transmit to illiterate others "undesirable" anticolonial and communist material. Furthermore, the onset of the Cold War challenged and changed Colonial Office attitudes toward newspapers in the colonies, and official concerns that Cold War politics had arrived in West African colonies led to a new, two-pronged approach whereby imported publications were rigorously censored, on the one hand, and local editors were subjected to proimperial public relations materials, on the other hand.

West African reading cultures depended upon the creation and maintenance of print-oriented subjects, as well as upon the availability of machinery, materials, and techniques for mass production. African newspaper publics did not simply exist "out there" in society or emerge out of oral local cultures, primed for the appearance of printed texts. Readerships had to be renewed, continuously convened and reconvened around particular local presses.[50] Yet print was a source of discomfort as well as empowerment for many local readers. Between the 1880s and the 1940s, the African-owned newspapers offered local readers numerous opportunities to contribute to printed debates, but print represented a highly visible and apparently permanent record of an individual's opinions and (dis)loyalties, as well as a vital channel for the expression of political and social demands. A court case brought against the *Gold Coast Leader* by Rev. Jacob Benjamin Anaman of the Wesleyan Church illustrates the importance of anonymity to the editors and proprietors of newspapers in the colonies. In his quest to discover the identity of "Abu," a correspondent who had openly criticized him on the letters page in September 1902, Rev. Anaman sent a local barrister to the offices of the *Leader*. The colonial court heard how the editor, Samuel Harrison, "politely thanked" the barrister, saying that "he would under no circumstances whatever, give him the name of his correspondent, rather than that, he was prepared to undergo anything."[51] Reflecting on the case after their victory in court, the proprietor—Fynn Egyir-Asaam—and Harrison reiterated the cardinal principle of their newspaper: "To give up the name of a correspondent was a thing we would never *dream* of doing as we considered such a thing a flagrant breach of 'editorial etiquette.' . . . Here let us remark to our correspondents and intended correspondents, that it is our earnest wish that the Public should have implicit confidence in us."[52]

As this court case demonstrates, the reasons for a contributor's decision to use pseudonyms were sometimes spiteful and libelous, rather than political or ethical. This illustrates a malicious use of anonymity with a long and controversial history. Anonymous journalism was regarded by the philosopher Arthur Schopenhauer in the 1850s as a form of "rascality" that "must be completely stopped" and by Daniel J. Solove, in his recent study of gossip, rumor, and privacy on the Internet, as enabling people to be "much nastier and more uncivil in their speech," less responsible in their comments, and more defamatory and invasive of the privacy of others.[53] Closer to home, G. K. Tsekpo, owner and editor of the 1950s Ewe-language newspaper *Mia Denyigba* (Our Homeland) in British Togoland, had such a distaste for pseudonymity that he described it as the vehicle for "falsehoods and bad conscience."[54] As Tsekpo was aware, when immersed in print and cut free from physical surveillance some people would exploit their invisibility to launch vitriolic attacks on local personalities or on other correspondents.

Pseudonymous letter writers frequently criticized one another in an intensely personal way on grounds of poor literary style, revealing in the process that newspapers were often regarded by readers and correspondents as a type of *literature* rather than as a form of ephemera. From the earliest days of West African press activity, the literary value of a journal was as significant as its content to readers. Throughout the colonial period, one finds correspondents using self-consciously "literary" turns of phrase, ranging from a comment by "S. H." in 1885 that "idle phantasms and dreaming sentimentalisms of local objectionists are ridiculous. Some only look strabismus and consequently must be periphrastic"[55] through to A. H. Filson's high-blown descriptions of his efforts to produce writing with literary value during World War I: "In fact, I feel diffident because cognizant as I am of the nature of the argument veritably bearing the inscription of 'To the most Intelligent' like the mythical 'Apple of Discord' it is my expressed wish that patience should be exercised."[56]

Readers did not hesitate to patrol the boundaries of English grammar and style in order to determine who had the right to see his or her text in print. A writer's mode of articulation was a clear sign to other readers of his or her social status and authority.[57] As "K. A." warned "Robertus" after the latter's article on English literature was published in the *Gold Coast Nation*: "It is not meet for Mr 'Robertus' to employ illogical and ungrammatical terms in his advice and to support same with a host of irrelevant quotations from Hymn Books, etc, thus to expose us to the bitter ridicule of other colonies."[58] Thus, pseudonymous writers abused other pseudonymous writers, reveling in the criticism of their chimerical enemies and, at the same time, asserting their entitlement to participate in the colonial public sphere (see chapter 1).

While articulating the opinions and desires of literate elites, these scathing letters also recall older, established oral traditions of protest and abuse in Africa in which socially inferior individuals or groups used song, dance, poetry, and other genres to convey their complaints against figures of power in society while carefully avoiding customary slander and defamation laws. In their influential study entitled *Power and the Praise Poem: Southern African Voices in History* (1991), Leroy Vail and Landeg White point out that "the various forms of oral poetry in sub-Saharan Africa are licensed by a freedom of expression which violates normal conventions": through a variety of socially recognized poetic genres, "chiefs and headmen may be criticized by their followers, husbands by their wives, fathers by their sons, employers or overseers by their workers, officials or politicians by their underlings, and even Life Presidents by their subjects, in ways that the prevailing social and political codes would not normally permit."[59] To some extent, the letters pages of colonial newspapers can be regarded in a similar manner, furnishing a genre in which disgruntled, pseudonymous "nobodies" in colonial society could find opportunities to air grievances, express rage, and make demands without naming, shaming, or physically exposing themselves. Editors carefully patrolled these spaces, however, rejecting any material that appeared to go too far.

One way in which editors separated authorial attribution from the contents of texts was through the composition of fiction, and several chapters of this book examine narrative prose by pseudonymous African writers. Focusing upon two editors from Nigeria, Isaac B. Thomas of the Yoruba-language *Akede Eko* (1929–53) and James Vivian Clinton of the English-language *Nigerian Eastern Mail* (1935–51), chapter 5 shows how their writing activities were not confined to political commentaries and editorials: these men also wrote fiction for publication in local and international journals. The reasons why Thomas and Clinton chose to ventriloquize as women in their choice of pseudonyms and first-person narrators is examined in the chapter, which addresses the relationship between print, gender cross-vocalizations, and the cultural dynamics of gender relations in different parts of colonial Nigeria.

If newsprint served an anonymizing function for West African journalists and creative writers in the colonial period, helping to mask the markers of social identity, in no sense was it gender neutral. The final two chapters of this book are dominated by the discussion of gender and pseudonymity. The participants in the publishing activities and print cultures described in this book were generally male members of Christian, professional elites and educated minorities, primarily located in colonial towns and cities.[60] Except for a tiny minority of elite-born and well-married individuals, West African women did not participate in newspaper production and consumption until the 1940s and 1950s.[61] Faced with the problem of identifying the gender of long-lost pseudonymous authors and in an effort to avoid speculative attributions of gender based upon the extent to which textual content manifests empathy or lack of empathy with women, chapter 6 asks about the ways in which the few *known* women journalists in the colonial period positioned their material in relation to the plethora of male-authored stories and articles containing familiar female character types and marriage scenarios.[62]

The pervasive use of pseudonyms in the colonial press considerably complicates any effort to "restore" the work and life-stories of early women writers, and these chapters highlight the difficulties of extrapolating—or presuming to know—an author's gender simply by interpreting the contents of published articles. Nevertheless, questions of authorship are all the more pressing given the "masculine" gender bias of a great deal of pseudonymous material and given the manner in which, in the cases examined in chapters 5 and 6, feminine masks were donned in order to perform moral judgments about marriage roles that were oriented against women.

Although a pseudonym hid a writer's identity from influential figures in the community and, of course, from the colonial state, the preceding examples demonstrate that not all pseudonyms were adopted for overtly political or anticolonial ends. Unsigned and pseudonymous articles were not always brimming with politically incendiary opinions in the colonies. Many writers were playfully mischievous, experimental, or didactic in their work. For instance, one writer for the *Gold Coast Nation* chose the name "Won Hu Nos" for a lengthy series of moralistic articles on West African education and the workplace. Described by the editor as "provoking us to jealousy, to wrath, to love and to good works," Won Hu Nos chose a name that was a transformation of the pseudonym "One Who Knows," also used by someone—perhaps the same individual—who contributed to the *Gold Coast Nation* in previous months.[63]

Given the predominance of pseudonymous writing in the colonial West African press, the reasons why some authors *did* wish to be publicly named should not be ignored. Did the content of named items differ in some way from that of anonymous and pseudonymous items? Were named items associated with religious or improving material, as with such pieces in Elizabethan and Jacobean England?[64] As will become clear in the case studies on the rise to celebrity of Wallace-Johnson and Azikiwe, one cannot ignore instances of named authorship in relation to unnamed material. This is especially significant given that the appearance of "proper names" on newspaper articles carried legal consequences in colonial courts, where legislation existed to prosecute named individuals for printed libel, defamation, and sedition and where official inquiries required the identification of named individuals as responsible for particular texts. The second case study in chapter 3 shows how Wallace-Johnson mocked and perverted British colonial systems of attribution, continuously slipping away from his inquisitors' efforts to identify him using English legal processes, while simultaneously generating celebrity status around his very name. Wallace-Johnson made a mockery of the colonial judicial system with his exasperating pedantry and refusal of sincerity. He outwitted his legal interrogators at every turn and used techniques inspired by oral naming conventions to undermine the process of "proper" naming upon which the British court depended.

In attempting to understand the social and political role of African newspapers in the colonial period, however, it is necessary to avoid the temptation to produce too rigid or oppositional a periodization of the press. In locating the emergence of new naming practices in the postwar period, for example, we risk erasing vital currents and continuities from earlier decades. The identification of an era of pseudonymity over and against a new era of self-naming and celebrity in the nationalist 1930s and 1940s produces a distorted, overly teleological model of African press history, not least because the notion of celebrity has a long history in Africa and because newspaper editors and journalists such as Azikiwe and Wallace-Johnson did not suddenly emerge as political celebrities in the 1930s.[65]

Nonetheless, there is a reason why Fred Omu's classic study of Nigerian newspaper history stops in 1937, with the arrival of Zik's *African Morning Post* in Nigeria, and why *The Power to Name* also ends in the 1940s. Through their achievement, first, of celebrity status among their supporters and, second, of notoriety and persona non grata status among their opponents, Azikiwe and Wallace-Johnson facilitated a rebirth of the African journalist as a named entity. In this, the two men mark a turning point in the politics of naming in West African newspapers. Unlike their pseudonymous predecessors who played with the anonymity of print, both men enabled authorial intention to be reconnected with public attribution: in other words, even when they used nicknames and pseudonyms, they generally *wanted* readers to attribute the content of their columns to a physically present, politically active person who circulated around the colonial public sphere producing a new, assertive political agency among local populations.

As indicated already with reference to slave names, for several historical and social reasons in the colonial period names were considerably more meaningful and mobile than names as traditionally conceived in Europe. In the opening two decades of the twentieth century, numerous people Africanized their "Christian" names, partly in response to the international rise of pan-Africanism alongside local cultural nationalisms that opposed the mimicry of English cultural forms and partly in opposition to the intensification of racism and the rise of "new imperialism" in Britain. As a consequence, in the 1890s and 1900s the African press carried increasing numbers of advertisements containing public announcements of name changes by deed poll. Names that carried particular social histories from the nineteenth century, including slave names, were transformed into new—or rather, precolonial and "traditional"—African names: thus, the surname "Solomon" became "Attoh-Ahuma,"[66] and "Macaulay" became "Ajasa."[67] "Adam L. Jacobs" of Lagos became "Adeoye Desalu,"[68] "Thomas William Waters" of Anamaboe (Anomabo) became "Kwamina (Waters) Ayensu,"[69] and "Isaac Augustus Johnson" of Freetown became "Algerine Kelfallah Sankoh."[70]

Particularly in Lagos, the period between 1906 and 1922 produced a bumper crop of name changes.[71] Throughout West Africa, all of the name changers were men, and sometimes entire families underwent the process: in 1914, for example, eight men in the Morgan family of the Gold Coast collectively changed their surname to Torto, and those brothers with European middle names also formalized their African names (see fig. 1).

CHANGE OF NAME.

"TORTO" FOR MORGAN.

We the undersigned beg to inform the public that from and after the 1st of January, 1914, we shall discontinue the use of the surname "Morgan," and substitute therefore the name "Torto," and our full names, individually, will in future be as given below.

Any documents, letters or papers bearing the name "Morgan" previous to this notification must nevertheless be regarded as valid.

W. Tchisampa Torto	instead of	W. S. Morgan
J. G. Tetteh O'Bak'ar Torto	"	J. Godfrey Morgan
S, Laryea Torto	"	S. Laryea Morgan
Frank Aja Torto	"	Frank Aja Morgan
S. B. Torto	"	S. B. Morgan
Frederick Obodai Torto	"	Fred. Morgan
J. E. Mensah Torto	"	J. E. Mensah Morgan
Ishmael Quarshie Torto	"	Ishmael Quarshie Morgan

Accra, Gold Coast.
December 29th 1913.

FIG. 1. "Change of Name: 'Torto' for Morgan," from the *Gold Coast Leader*, 10 January 1914, 2

Yet as figures 2 and 3 reveal, some of these name changes were more ambiguous, mediated, and ambivalent than implied by notions of nationalist assertions of Africanity. Not all name changes represented deliberate Africanizations of identity, especially in Sierra Leone: thus, in 1906 Maximillian Eugene Hamelberg of Oxford Street, Freetown, advertised a change of surname to Dawson,[72] and Moses Athanasius Taylor of Fourah Bay Road, Freetown, "absolutely renounced relinquished and abandoned" his middle name, without tampering with his first and last names (see figs. 2 and 3).

The newspaper was an essential vehicle for the communication of these new and self-conscious identities. Apparently ordinary family names such as Jacobs and Johnson and the ways in which African names were spelled were exposed as loaded with social and political implications, containing commentaries on a history of violent European

FEBRUARY 29, 1908.

Change of Name

I AMADO TAYLOR heretofore called and known by the name of MOSES ATHANASIUS TAYLOR of 65 Fourah Bay Road Freetown in the Colony of Sierra Leone hereby give Public Notice that on the 12th day of February 1908 I formally and absolutely renounced relinquished and abandoned the use of my name Athanasius and then assumed and adopted and determined thenceforth on all occasions whatsoever to use and subscribe the name of AMADO instead of the said name of Athanasius.

AND I give further notice that by a Deed Poll dated the 12th day of February 1908 duly executed and attested and registered in the Office of the Registrar-General of the Colony aforesaid I formally renounced and abandoned the said name of Athanasius and declared that I had assumed and adopted and intended thenceforth upon all occasions whatsoever to use and subscribe the name of AMADO instead of Athanasius and so as to be at all times thereafter called known and described by the name of MOSES AMADO TAYLOR exclusively.

Dated the 13th day of February 1908.

MOSES AMADO TAYLOR,
late MOSES ATHANASIUS TAYLOR

FIG. 2. *(left)* "Change of Name," from the *Sierra Leone Weekly News*, 29 February 1908, 10

FIG. 3. *(below)* "Change of Name," from the *Lagos Standard*, 29 December 1915, 7

CHANGE OF NAME.

It having been brought to my notice that people experience difficulty to understand the reasons actuating me for changing my name I beg to explain as follows:— My late father was a great and successful fisherman and was therefore called "Whehuto" which was a nickname and subsequently reduced to Fisher but that not being his real name I bethought myself to discard it and assume Godonu (Babatunde) Midegbepo (Weniwon). As however my people are not quite satisfied by my dropping the name Fisher I should from henceforth be addressed as follows.

Godonu Midegbepo Fisher
lately known as
S. G. Midegbepo.

Anonymity, Pseudonymity, and the Question of Agency ≈ 19

contact, but also lively local political contexts and debates about Africanity and Englishness.

One printed genre in which authors are always named—not discussed in detail in this book—is the memorial poem, a genre that flourished in the early twentieth century. Lay writers used the medium of print to memorialize loved ones and insert them into history. The authors and subjects of memorial poems were often named many times over, and the poems themselves frequently took the form of acrostics, giving thickness and textual form to the names of the deceased (see fig. 4).

From the 1880s onward, the writing of death became increasingly commercialized. In December 1885, *Sawyerr's Bookselling, Printing and Stationery Trade Circular* advertised "The Penny Packet of Mourning Stationery," containing three sheets of black-bordered notepaper and three matching envelopes.[73] Biographical writing also prospered after the 1880s, particularly the genre of newspaper obituaries of "great men of affairs" in which (dead) subjects were fleshed out in print by

---

IN MEMORIAM.

In loving memory of the two brothers who died respectively on the 16th June 1914, and on the 10th July 1914.

C hildren's father Charlie is gathered to his fathers.
H ow beneficent and benevolent was he!
A las the day! since Job's news unexpectedly
R eached his brother Joe, Joe never smiled again.
L ast time that they bade Good-bye to each other, only
E arth forboded that they would meet again only in her bosom.
S uddenly and silently did he shuffle off the mortal coil.

A t my house that he last visited and conversed with me,
N o man could make me believe that it was valedictory.
D eath, to be the last enemy that shall destroy, is God's truth,

J uly, O hone! brought Job's news to the House-of-mourning.
P oor brother Joe was summoned to follow his brother Charlie.

B arrister well-experienced, popular, and munificent was he.
R emember, O earth, how he held his advocacy to excellence!
O h! who could fathom the weird that they respectively dread,
W hen shall I behold their loving faces once more?
N ot on earth but in heaven at last I know.

P atiently am I biding my time to meet them there where they are biding tryst.

O , may the Creator and Redeemer accept the souls of the two
B rothers, and let them have an eternal joy, and
E verlasting bliss, and peace, to sound His praises; and, in the
E nd, let me meet them Home, when I cross over Jordan!
                                SAMUEL ASAAM QUAGRAINIE.

Appam, July 1915.

FIG. 4. "In Memoriam," from the *Gold Coast Leader*, 17 July 1915, 2

named authors; the genre of newspaper profiles of African heroes also flourished at this time.[74]

People's regional and political identities in the colonial period were characterized by great elasticity. An individual might identify as part of a local ethnoregional nation such as the Fante or the Yoruba, *and/or* as part of the British West African nation stretching from Nigeria up to the Gambia, *and/or* as part of the global pan-African nation reaching from West Africa to the Caribbean, London, and North America, *and/or* as an imperial citizen, loyal to the British Crown. Consequently, the central idea behind studies of anonymity and pseudonymity in Europe—that a person possesses a singular "true" and discoverable name over which a mask is placed—is anachronistic when applied to colonial West Africa, where names were compound and mobile.[75] Over the course of an individual's life, he or she would accrue a variety of names and titles depending upon and reflecting social status, gender, generation, religious beliefs, achievements, and standing in the eyes of the community.[76] Replete with content and commentary, West African names, including Christian names and the names given to people at their funerals, thus spoke volumes about individuals' social position. Viewed from this context, the pseudonyms to be found in the colonial newspapers can be regarded both as part of a public commentary and as part of an established West African tradition where nomenclature reflected a person's public standing. As Likaka comments of naming in colonial Congo, "Renaming and name changes were in reality continuous practices throughout the life of a person. They occurred often and appeared vital because they altered the personality and restored harmony in the body and psyche of the name-bearer."[77]

Though this book focuses on newspapers rather than on anonymity and pseudonymity per se in colonial West Africa, the types of oral naming practices identified by Likaka and others—including abusive names, nicknames, praise names, evasive names, and slander and defamation in customary law—cannot be excluded from the field of study. As indicated earlier and as argued in several chapters, an understanding of customary contexts for naming is vital to an appreciation of the ways in which printed names were deployed in West African newspapers. Indeed, to do justice to the local cultural contexts for pseudonymous practices, two other interconnected dimensions of orality need to be considered prior to a discussion of printed materials. The first is the relationship between oral genres and naming, including those oral genres that license the performer to make a political or social critique and to ventriloquize across gender and rank, mentioned briefly in the preceding pages and discussed in part 3. The second is the mobilization of oral genres within the press.

Large numbers of anonymous folktales found their way into print, often reworked for political and moral ends. Throughout the 1910s and 1920s, newspapers such as the *Gold Coast Nation* published folktales in which a political moral was extracted from a familiar parable, and realist narrative techniques were used to draw lessons from nonrealist tales. Chapter 4 analyzes the dynamic status of these anonymously authored folktales, together with their power to absorb contemporary moods, opinions, and representations. Newspaper folktales and folklore in the colonial period were characterized by a plurality of uses, styles, influences, and orientations. Even the most familiar Ghanaian Ananse Spider story would often be narrated *through* "untraditional" or "imported" texts such as *Pilgrim's Progress*, Aesop's fables, Shakespeare's plays, and biblical parables.

Not all folk stories were anonymously authored. Chapter 4 also considers an array of fully attributed tales in terms of how they might or might not differ from the unnamed material. The chapter asks whether named tales were politically less critical than anonymous stories, as one might expect if one adheres to the Eurocentric model of anonymity-as-masking. Examining a range of tales from Ghanaian newspapers in the early twentieth century, the chapter attempts to explain the surprising discovery that the most politically critical tales were in fact written under so-called proper names or barely concealed abbreviations.

Besides folktales, an additional but rather different and more abstract type of anonymity can be found in the colonial West African press, relating not to the disguise of individual writers but to the ontological status of print. Again and again, editors insisted that the medium of print allowed the text to be disconnected from the writing body. They made every effort to de-personalize writing, to de-scribe it in order to press ahead and, in the words of "Atoo" (also known as "Attoo" and "Atu") in the *Gold Coast Leader*, "call a spade a spade—whether it be a *Governor spade or a Subject spade*."[78] In the process, another form of anonymity emerged in the press, one that is inextricable from the history of print in the colonies.

One way in which editors attempted to remove themselves from the printed page as named individuals with biased personal opinions was through their regular commentaries on the role of the press as a mouthpiece for Africans in the absence of an electoral system and democratic representation in government. Chapter 2 details the near-obsessional preoccupation of editors with describing the role and function of newspapers. On each occasion, editors maintained that their newspapers represented the public, at a far remove from individual personalities, including their own. In an "Open Letter to His Excellency Sir Matthew Nathan," the editor of the *Gold Coast Leader* carefully negotiated this impersonality: "In humbly cooperating with your Excellency in the administration of this Government we shall be called upon as the mouth-piece of the people over whom your Excellency is appointed to rule, to criticize where criticism offers itself."[79]

Atoo, who wrote a regular column for the *Gold Coast Leader* for many years, exemplified the principle that personal feeling should be separated from journalistic reportage: "The duty very often falls on us loyal sons of the country to set aside all feelings" in the reporting of actions that "[are] offensive and dangerous to the safety and welfare of the public."[80] This was not "to engage in personalities" but to protect the public's "rights, liberties and lives."[81] Atoo's argument on this occasion set the *Leader* on a collision course with its archrival, the *Gold Coast Nation*, but both journals operated according to a similar ideology in which the opposite of the public sphere was not so much the private sphere as the sphere of personalities. Thus, the editor of the *Gold Coast Nation*, Attoh-Ahuma, was vehement in his assertion that his journal was innocent of "rioting in personalities."[82] Indeed, on one occasion Attoh-Ahuma defended the very dullness of his paper on the grounds that its lack of interest to readers and "circumspect" approach to politics should be interpreted as evidence of its integrity as the "official organ" of the Aborigines Rights Protection Society (ARPS), over and against the *Leader*'s scandalous, gossipy style.[83] In support of this position, he published a letter from the general superintendent of the Wesleyan Methodist Mission, W. R. Griffin, praising the "high tone" of the *Nation*.[84]

One result of the editors' repetition of the principle that their newspapers expressed opinions cut loose from personal identity, or personality, was the magnification of the status of the printed word. Anonymous and divorced from the pen-holding hand, the printed page seemed to take on an activist subjectivity of its own in the minds of correspondents. Print was regarded as discursive yet also as impartial and public. As

"K. S." wrote in an article on "Journalism on the Gold Coast" in 1903, "Consider such memorable works as the *Bible*, *Pilgrim's Progress* and many others that have served to help more men to heaven than what their authors could do by human agency."[85] The printed page conferred anonymity and independence on correspondents, removing human agency and thereby turning individual writers into members of a public that could exercise its "right to take notice of anything that affects it, whether morally, socially or otherwise. It has a right to complain of or praise the actions, or conduct, of any person or a community of persons when such action or conduct is beneficial or otherwise to it."[86]

An illuminating early example of this emphasis on the independent textual agency of print can be found in *Sawyerr's Bookselling, Printing and Stationery Trade Circular; and General Advertising Medium*, a newspaper published in Freetown, Sierra Leone, in the mid-1880s by the trader and bookseller T. J. Sawyerr. In spite of the fact that its title carried the name of its proprietor,[87] *Sawyerr's* was one of the earliest West African journals to define its journalistic content as separate from individual authorship or personality. In a front-page editorial in February 1886, Sawyerr insisted that "public interests" were served by the journal together with the interests of "the clientele of the business it advertises."[88] "The individualism wherewith our title is interwoven is *limited to the advertising phase of the 'Circular' and operates no further in its influence*," he insisted, adding that in contrast to the "advertising phase" of the journal,

> the "Circular" dances to no special piper. . . . Whilst discountenancing whatever is scurrilous or defamatory, we allow no spurious delicacy or fear of man to influence our exposing whatever we believe to be detrimental to the public interest or our bringing to notice whatever we believe might tend to the general well-being of the community. We can neither cringe nor fawn: we neither court the approbation nor fear the frowns of any, and the travailing of carping critics we regard with the utmost indifference. . . . Though seemingly only a Trade circular in an insignificant settlement, we shall never look on lamely while oppression and villainy are rampant.[89]

Sawyerr's ideas about "the community" and "public interest" were bound up with the withdrawal of his "self" from the printed page.

Disavowing individual bias and a personal agenda, he seemed to believe that self-interested commercial discourse could be separated from neutral journalistic discourse, even though both discourses flowed from the same person's pen. In spite of West African newspapers' masculine orientation and elite bias, Sawyerr's insistence on the independent, social character of print—his invocation of a public sphere, in other words—was echoed many times over in the West African press between the 1880s and the 1940s. Correspondents and columnists were regarded as equal to one another in the public anonymity of print, and West African newspaper correspondents were often subjects whose identities were constituted through print, rather than prior to print.

A description and discussion of a *colonial* public sphere is therefore necessary in order to understand the assertive, self-idealizing presence of the region's fourth estate, at least until the media transformations and political upheavals of the period after World War II. Newspaper editors—often also political agitators—continuously and sometimes disingenuously reiterated liberal newspaper principles about the public sphere, insisting that they used the press to "discuss public affairs fully and freely."[90] With this in view, the next chapter debates the contradictions and (im)possibilities involved in attempting to refract colonial West African newspaper history through the lens of Jürgen Habermas's notion of the public sphere, for if a government is not answerable to or elected by a country's citizens and if political institutions ignore the presence of civil society in their ordinances and statutes, it is necessary to question the extent to which newspaper readers in colonial settings can gain access, through the press, to any kind of conventional, anonymous, or ideal public sphere.

PART I

Newspapers in Colonial West Africa

1 ⤳ The "Fourth and Only Estate"
Defining a Public Sphere in Colonial West Africa

IN HIS work on the evolution of the public sphere, Jürgen Habermas identifies a brief utopian moment in European history. In the early eighteenth century, he writes, a bourgeois space emerged that "mediate[d] between society and state, in which the public organize[d] itself as the bearer of public opinion."[1] Comprising coffeehouses, salons, and social clubs and including printed materials such as novels, periodicals, and pamphlets, this "public sphere" is defined by Habermas as a nonhierarchical environment in which consensus was built through processes of free, critical, rational dialogue between bourgeois citizens as they emerged from feudal hierarchies in early modern Europe.[2] By the early nineteenth century, however, this liberal public sphere had waned, a victim of increasing state interventionism and the intrusion of private corporations into the dynamic space between state and society.[3]

Whether or not this idealistic assessment accurately reflects the beginnings of modern bourgeois cultures in Europe and whether or not an emergent class can ever be status free in the manner described in the foregoing précis, one exception to the rule of bourgeois reason stands out immediately. Nothing could be further from Habermas's notion of democratic public dialogue than European imperial expansion. If the eighteenth century spawned the idea that individuals of reason could produce civil society and the common good, it also spawned reactionary, evolutionist myths of non-European irrationality and tribal subhumanity epitomized by "aboriginals" and Africans.

Unlike Habermas's exemplary citizens who were "stripped of status ... the strength of their rational arguments being more important than their position in society or personal wealth,"[4] Africans for much of the colonial period were widely regarded by their rulers as incapable of reason or civility, requiring intervention and tutelage from men of modernity and enlightenment.[5] Interestingly, however, as this chapter will suggest, nothing could be closer to West African newspapermen's definitions of the role of the press between the 1880s and World War II than Habermas's utopian model of the public sphere. Unlike other types of local publication, such as ethnic histories, missionary periodicals, and town histories, which were often anything but egalitarian, newsprint made possible the imagination of a new type of public, conceived as anonymous, detached from personal and familial affiliations, and capable of expressing public opinion for the first time in the new public space constituted by African-owned newspapers.[6]

AFRICAN-OWNED NEWSPAPERS AND WEST AFRICA'S PUBLIC SPHERE

In April 1905, the proprietors of the *Gold Coast Leader* were prosecuted for publishing a defamatory article by a correspondent using the common pseudonym "Veritas," in which police superintendent Isaac Emmanuel Quist of Kumasi was accused of the double rape of a pregnant woman. Quist was well known to the *Leader*. Only the previous year, his marriage to Regina Azu was announced in the columns, and in July 1904, the editor had wished him a "speedy recovery" from illness.[7] But by October 1904, allegations of Quist's professional misconduct had started to surface on a regular basis in columns by contributors such as Veritas, "Scrutineer," and the popular Attoo, to the extent that he became known in the press as the "lawless lord" and the "god of Kumasi."[8] On an almost weekly basis, pseudonymous staff on the *Leader* started to allude to rumors of Quist's use of terror tactics and violence, taking no care to avoid the publication of libelous and defamatory material. In particular, Quist's European bosses were said to have taken no action to control their officer's all-too-public misdemeanors. Here was an African colonial official who, to the pseudonymous Attoo at least, was "worse than a lunatic with a firebrand in his hand."[9] The Quist case was a time bomb waiting to explode, testing recent colonial newspaper regulations designed to deter editors and proprietors from sheltering behind others' pseudonyms when charges of defamation or sedition arose.

In the wake of their victory against the Crown, the managers of the *Leader* published an editorial entitled "Our Fourth and Only Estate," in which they triumphantly inscribed the trial into posterity as "The Great Criminal Libel Case" of 1905.[10] Rather than reinforcing their faith in the freedom of the West African press, however, or in the fairness of the colonial judicial system toward pseudonymously authored disclosures, the victory in the libel case highlighted another matter: the peculiarly distorted and unreasonable relationship that arises in colonial settings between governments and the "native" press.

Although Quist was arrested after the hearing and subsequently found guilty of the rapes, staff on the *Leader* felt that the hand of luck, rather than the hand of justice, had brought about the positive result.[11] During the trial, some British commentators had raised the possibility of strengthening press censorship laws in the Gold Coast to prevent potentially defamatory material from appearing in newspapers in the first place.[12] In a similar spirit of suppression, two colonial magistrates in the case, Dr. Tweedy and Major Davidson-Bouston, obstructed evidence of Quist's misdemeanors by dismissing complainants without taking statements from them.[13] Even the presiding judge in the case, Mr. Justice Smith, allegedly made "rude remarks" about the *Gold Coast Leader* in summing up the evidence in court.[14]

For staff on the *Leader* at the conclusion of the trial, these various negative official reactions to the role of African newspapers carried at least as much weight as the fact that the supposedly libelous story was found to be accurate by the judge. In other words, the newspapermen experienced the trial as an instance of the frustration or prevention of the emergence of a genuine public sphere in Britain's colonial territories.

Two types of public men were at loggerheads in the trial: first, government officials or colonial civil servants such as Quist and his managers, who were exposed for having abused their authority under the protection of the state; and second, journalists as citizens, who were setters of public opinion in the space between state and society. The locking of horns between these two groups typified West African press relations throughout the colonial period, creating political effects that are discussed in several chapters of this book. In reflecting on the case in "Our Fourth and Only Estate," the editor of the *Leader* pointed out that in England, Australia, New Zealand, and Canada, there "[are] parliaments and other assemblies wherein the people give effective voice to their wants and have the means of securing them."[15] In colonies such as the Gold Coast, by contrast, "the people . . . have only one Estate, and that is the Press."[16] In a pointed quotation from the liberal republican philosophy of the European Enlightenment, the editor continued on to note that "the reign of might over right [dominates]" people's lives in Britain's West African colonies and that except for the press, "we have not the instrument that cries halt! to tyranny, oppression and wrong."[17] If there was no social contract and if indigenous political representation was absent from or partial and compromised in the other three estates, this editorial demanded that readers ask about the function of the fourth estate in colonial settings. What happened to the notion of the fourth estate and to the wider concept of the public sphere if the other three estates actively discriminated against those who take ownership of the fourth?

This notion that the press was West Africa's only estate was not unique either to the *Gold Coast Leader* or to English-language newspapers in the region. Although this view appears to ignore other types of public space such as clubs, unions, customary forums, and associations, West African editors and proprietors insisted again and again that the citizens of the colonies only had access to one sphere for self-expression: the newspapers. In contexts where governments did not represent their citizens through a consensual social contract, Africans had "no other means of defending our rights," as Gold Coaster James A. Busum wrote in the covering letter to his petition against the Criminal Code (Amendment) Ordinance of 1934, an act that proposed severe penalties for the reproduction and possession of seditious publications in colonial Ghana.[18] "The Press," Busum continued, "a harmless organ, is the only means through which our cries are sometimes heard, and if our only and last armour for harmlessly voicing our grievances to the public [is curtailed], it is felt that a great injustice is being meted out to a very helpless people."[19]

These sentiments from the mid-1930s reverberate with late nineteenth-century and early twentieth-century African views of the press as holding power to account in a public sphere distinct from the state. As the Nigerian politician Hon. C. A. Sapara Williams stated in his opposition to the Ordinance for Regulating the Printing and Publishing of Newspapers, or Newspaper Ordinance (no. 10), passed in Lagos in 1903, the press was "the only medium for the people to express their grievances."[20] The press, West African editors and readers concurred, was the sole force through which British political authority could be monitored and colonial power held to account, in the absence of internal governmental checks and balances: it was, as Busum insisted in a contradictory metaphor, a "harmless weapon" for Africans "in defence of our rights."[21] In the words of the editor of the *Sierra Leone Weekly News* thirty years earlier, "No Governor can get Native opinion from his Council (where the Native Members are, as a rule, from a wealthy class) as fully as from the local Press."[22] Newspapers, he added, "seek to improve the measures submitted to Legislative Councils."[23]

The role of newspapers in bringing news stories to light was therefore seen to be coterminous with the struggle for political representation. Print was the crucial medium for this process, making possible new ways of imagining the public. African intellectuals repeatedly asserted their belief in the liberties and social equalities made possible by newsprint. Half a century ahead of Habermas's utopian conceptualization of emergent bourgeois cultures in Europe, West African newspapermen seemed to adopt his model almost verbatim in their descriptions of the role of the press as a vehicle for status-blind debates. Editors repeatedly insisted on the position of their presses as what newspaper historians John Hartley and Alan McKee term "the *locus* of the public sphere," as "primary and central institutions of politics and idea-formation," with correspondents serving the pursuit of "freedom" and "democratic politics" in the manner or European and North American journalists.[24] "Our columns are open to all, irrespective of creed, colour, or race," declared the first editorial of the *Western Echo* of Cape Coast, Ghana, in 1885, setting the tone for numerous future newspaper initiatives: "Do not fear to speak through us; we will not fear to make generally known your wants."[25]

Adhering to classic liberal definitions of the freedom and impartiality of the press, popular since Thomas Jefferson described American republican ideals in the late eighteenth century, West African newspapermen demanded their right to occupy the *same* type of public sphere as that inhabited by European and American journalists. This was rather different from the mode of authority asserted in the other types of printed literature circulating in colonial West Africa between the 1880s and 1940s, such as missionary publications, official reports, pamphlets, and local histories, in which named authors made use of print to assert authority and expertise on a range of issues.[26]

Life in Britain's colonial possessions was anything but egalitarian and consensual, but from Sierra Leone to Nigeria and Ghana and from African-language to European-language newspapers, editors articulated a strikingly familiar model of rational press citizenship alongside ideals for democratic public participation, regardless of race, gender, or social status: "Our motto is 'TRUTH WITHOUT FEAR,'" read the "Prospectus" column in the first issue of the *Western Echo*: "We shall endeavor to preserve through each series a firm and free tone. . . . A newspaper is a worthless institution if it is afraid to speak out."[27] Decades later, an editorial in the *Gold Coast Leader* on the "high calling" of journalism declared, "The object of a newspaper writer should . . . be that of a fair-minded impartial judge of facts and affairs, and to set forth his considered views upon them without malice and without fear or favour."[28]

The African-owned newspapers thereby explicitly attempted to produce an egalitarian public sphere and to generate a form of civil society on paper that was activated through participation and debate and, crucially, through print. African-language newsprint culture was no different from English-language print culture in this respect: as Karin Barber demonstrates in her study of Yoruba print culture in the early twentieth century, Yoruba newspapers in 1920s Lagos played an essential role in the project to convene a progressive citizenry, equal in status on the printed page.[29] Similarly, with reference to Yoruba and English pamphlets published by Lagosian elites between the 1880s and 1920s, Nara Improta comments: "Debates transcended barriers of language and genre (and also media, place, social class etc). Many debates crossed over the two languages with no interruption in the line of reasoning. The pool of intellectual production, even with some differences that have to be pointed out relating to language and audience, was the same pool" (personal communication).

Anonymity and pseudonymity were vital to the imagination of an egalitarian public sphere. Under pseudonyms, members of educated elites, school-leavers, clerks, men, women, and youths could participate in the formation of public opinion. With a print bias typical of editors and examined in more detail in the next chapter, readers were informed that *only* through print could they engage in free dialogue between equals. From the 1880s onward, editors protected their contributors from exposure to surveillance or assimilation by the state: "Do not for a single moment doubt us when we say that no one need fear that his name will be given up as the writer or any letter or article," they reassured correspondents.[30] "In a country like ours, where one is not at liberty to say what he pleases in the Press," wrote the pseudonymous "Druboh" in the *Gold Coast Leader,* people naturally make use of "many *nom-de-plumes* or initials," and therefore, any efforts at "fishing out [the real identity of] correspondents to the Press is one of the worst things one should ever attempt to do."³¹

The cloaking of contributors' real names behind pseudonyms can be interpreted as an egalitarian gesture to erase the signs of self that would have revealed their social status and to challenge official codifications of identity in what Neeladri Bhattacharya describes as the "public classification and categorization of individuals" that occurred under colonial regimes.³² West African editors and columnists—all men, with few exceptions (see chapters 5 and 6)—used the press to hide existing hierarchies and to yearn for freedom of expression and political representation. Throughout British West Africa from the 1880s on, newspapers presented themselves to the public as consensus-building, deliberative spaces for the emergence of rational debate between citizens without self-interest. Shaping public opinion, stimulating debate, questioning the legitimacy of colonial authority, airing grievances, and exposing "evils," the African-owned newspapers emphatically endorsed post-Enlightenment notions of the social contract; yet they did so in colonial settings marked by local gender, generational, and economic hierarchies.

At this point, a crucial distinction must be made between the notion of the bourgeois public sphere as formulated by Habermas and that of the colonial public sphere within the British Empire. For Habermas, citizens' liberties were protected by the framework of democratic nation-states. For West African newspapermen, by contrast, in the absence of representative national governments the press was one of the few vehicles to convey citizens' complaints to legislative councils and the metropolis, providing the means for local people to communicate with the rest of the world. Their printed articulations were imbued with a sense of the world. As Barber writes of Isaac Babalola Thomas, editor of the Yoruba language newspaper *Akede Eko,* "Thomas loved the idea of print's ability to reach a vast, unknown, indefinitely extensive public: 'the four corners of the world,' as he frequently puts it."³³ In corners of the world where locals were excluded from national self-government and where they struggled to progress through institutional hierarchies, one of the few remaining modes for public self-articulation was the press.

IMPERIAL NETWORKS AND THE COLONIAL PUBLIC SPHERE

The account thus far is thoroughly biased toward print. The circulation of newspapers was largely limited to educated elites in the colonial period. Elite African spokesmen for the press often failed to acknowledge the fact that, in addition to newspapers, many other potential public spheres could be identified in West Africa, including town and village associations, singing bands, church prayer groups, funeral cooperatives, masquerades, military groups, and a multiplicity of other social organizations that created spaces separate from the family and the state. Many of these predated colonialism and newspapers in Africa by many decades, and they were independent of chieftaincy structures.[34] By Habermas's stringent definitional criteria for the public sphere, however, the majority of these associational activities would be regarded as socially divisive rather than publicly unifying, serving the interests of their members rather than the common interests of the "nation."

With similar problems in view, historians of empire have generally avoided the temptation simply to apply Habermas's model to colonial contexts, for as Bhattacharya points out—as did Habermas himself[35]—the concept of the public sphere is historically situated in Europe, applicable to the emergence of the bourgeoisie and nation-states in the eighteenth century rather than to public discourses in precolonial and colonial societies.[36] But given editors' strikingly "Habermasian" insistence on the role of newspapers in colonial West Africa as vehicles for the public will, it is necessary to develop an inclusive understanding of the colonial public sphere, one that acknowledges newspapers' articulations in the context of imperial power.

Scholars have developed a variety of subtle models to understand the networks of cultural and political exchanges that emerged in the imperial world and to appreciate the shifting publics generated by colonial encounters. For Alan Lester, in his study of the white settler press and the movements of British citizens in and between the Cape, New South Wales, and New Zealand, "a trans-global British settler identity" was forged along the networks opened up by the imperial transport infrastructure in the mid-nineteenth century.[37] Ideas of Britishness were negotiated and sustained through these imperial circuits, Lester argues, especially via the printed artifacts—letters, diaries, telegrams, and memoirs, as well as newspapers—that circulated around Britain's far-flung colonial possessions.[38]

British imperial networks and concepts of Britishness are also at the center of Mrinalini Sinha's discussion of the colonial public sphere in India. Influenced by the Subaltern Studies Group, Sinha explicitly addresses the topic of the public sphere in the British Empire, concentrating on European social clubs in India, with their class biases and policies of whites-only membership.[39] "The colonial public sphere needs to be distinguished from both the classical bourgeois public sphere studied by Jurgen Habermas in the metropolitan European context and the emergent colonial Indian 'publics' studied more recently by scholars of South Asia," she writes, insisting upon the maintenance of a clear distinction between "colonial" and "Indian" public spheres as separate spaces within imperial social formations.[40] With this remit in view, Sinha does not discuss Habermas's concept of the bourgeois public sphere and its applicability to British India. Instead, her focus is upon the production of visible differences in the colonial public sphere, differences relating to race and whiteness, to gender and Englishness, to concepts of social inclusion and categories of social ineligibility or subalternity.

Sinha's detailed social history of "the club as a central institution of the colonial public sphere" is designed to develop the study of Eurocentrism in colonial settings.[41] She shows how European social clubs helped to produce racialized identities and to reinforce class and gender politics: these contributed to a "colonial" public sphere where the term *colonial* stands clearly for European male bourgeois power.[42] For Sinha, as for Lester, that word is therefore used to refer to European discourses and spaces, to the assertion and effects of racial whiteness as an ideology and organizing principle. For both scholars, therefore, *colonial* describes a network of allegiances, movements, and self-definitions in European-controlled spaces. Such a network, for Sinha at least, operates in contrast to the "Indian public sphere."

To use the term *colonial* as a synonym for *European* artificially excludes the diversity of encounters made possible by colonial rule, however, and segregates indigenous public spaces from the colonial public sphere in a manner that assumes few overlaps between stratified populations in colonial societies.[43] As with Lester's work on imperial administrators, Sinha's racialized opposition of *colonial* versus *Indian* neglects the plurality of encounters *between* colonizer and colonized, the numerous crossings and articulations of people, commodities, texts, and ideas to and from colonial spaces throughout the imperial world. Such crossings and encounters occurred both alongside and as a consequence of the rigid, exclusionary structures of colonialism. To understand the literary and debating clubs that proliferated in colonial Ghana in the 1920s and 1930s, for instance, one needs to position their activities both beside and beyond the British presence in the region, to see them as an effect of colonialism but not as its direct product.[44]

In addition to the problems that arise with simply applying Habermas to colonial settings, many critics have pointed out that Habermas's notion of the public sphere does not do justice to the complexities of—and the inequalities within—public cultures as they emerged in bourgeois democracies in the West.[45] In particular, Habermas's belief in the emancipatory potential of rational consensus neglects historically entrenched inequalities between men and women and between different social classes and groups. His notion of the public sphere also disallows the productive potential of supposedly "irrational" or antagonistic beliefs, passions, and opinions, labeling them inadmissible.[46] Additionally, as Hartley and McKee write in their study of newspapers and the public sphere and as indicated at the start of this chapter, the Enlightenment project of modernity was itself flawed, for the European Age of Reason was "dogged by grotesque shadows—gothic, fascist, bureaucratic; comfort was unevenly distributed; universal brotherhood was ditched on the grounds of sexism and racism."[47]

Newspaper correspondents in colonial West Africa faced these shadows on a daily basis, and yet a self-justifying language of rationalist citizenship permeates their journalistic discourse. A cynical interpretation of the idealized public sphere they articulated between the 1880s and the 1930s might suggest that the educated elites, intellectuals, and businessmen who set up printing presses in the colonies were deliberately masking their class and gender interests in the language of ethical universalism, rationalism, and freedom of expression, interests that are manifest in other types of publication.[48] Similarly, in their obvious bias toward print as the vehicle for reasoned debate, they largely ignored the power of customary authorities in West Africa, a zone of exclusion that also denied Britain's growing political investment in local chieftaincy structures under the system of Indirect Rule.[49]

Furthermore, their explicit and repeated endorsement of a bourgeois, rationalist project shows them to be caught within a Eurocentric epistemology that was underpinned, in the colonial world, by stereotypes of Africans as irrational, superstitious, and premodern.[50] Presented as universalizing, their notion of the public sphere thus concealed the "social moorings" of its promoters and failed to recognize the legitimacy of other publics.[51]

Yet for numerous West African newspaper editors, the articles they published on political and social topics and their appeals for readers to engage in correspondence and debate served to harness the printing press to a new, participatory style of politics, implicitly in opposition to a bureaucratized, hierarchical, and paternalistic British colonial power. The very blind spots identified by critics of Habermas—his neglect of existing power structures and historical inequalities—formed the criteria for West African journalists' utopian vision of newsprint as an expressive medium that erased identity in otherwise undemocratic public spaces. The fact that all of the newspapers discussed previously strategically ignored women and the intensely stratified character of colonial West African societies does not dilute the editors' investment in ideas of the public value of newsprint. Operating within imperial circuits of information and opinion, without the scaffolding of the nation-state, their efforts reveal the complexities and complicities of a distinctly *colonial* public sphere, the definition of which must be expanded to acknowledge surveillance operations by colonial officials but should always, in addition, remain inclusive of the colonized populations.

THE PUBLIC SPHERE IN THE "STORMY 1930S" AND AFTER

The historian Dwayne Woods argues that in the period leading up to independence, "what transformed African urban centers briefly into a constituted public sphere was the role that African intellectuals had in providing a normative framework for associational politics."[52] Over and against competitive or inward-looking associations such as credit unions and town guilds, Woods suggests that African intellectuals played a key role in "mobilizing and shaping public opinion" in the 1940s and 1950s, drawing upon the spirit that motivated grassroots organizations and groups in previous decades and channeling it into a new nationalist consciousness that exemplified the Habermasian ideal.[53] Just as Habermas identified a process of refeudalization by the forces of state interventionism and private interests in the early nineteenth century, however, Woods sees the nascent, democratic public sphere produced by literate and aspirational African intellectuals in the late colonial period as a short-lived phenomenon: for him, its demise occurred in the period immediately after independence, with the appearance of authoritarian postcolonial regimes whose attitudes to the continent's publics and public spheres were anything but liberal.[54]

If we accept Woods's broad definition of the "constituted public sphere" as a Habermasian space in which public opinion could be mobilized and shaped outside state control, then African-owned newspapers from the 1880s onward can be regarded as essential to the transformation of associational politics into a collective consciousness. Owned and edited by African intellectuals, mediating between competing social activities, defining public interest over and against gossip or "personalities," and hailing diverse constituencies of reader, West African newspapers offered a clear expression of civil society, and they helped to demarcate an as-yet-unavailable public sphere for free, critical dialogue between literate citizens. They moved easily between estates, offering pulpit-style sermons and printing transcripts of court cases and judgments, making space for the interpretation of legal proceedings and colonial ordinances as well as the articulation of a Christian morality.

There is a great deal of value in Woods's historical framework—particularly with reference to the rise of nationalist movements spearheaded by African intellectuals in the postwar period—but he does not discuss the cultural and political roles of African intellectuals prior to the 1940s. Furthermore, he does not address their many newspapers and publications or the ways in which colonial rule militated against the emergence of a genuine public sphere in the British Empire. With such matters in view, one might question whether a public sphere was "born" at all in colonial West Africa. Numerous newspaper editors and proprietors became major political leaders involved in power struggles and party politics across the region. They included J. E. Casely-Hayford, who started his journalistic career on his uncle's *Western Echo* in the 1880s, and John Payne Jackson, whose *Lagos Weekly Record* (1891–1930) contained an "arsenal of ideas from which opponents of the government took their weapons,"[55] as well as J. B. Danquah and Nnamdi Azikiwe in Ghana and Nigeria, who professionalized journalism in the decades preceding independence but also used the press for party political campaigning.[56] In spite of their insistence on journalistic impartiality, from the 1880s onward their newspapers played a central role in their political campaigns, to the extent that the fourth estate arguably remained firmly welded to the other three estates well before the negative postcolonial transformations described by Woods.[57]

In simultaneously yearning for a public sphere and acknowledging its absence under colonial rule, the region's literate elites found themselves stepping continuously into party political shoes, treading across the other three estates even as they attempted to use newspapers to generate a spatial separation between society and state. If a defining feature of the public sphere is its independence from party political interests, the West African press did not realize a mediating function in the colonial period. As a consequence, in colonial West Africa "matters appertaining to the Press" included legal and legislative issues, such as the need to "maintain our laws and customs and properly safeguard our constitution,"[58] as well as the common Jeffersonian principles of press freedom and the "liberty to ventilate our grievances."[59]

"It should not be impossible for a Governor to understand that the criticism of an Editor may be solely for the purpose of improving proposed Legislation, and not in the slightest degree from being actuated by a spirit or hostility or fault-finding," stated the editor of the *Sierra Leone Weekly News*, taking on the mantle of political critic in the very act of disavowing political involvement.[60] In defining their own legitimacy and in attempting to enforce institutional transparency, somewhat paradoxically they tended to shadow and emulate the church, the law courts, and the government. Across the political spectrum, West African editors used their newspapers to attempt to influence government policy and legislation. They became something of a parallel government, using print to define the portfolios of colonial civil servants and to oversee the transformation of local and municipal events into public opinion.[61] Nevertheless, these journalists distanced themselves from the institution of colonial government in favor of a print-mediated mode of democratic participation and critique: they thus created for themselves an exemplary public sphere that was also, simultaneously, an exemplary parliamentary sphere in its democratic, discursive, and egalitarian orientation.

In some sections of the press, however, government was regarded as little more than "a farce . . . a snare, and a delusion."[62] Always facing away from the people, hidden and duplicitous, colonial power was seen by the most radical editors to take the form of a system of entrapment. Newspapers, in such a setting, became the surrogate representative body through which journalists could make the government visible, rather than the means to mediate *between* the state and society in the manner described by Habermas.

Despite this, the liberal ideal remained robust. In a petition to the secretary of state for the colonies in 1946 accusing the Nigerian governor, Sir Arthur Richards, of victimizing his newspaper group and other far more serious crimes, Nnamdi Azikiwe articulated the ambivalence of the space inhabited by local newspapers: "The newspapers owned by our Company are willing to offer helpful and constructive criticism of Government policy as occasion demands," he wrote.[63] But Zik's reiteration of West African journalistic principles looked rather archaic and contrived, for it occurred toward the end of a stridently political list of ideals for the newspapers owned by Zik Press Ltd., including: "1) being uncompromisingly opposed to privilege in any form, whether among/between Africans or non-Africans; 2) insisting that African and non-African leaders should live up to the standard which they profess; [and] 3) believing in efficiency and remuneration according to a person's worth, irrespective of race, colour, creed, sex."[64]

The space occupied by the press in West Africa was under constant scrutiny by antagonistic officials who had other interests at heart. Paradoxically, through the exercise of their liberty African-owned newspapers furnished colonial officials with information about the educated elite's political campaigns and aspirations. This regime-level readership is revealed by the fact that "His Excellency the Governor" is the delivery name scrawled across the top of the majority of colonial West African newspapers in the British Library's newspaper collection.[65] As a consequence, the "native" press was generally tolerated for its value as a tool for the surveillance of African elites by colonial officials.[66]

Editors' repetitive comments about the public role of newspapers can be seen as utopian efforts to bring into being the very public sphere that was denied to the inhabitants of colonial societies by antidemocratic imperial governments. Until the emergence of sensational popular newspapers such as Azikiwe's *West African Pilot* and *African Morning Post* in the mid-1930s, in thinking about the function and value of newsprint the politically engaged elites who owned and wrote for the press envisaged it as a radically egalitarian space for rational expression between anonymous citizens. As late as the 1920s, editors and proprietors insisted—often disingenuously—that "the object of a public writer should not be to vent his own spleen against individuals, or bodies, or organisations, under cover of the editorial chair since to take that course would indicate a cowardly nature which . . . takes cover in print."[67] As a result of the dramatic mismatch between colonial political structures and local journalists' utopian representations of the function of the press, the idea of the colonial public sphere in West Africa should thus be regarded as coterminous with print, as generated in print, by and for print-consuming, print-producing colonial subjects.

As the stormy 1930s gave way to the nationalist 1940s and 1950s, however, many newspapermen used the press to launch anticolonial political movements and themselves as political leaders. Although this was not a new phenomenon—for editors had used their newspapers to engage in political campaigns since the 1880s—the late 1930s marked a new era of mass politicization through the press.[68] The "real trouble in West Africa," British officials knew, would "begin after the inhibitions arising from war conditions have been removed and when Government will be expected to redeem its rather vague promises in concrete form and in the shortest possible time."[69] Azikiwe's youth movement and Wallace-Johnson's provocative anticolonial activities emerged in this period of mass politicization, but many other West African intellectuals and nationalists, including J. B. Danquah, Kwame Nkrumah, Ernest Ikoli, and Duse Mohammed Ali, became wholeheartedly party-political through the newspapers they edited in the 1930s and 1940s. In short, the bourgeois public sphere to which African newspapermen aspired in the early and middle colonial periods never was—and, as a result of colonial rule, could not become—translated into a "real" social space that mediated between the state and civil society in the manner imagined by Habermas for eighteenth-century Europe. Nonetheless, for West African editors and literate elites newsprint made possible the imagination of a new audience: whether articulated in African or European languages, public opinion was regarded as a new type of discourse synonymous with newspaper writing.[70]

2 ⇝ Articulating Empire
Newspaper Networks in Colonial West Africa

THE FIRST newspapers in West Africa date back to the early nineteenth century, when Christian-educated, liberated slaves from diverse parts of the world returned to Sierra Leone and Liberia and set up their own printing presses.[1] From this moment of inception, the region's newspapers were entwined with the cultural histories of African diasporas, African elites, the spread of Christianity, and the consolidation of the colonial state. Any history of West African newspapers in the colonial period will also, therefore, form part of a wider history of local elites in the British Empire.

By the late nineteenth century, newspapers were a common feature of West African elite cultures, particularly along the coastal belt connecting the Gambia with Sierra Leone, Liberia, Ghana, and Nigeria. Newspapers provided vibrant discursive spaces in which people of different social ranks and literacies could offer commentaries on culture, colonialism, and current affairs. The English-language press in West Africa helped to produce and sustain one particular new public: a transcolonial reading public, politically articulated and composed of individuals joined by their shared identity as members of the British Empire but separated ideologically in many other ways. Literate elites throughout the colonial world were able to connect, via print, across many thousands of miles, participating in the formation of a panimperial "imagined community" that far surpassed Benedict Anderson's nation-centered model of print capitalism. Through the medium of Reuters telegrams, local readers in Accra or Freetown or Lagos could access information about Home Rule campaigns in India and Ireland, the Ku Klux Klan in North America, Japan's economic transformation, and the emergence of racial segregation in South Africa. Throughout the empire, readers were thus articulated—connected together, spoken for, and speaking for themselves—in new ways by their English-language newspapers.[2]

As a consequence of these connections, extensive new political networks were made possible by the press as readers in one location forged links and made comparisons between themselves and others. Reuters reports about Irish "agitation" and about Boer demands in South Africa inspired supportive editorials in the *Gold Coast Leader*, where comparisons were drawn between the political rights of imperial subjects in British colonies globally and the situation in West Africa.[3] Similarly, the introduction of repressive ordinances in one colony often generated critical editorials, telegrams, petitions to the secretary of state, and letters of protest from pressure groups in a multitude of other locations. Sir Douglas Jardine's attack on press freedoms in Sierra Leone in 1939, for example, stimulated petitions and protests from as far afield as the Negro Welfare Cultural and Social Association in Trinidad, George Padmore and the International African Service Bureau in London,[4] the Independent Labour Party (Saltcoats Branch, Ayrshire), the League of Coloured Peoples in Sierra Leone, the Women's Auxiliary of the West African Youth League in Sierra Leone, and the Committee of Citizens on Behalf of the Inhabitants of Sierra Leone (Colony and Protectorate).[5] Though Governor Jardine's Sedition Ordinance and his Undesirable Literature Ordinance passed into law, the international opposition they generated demonstrated the presence of coherent transcolonial political networks that made use of the press to respond rapidly with organized opposition focused on specific local sites of colonial power.[6]

Networks of loyalty and trust often remained robust between newspapermen for many decades. In one letter describing a dispute in the mid-1960s between Nelson Ottah, editor of the Nigerian *Drum*, and Tom Hopkinson, the London-based editor of *Drum* magazine, over whether to publish one of his detective stories, the veteran newspaperman James Vivian Clinton remarked that Ottah was "trained by me on my weekly newspaper in the thirties."[7] Although the London editor "refused permission to publish," Clinton noted that the Lagos editor "had already paid me . . . on his own opinion of the merits of the story."[8] This account reveals the resilience of journalistic affiliations and networks but also the disagreements over content and quality between metropolitan editors and their "satellite" stations.[9]

Comparison and competition, rather than solidarity and cosmopolitanism, were sometimes at the core of these transcolonial networks of articulation. Editorials in the West African press frequently mentioned the unequal resources and preferment given to "other colonies" such as Trinidad and Mauritius over the home colony.[10] Lagos and Cape Coast were archrivals in this respect, as editors closely monitored British investment in schools and municipal services in one another's cities, complaining vociferously about perceived inequalities.

Particular print-mediated subjectivities emerged in locally owned newspapers in colonial West Africa. Significant processes of textual production can be found in the press in the form of readers' articulations. The binary opposition between the reader and the text, or the consumer and the commodity, which tends to dominate Euro-American literary criticism, is inaccurate to describe these colonial (con)texts and subjects, for if one privileges the contents of a text above its consumption or official documents above supposedly ephemeral texts, an entire field of articulation is erased from the literary map.

Stuart Hall, Richard Middleton, and other cultural theorists have used the concept of articulation to describe the processes whereby social classes "speak forth" from particular socioeconomic positions, connecting cultural elements together but never being wholly fixed within the parameters of class. An articulation, Hall stated in an interview, is "the form of the connection that *can* make a unity of two different elements, under certain conditions. It is a linkage which is not necessary, determined, absolute and essential for all time. You have to ask, under what circumstances *can* a connection be forged or made?"[11] Building on this concept of articulation as a series of cultural connections, as a clearly voiced argument, and also as an encounter that takes place within dynamic social parameters, this chapter will challenge critical frameworks that set local (or indigenous) readerships against global (or colonial) texts in fixed oppositional relationships.

Throughout colonial West Africa, African newspaper editors consistently encouraged readers—especially the newly educated subelites living in and around the region's expanding cities—to put their literacy to good use and to write in on a wide range of issues. In the first weeks of a newspaper's existence, readers were frequently invited to send in "anything, even in the shape of extracts or notes from whatever papers or

Journals you may have read."[12] This, in turn, sustained the sales of particular titles as readers became centrally involved in textual production, purchasing newspapers in order to follow and participate in the progress of topical debates. African readers actively helped to set the agenda in the newspapers, responding eagerly to the invitation of editors to "freely express their views and intelligent opinion" in the letters pages.[13] As well as consolidating the power and political networks of established elites, then, the newspapers generated new cultural circuits and new identities for readers. In increasing numbers, particularly from the 1920s onward, newly literate groups became centrally involved as participants in the production of material, and their output reveals a great deal about local attitudes toward literacy and print in the colonial period.

As the profile of readers shifted from university-educated "gentlemen" born into established families in the late nineteenth century to newly literate locals—clerks, teachers, catechists, and white-collar workers, including women—who emerged into West Africa's public spaces after the 1920s, the content of newspapers also changed to reflect the opinions and aspirations of the social groups that benefited from colonial mass-education policies. The expanding colonial education system produced growing numbers of ambitious, energetic young men—but fewer women—keen to put their reading skills to further use.

Colonial West African newspapers were not homogeneous or coherent, as suggested by some media historians. In her study *The Press and Political Culture in Ghana*, Jennifer Hasty writes, in a survey of the colonial period, that "news media in Africa emerged as expressive local forces of indigenous resistance against the globalizing forces of colonial repression and exploitation."[14] By placing "indigenous local resistance" over and against "globalizing colonial repression," Hasty follows other press historians in assuming that newspapers offered sites of strategic African resistance against colonialism; that local forces can be clearly differentiated from and set against global forces; and that indigenous newspapers conveyed a coherent, homogeneous, oppositional ideology.

Print cultures did play a fundamental role in articulations of resistance to colonial power between the 1880s and 1950s, but the representation of these processes is often clouded by two assumptions made by newspaper historians: first, that nationalism was the driving force of press activity for the entire colonial period,[15] and, second, that newspapers expressed a homogenous imagined community and represented a democratic public sphere.[16] Though the African-owned press was one of the few available vehicles for political resistance, this teleological, nation-centered approach needs to be modified to accommodate the region's complex cultural histories of reading and authorship.

If one supports the idea that the rise of print capitalism and the emergence of a public sphere in the colonies were inextricable from the rise of nationalism and democratic self-assertion, as proposed by Anderson and Hasty, one gets a partial, distorted picture of newspaper readerships in West Africa. Anderson argues that heterogeneity is a fundamental characteristic of newspapers, but the heterogeneous readers of—and the heterogeneous columns in—West African newspapers lacked the pivotal idea of a shared "national" identity that, in Anderson's model, glues the imagined community together.[17] Indeed, until the mid-1930s in West Africa, the very word *nation* was used to describe complex and diverse identities and affiliations, including identities that historian Frederick Cooper describes as "deterritorialized forms of affinity," such as pan-Africanism, Christian humanitarianism, and proletarian internationalism as well as "pro-colonial" and reformist imperial allegiances.[18] Partha Chatterjee also criticizes Anderson for ignoring the various forms of community imagined locally and for ignoring the diversity of local nationalisms to be found in the colonies.[19]

In West Africa, a single issue of a newspaper could articulate several "deterritorialized" forms of affinity side by side. As suggested already, when the term *nation* was used in the early to mid-colonial press (1880s–1920s), it generally included local affiliations alongside colonial and pan-African identities. Anderson's definition of print nationalism is anachronistic in the context of these heterogeneous "national" times, spaces, and identities. West African newspapers did not *require* the homogeneous temporality that characterizes newspapers and the idea of national identity for Anderson and his followers.

Newspapers from colonial West Africa were fragmentary and varied and less politically coherent than the nationalist model assumes, and as the last chapter suggested, they did not simply conform to a Habermasian model of the public sphere as a space for democratic, rational debate and self-assertion in liberal democracies. Until the industry was professionalized by press entrepreneurs such as Azikiwe, who introduced technologies of mass production in the mid-1930s, a multitude of genres and an eclectic set of identities could be found in the press. In a single "General News" column of the *Gold Coast*

Leader from 1902, "poetical effusions" by local writers could be found together with fragments of general knowledge about the Arab world, quotations from Shakespeare's *Hamlet,* and news of local police violence against women in the town of Cape Coast.[20] In other papers, with little apparent conflict of interest, popular imperial romances such as Amy Baker's novel *Never Laugh at Love* would be serialized next to fiercely pan-Africanist publications from West Africa and the United States. Beside these were publications from Britain, such as the racially offensive anti-Liberian pieces by Sir Harry Johnston in the early 1920s.[21] What linked these items together as colonial articulations was their interest in Africa and race, not any ideological agreement about the issues they addressed.

Moreover, printed texts that appeared to critique the British government too aggressively caused a great deal of concern on all sides in the colonies, often arousing as much consternation among African newspaper editors as among colonial officials. African migrants and university-educated professionals aroused particular suspicion among officials as purveyors of seditious material. Aware of their status as prime suspects, these elites were quick to defend their presses and to rearticulate (with) the British Empire, sometimes at the expense of local readers. Thus, in an early issue of the *Gold Coast Nation,* the following warning was issued to contributors: "We consider it an Act of Christian Charity to forewarn some of our Correspondents . . . who are in the habit of rioting in personalities whenever the whim seizes them, that there is such a thing as Libel in the Criminal Code."[22] The editor cited colonial legislation and reminded readers that the penalties were six months for negligent libel and two years for intentional libel. Finally, using a striking sexual metaphor, he informed "our disappointed Correspondents [that they] should therefore see with us when the *Nation* refuses to soil its virgin columns with slanderous and libellous communications."[23]

Similarly, pseudonymous creative writers frequently anticipated accusations that their fictional creations contained libelous material. If authorial anonymity was an unquestioned convention in West African newspapers, the very hiddenness of writers sometimes gave rise to suspicions that their stories disclosed a different, more scandalous type of biographical information. Anticipating suspicions that the story "His First and Only Love" depicted the romantic entanglements of actual local personalities, rather than fictional characters, the Sierra Leonean author "Erne's Friend" insisted, "I . . . ask you not to attempt to personalise my characters, or fancy this or that living person is Philip Thompson, or Myra Williams, &c, for you surely would be wrong."[24]

Editors in West Africa regularly expressed concerns that the authorities would attempt to shut down their presses and stifle printed criticisms of colonial regimes. "Wild speculation is rife," wrote the editor of the *Gold Coast Nation* in 1912, that "the local press is to be gagged and the Editors thereof deported for their impertinence and impudence."[25] One consequence of this nervousness was the conservative reaction of some pressmen when one of their fellows was in trouble for flouting colonial sedition ordinances. When James Bright Davies, the veteran West African journalist and flamboyant editor of the *Times of Nigeria*, was imprisoned for six months in November 1916 under the wartime Criminal Code for seditious libel by "exciting disaffection" against the Nigerian regime, fellow editors did not express unconditional solidarity with him.[26] Influential Lagos newspapermen such as Kitoyi Ajasa and Thomas Jackson fought hard (and successfully) for the old man's release, but at least two editors—of the *Lagos Standard* (Nigeria) and the *Gold Coast Nation* (Ghana)—made use of the incident to criticize allegedly seditious and libelous journalism in general. Without actually naming Davies, the editor of the *Lagos Standard* declared, in a potted history of West African newspapers, that the old 1880s papers, in which the prisoner was a leading figure, contained "sensationalism and the use of violent and unmeasured language" as well as "vicious and unnecessary attacks on the character of individuals."[27] The editors of these 1880s newspapers, the *Standard* continued, "made themselves objectionable, pandered to public prejudice and rendered themselves ready and willing tools of a loud and empty headed section of the community insistent on the sensational and the vulgar."[28] Turning finally to the case of Davies, the *Standard*'s editor declared that the veteran pressman "had the fairest of trials at the hands of the Chief Justice Sir Edwin Speedy" and that "the lessons to be learnt therefrom will not be lost on West Africa's natives."[29]

This editor's defensive allegiance to the British Empire was not the isolated response of a lone African loyalist. The *Lagos Standard*'s article was transported to Ghana and reprinted in full in another conservative newspaper, the *Gold Coast Nation*. In an editorial on the topic, the *Nation* added its own imperial articulation to that of the *Standard* on Davies's imprisonment. "Overzeal for the welfare of his country has brought this trouble upon him," the editor declared, extrapolating immediately from the case to comment on the tactics of "some West African journalists" who, of late, "[have] lent themselves to a habit of launching attacks devoid of decency, on individuals—Africans and Europeans"; in conclusion, he wrote, "these journalists will do well to bridle their sledgehammer attacks in discussing matters of public interest."[30]

In addition to their consciousness of surveillance by colonial officials and other hostile readers, such editors were self-conscious about the presence of new readers, which gave rise to incessant commentaries about the correct and proper ways for readers to write for publication in the local press. In this manner, those working for the newspaper—often themselves also engaged in full-time careers as lawyers, doctors, entrepreneurs, and teachers—asserted their own authority and professionalism as writers and carefully patrolled the quality of material submitted by readers. At times, newspapers resembled handbooks of journalistic and literary style. Potential contributors were offered regular advice and feedback on how to compose publishable items for submission. Thus, the *Gold Coast Leader*, a newspaper aimed specifically at young and newly educated readers in Ghana, "invite[d] all classes to write" but advised prospective contributors to "be yourself, imitate no one, say what you wish to say in your own way and leave it there: you need not ransack tomes of dictionaries for words to suffocate your readers with."[31] This statement symptomized the aesthetic preference of the editor for contributions written in simple English style, a topic about which there was considerable debate in the press. Throughout colonial Ghana at the time, pomposity and imitativeness were frowned upon by highly educated Africans; in particular, the use of bombastic English was considered to be a hallmark of the "semieducated" classes, regarded not as a sign of intelligence but as a mark of a person's overinflated ambition and illegitimate social aspirations.[32]

In a lengthy follow-up article addressed "To Our Intending Contributors (continued from our last)," the editor wrote:

> We are positively thirsting for materials that will be talked about, at the store, office, a social gathering or at home, and if some energetic contributor sends us an article bearing on this, written as best as he could, with a modicum of common sense in its treatment, the chances are ten to one that we will pass it for publication while we may return to its author an essay on something that had happened some weeks, months or even years, previously, and

this is because the first essential of newspaper articles is that they must deal with some topic of the moment.³³

The *Leader*'s editor was always courteous and inclusive toward new contributors, but other editors were less polite in their printed statements about why items were rejected. A censorious item entitled "Answers to Correspondents," published in the *Gold Coast Nation* in July 1915, supplied a revealing set of reasons for the rejection of particular contributions from local readers, and, in the process, tapped a rich seam of information about attitudes toward journalistic content and style at the time. To "Retired Catechist, Tarquah," the editor commented, "Your article re: the morals of our young people is admirable but you clothe it in such language that we are unable to give publicity to it."³⁴ The response to "J. R." of Saltpond gave insights into what was considered newsworthy and how a reader might find publication by developing a wider discussion of racial discrimination from an otherwise "personal" experience: "Your letter re: Mercantile Agent is too personal and unsupported by facts. Please note that our columns are not open to the ventilation of private and personal grievances but to what is generally of public interest. If you have any complaint against the head of your firm make representations to the proper quarters. If he is a negrophobist and his acts are against public interest and the race, supply us with all the necessary facts and leave the rest to us."³⁵

These warnings indicate that even though West African newspapers were heterogeneous, providing spaces for literary experimentation and for the articulations of new readerships, they were not radically open, unregulated forums for anybody who could write to find publication. In submitting contributions, readers risked criticism and public rejection from editors. Indeed, in one article for the *Gold Coast Nation* advising potential contributors on journalistic content and style, a regular pseudonymous contributor called "The Man in the Street" proposed that readers should simply "send to the editor the substance of an article to be rewritten by him, rather than to write the article himself in unworthy English and insist on its being printed exactly as he wrote it."³⁶

Unsurprisingly, given that newspaper proprietors were members of Christianized, highly educated male elites, such attitudes echoed governmental and missionary debates about how to limit the excessive self-confidence of new readers in the colonies.³⁷ As the Sierra Leonean newspaperman and bookshop owner T. J. Sawyerr argued in 1886, "We want all the talkers in this community to be useful talkers, and to be so, they must store their minds with useful information. Let them read good books and good magazines, and endeavour to digest every good thought."[38] To this end, Sawyerr's bookshop stocked titles to rival those of any Christian missionary educator, including morally improving nonfiction and etiquette books such as *Ready Made Speeches, Character and Culture*, and the best-selling pamphlet *Don't*, alongside novels by George Eliot and Louisa May Alcott and a plenitude of religious texts.[39] The history of reading in West Africa is intimately connected to the rise of "good books and good magazines" and to the moral debates provoked by such texts.[40] Newspaper editors' erasure of the Eurocentric dichotomy between readers and texts was not, therefore, an erasure of the social hierarchies separating the highly educated elites from correspondents and lay contributors to the press. Indeed, editors' perceptions of themselves as moral and political leaders in the community often found expression through their public advice on literary content and journalistic style.

Imperial subjects one and all, these missionary-trained newspapermen voiced the contradictions of existing "after Empire" in their simultaneous expression of unhesitating loyalty to the British Crown and their identification of the newspaper as the sole vehicle for the expression of complaints about colonial rule. The inaugural issue of the *Gold Coast Leader*, in June 1902, established this double articulation of colonial identity.[41] On the front page, the editor reacted to the news of King Edward VII's illness: "As His Majesty's loyal subjects, we would most humbly and respectfully tender our heartfelt sympathies to His Majesty's government, here and in the mother country. . . . We shall ever shout God Save the King."[42] But in the same column, the editor attempted to generate a sense of shame among British officials by describing the poor state of Cape Coast as if witnessed through the eyes of a foreigner in town: "Any foreigner learning the length of time this ill-starred Town has been in the possession of the English will hardly give credence to what he will be privileged to be an eye-witness, as to its sanitation, and general condition."[43] At least three different colonial readerships were included in the remit of this editorial: first, "we," the educated Africans in Cape Coast; second, the British colonial authorities who were responsible for municipal development; and third, metropolitan and "foreign" readers with no knowledge of the locale.

Many years later, in 1939, a committee of Sierra Leonean political activists adopted a similarly double mode of articulation, juxtaposing an acceptance of British colonial rule with a protest against the plethora of repressive new press ordinances introduced to the colony by Governor Sir Douglas Jardine. Their position, however, demonstrated the extent to which elite African attitudes had transformed in relation to the definition of so-called useful literature, moving away from the missionary morality of Sawyerr's booklists and toward a liberal, secular model of literary freedom.

Journalists and readers regarded members of the press as playing not only a political role but also a vital intellectual role in West Africa, providing factual historical information and reference material to help readers with research, essay writing, correspondence, and articles. In an editorial in 1885, Sawyerr instructed readers: "*Kindly keep this number as you will require it for reference when our next number is published.*"[44] Thirty years later, as if to prove the longevity and usefulness of Sawyerr's instruction, the editor of the *Gold Coast Nation* regularly cited from his personal collection of 1880s newspapers, including the *Gold Coast People* and the *Western Echo*, in order to urge readers to remain loyal to the region's history of political assertiveness and to continue their tradition of pressing the colonial regime for self-government.[45] Keen readers would cut out and preserve articles and correspondence from a wide array of journals.

As a result, a particular mode of historical writing, or history making, emerged over time. Editors and correspondents used the medium of print to print a version of history. Correspondents cited previously published newspaper articles rather than political speeches, oral histories, or monographs, and editors reprinted articles from decades-old West African newspapers or extracts from letters written in the late nineteenth century to draw comparisons and establish continuities with Africans' political demands in the present. Narcissistically, the newspaper was offered to readers *as* posterity, as the vehicle for history. As K. S. put it in an early issue of the *Gold Coast Leader*, "The *Newspaper* [is] . . . the weekly or daily history of the world."[46]

In other instances, as with the serialized "Ongoing Review of the Years 1910 to 1913," published in the *Gold Coast Nation* in April 1914, newspapers produced a form of living history in columns that reflected upon current times and the immediate past for the benefit of posterity.[47] This style occurred most obviously during the opening months of World War I. As early as 10 September 1914, a series of editorials entitled "Abridged History of the Great European War" appeared in the *Gold Coast Nation*, containing snippets of information from the English press that were cut and pasted into a coherent narrative. "We have to acknowledge our indebtedness to the *Times*," the editor commented in the first of this series, which was offered to readers as "a historical compendium to our schools and the general public alike."[48] All of these examples indicate that editors, contributors, and readers alike regarded printed material as factually correct and historically accurate. Newspapers were worth keeping, the editors insisted, positioning their products as constitutive of history and the opposite of ephemera.

Yet on more than one occasion, articles from other journals were reprinted in an effort to convey sentiments that would have been unacceptably controversial had they stemmed from local sources. After reprinting an article from the London journal *Truth*, in which young people's enterprise and energy were promoted over and against the older generation's, the editor of the *Gold Coast Leader* commented, "What a hubbub there would have been, if *we* had ventured in any shape or form to have said anything like this—such a universal truth would have been [interpreted as] nothing but gross personality, etc."[49] Interestingly, the antagonists in this case were not the colonial authorities but Africans of senior status, such as chiefs and elders.

Editorial cut-and-paste work was not, therefore, simply a way to supplement local items with news or facts from further afield. The activity of "culling," as editors called it, was also a form of articulation that enabled them to ventriloquize challenges to existing hierarchies in the name of truth without attracting accusations of treachery or personal ambition.[50] On occasion, to doubly mask this political initiative, editors cross-culled material by reprinting items from the British press that had already been reprinted in British or West African journals. In this manner, they added links to the chain of imperial articulations.[51] Editors became readers of others' texts in order to provoke their own readers to produce further texts; the consumers of such items were always rereaders, aware of the status of the text as already published elsewhere.

In the process of citing articles from other newspapers, editors betrayed their loss of faith in oral forms of transmission and demonstrated a particularly print-biased method for compiling the story of the past. If West African newspapers were regarded as an archive or resource base by their readers at the time, the cut-and-paste method produced a type of historical narration that was distinctive to the press.[52] Print was far more than a medium for editors; they seemed to be convinced of the permanence and superiority of published texts over oral genres. A pervasive bias against nonreaders permeated West African newspapers from the 1880s onward: as one correspondent, S. H., wrote patronizingly in *Sawyerr's Bookselling, Printing and Stationery Trade Circular* in 1885, "A numerous body of local non-readers [exists]" in Freetown, preventing people from "be[ing] able to appreciate the schemes we are daily hatching up for their benefit."[53]

ORAL PUBLICS AND THE PRINT BIAS OF EDITORS

The history of reading in the colonies need not be confined to the history of readers, nor to literate elites who had passed through the missionary and colonial school systems. As Kate Skinner suggests in her study of Ewe-language newspapers in the early to mid-twentieth century, the "Ewe print sphere was in no way sealed off, either from Ewe speech and song, or from the oral or written texts that were produced in English and French in the coastal capital cities of Ghana and Togo."[54] No history of colonial readerships and print cultures should ignore the empire's nonliterate majority. What kind of public was constituted by those social groups that existed outside or beyond the imperial education system? Should we follow the bias of elite African pressmen from the period and position nonreaders, to quote the *Gold Coast Nation* from 1912, as "poor ignorant masses" outside "modernity"?[55] Clearly not gathered around printed texts, members of these groups—which cannot be seen as singular or homogeneous—organized their lives in their own ways and called upon elaborate, diverse cultural forms ranging from the oral to the written.

Oral forms are elusive and easily silenced in histories of African literatures, especially when written texts—newspapers, archives, libraries, and printed ephemera—provide the primary material for researchers. This problem is compounded by the preoccupation with education and literacy in the African newspapers themselves. Editors often used the medium of print to assert the supremacy of print over "illiteracy," as orality was demeaningly labeled. Oral forms of transmission were regularly dismissed as rumor and speculation, over and against "the light of [printed] knowledge."[56] For African newspaper consumers, progress, modernity, and "enlightened" subjectivity were inextricable from the ability to read. In the English-language press at least, other forms of knowledge were generally regarded as backward unless and until they were rendered into print.

Editors did not ignore orality, however: large numbers of folktales found their way into print, often reworked for political and moral ends. Throughout the 1910s and 1920s, the *Gold Coast Nation* published folktales in which political morals were extracted from familiar parables, and realist narrative techniques were used to draw lessons from nonrealist tales (see chapter 4). Considerable further research is required into this political engagement with literary realism, for such columns reveal the dynamic status of folktales and their power to absorb contemporary moods, opinions, and representations.

Editors and contributors also frequently expressed anxieties about "losing" African oral cultures as a result of the absence of printed versions of tales. In an article symptomatically entitled "National and Historical Research," the editor of the *Gold Coast Nation* exemplified the educated elite's unquestioning belief in print: "Those who possess information that will be useful to the student of the history and customs of our forefathers are often illiterate."[57] As a result, he concluded, "in 20 years' time much interesting and useful knowledge will have been lost to the nation if immediate efforts are not made to gather it now."[58] Such views reveal a seminal shift in West African attitudes to the narration and preservation of history. No longer able to trust oral historians for the transmission of the past, West African newspapermen emphasized a new ideology in which the production of history was inextricable from the printing press. The printed page was regarded by them as the sole means for preservation and articulation, a way to "embody . . . thoughts and ideas on paper in more or less permanent form."[59]

The intense, sometimes obsessive reflections on the topic of reading to be found in the African-owned newspapers might tempt one to believe that so-called oral communities occupied a separate "traditional" sphere, unfamiliar with and untouched by texts or textual knowledge. Outside the two-culture model, some Africans were able to lead "literate" lifestyles without embarking on extensive acts of reading.[60] Some social groups did not require *any* reading skills or primary texts in order to identify themselves as literary. For instance, when the new Asante elite returned home to Kumasi in central Ghana in the late nineteenth century after trading and accumulating wealth on the south coast, they asserted their distinctiveness by appropriating the mannerisms, clothing, and culture of the coastal intelligentsia, adapting them into a lifestyle of their own. These semi- or nonliterate entrepreneurs established themselves as "literary gentlemen" in their hometowns, setting up associations along the lines of the Cape Coast literary and debating societies. From this platform, they petitioned the customary authorities for reforms in their interests.[61] These Kumasi gentlemen demonstrated one of the creative ways in which book knowledge was reconceptualized to suit local power struggles.

Nevertheless, as indicated earlier, a particular type of subjectivity was convened through newsprint. Editors actively courted and produced readers, inviting them to send in letters on particular topics, to make suggestions for future articles, and to write about ethical and political controversies. In 1886, Sawyerr declared, "We shall at all times be pleased to receive suggestions which may tend both to improve this publication and increase its utility."[62] This inclusive attitude toward educated readers remained stable for many decades in West Africa, until at least the mid-1930s.[63] "Now, dear ladies and gentlemen," ran one reflective editorial in the *Nigerian Observer* in November 1931, "are these articles not interesting and educative when properly considered and put into practice and not just for mere reading sake?"[64] Operating in a tripartite manner as conveyer of news, educator of autodidacts, and platform for moral debate, newspapers did not exist "just for mere reading sake." Articles were expected to be educative and uplifting at all times. This public literacy was distinctly moral in orientation. As the editor of the *Gold Coast Nation* wrote in 1913: "The West African Press to do the most good for country and people should aim at the cultivation and dissemination of moral and spiritual principles more than anything else, at least for a good many years to come."[65]

These literary values were articulated in the 1930s with as much fervor as in the 1880s, and they continued to characterize attitudes toward print in postcolonial West Africa.[66] "The Press deserves its name," stated an editorial in the *Nigerian Eastern Mail* in December 1937, because "(1) it gives a chance to all to voice out their feelings. (2) It corrects some of our defects. (3) Its weekly publications are of the great[est] interest and educative value to the general public. A real instructor and director to the Africans."[67] In 1930, a letter to the *Nigerian Observer* of Port Harcourt from one "Jack Never Fear" insisted, echoing the early twentieth-century editors, that readers should subscribe to the journal "for the purpose of gathering better informations [sic] than theirs for the formation of their character whilst they also have got important subjects to forward to you for publication and general discussion which at the end may tend as pathway to moral and intellectual advancement."[68] The list of similar examples from the 1920s and 1930s is almost endless. Whether or not these "puffs" were written by editors rather than readers, they demonstrate that reader participation was one of the defining principles of the African-owned press.

AFRICAN READING PUBLICS

In work that expands and complicates Anderson's *Imagined Communities*, Michael Warner argues that modern media audiences are constituted in and through particular discursive moments. Publics "do not exist apart from the discourse that addresses them," nor do publics exist in isolation from "pre-existing forms and channels of circulation" in a culture.[69] Warner challenges reception theory models by reversing the conventional paradigm for reader-text relationality, in which readers are generally regarded as fully formed and rational entities, existing before texts and discourses. Publics come into being around texts, Warner insists, and not prior to them.

This idea that "texts constitute their publics" powerfully describes the reader-text relationship in early West African newspapers.[70] Newspapers contained an incredible amount of introspection on the topic of reading and writing. Particularly during the months after the launch of a new title, editors and correspondents became almost fixated with the subject of reading, returning to it more regularly than to news items in their bid to define journalistic etiquette and to justify their contributions according to principles of public interest.

The frequency with which these circular, self-reflexive "feedback loops" occurred can be explained in a number of ways.[71] Stark economic and practical difficulties surrounded the attraction of new readers to a paper. Editors were burdened with the considerable problem of how to extract remittances from subscribers who were reluctant or unable to part with their dues. They regularly appealed to subscribers to settle outstanding bills, and they begged nonpaying readers to support the emergence of an African press rather than to read secondhand copies borrowed from acquaintances. On several occasions, editors and letter writers pleaded with fellow readers to subscribe to—rather than to beg, borrow, or steal—the newspaper. "Dear Sir," ran one letter in the *Gold Coast Leader*, "Kindly allow me space in your valuable columns to speak of the behaviour of some scholars in town who have turned themselves into paper ('Leader') beggars. It is very strange and quite disgraceful to see respectable men of means imploring their friends to lend them the 'Leader' for their perusal."[72] In dealing with problems of this type, some editors attempted to shame errant subscribers into paying by threatening to publish lists of their names; others hailed local benefactors by name, inviting less exemplary members of the literate community to interpret the implications for themselves. The problem of attracting and maintaining a subscribing readership was a source of many press bankruptcies in the colonial period, but it also stimulated commercial, technological, and literary innovations among editors desperate to attract new readers from the expanding ranks of educated, salaried Africans. Spurred on by Zik's popular press, examples of such editorial innovations in the late 1930s included the publication of portraits of "great men," essay-writing competitions, and invitations to participate in debates.

New publics needed to be vigorously hailed, reinforced, and maintained by editors. To survive, the newspaper needed to be a magnet for new readers, and a failure to convene readers, or new publics, would result in the failure of the press.[73] A significant effect of these feedback loops, therefore, was the emergence of reading as a form of cultural production. Similarly, literary production was a form of consumption. The critical tendency in postcolonial book history to separate cultural production from cultural consumption is complicated by such articulations between editors and readers.

In spite of the comparatively small percentage of the population making up the literate community of particular colonies, there was no homogeneous reading public for editors to address: preconstituted publics did not exist autonomously and automatically, waiting patiently in the wings for the appearance of a new text or media commodity. In her groundbreaking work on the Yoruba press and reading publics in 1920s Lagos, Karin Barber shows how the linguistically and generically diverse Yoruba-English newspapers convened "a compound public, no layer of which was reducible or subsumable to the others."[74] No preexisting public sphere awaited the arrival of a newspaper in West Africa. Newspapers provided readers with a unique forum for literary and generic experiments, and they produced new reading communities, some more potentially "dangerous" than others.[75] Throughout colonial West Africa, these compound publics played significant roles in shaping the content and structure of newspapers: if newspapers convened publics as Warner suggests, Barber shows how publics also played a seminal role in producing literary experiments and genres.

⌒

The circulation of African newspapers—and local editors' organization of readerships as carriers of public opinion—often aroused sensitivities among government officials in the colonies, especially with the emergence of an increasingly literate urban workforce alongside a politically vociferous press after World War I. At the same time as new classes of readers were produced by the expanding colonial education system, an influx of "unpalatable" foreign publications and the rise of media enterprises such as Zik Press Ltd. in the mid-1930s led several governors in the region to attempt to introduce repressive measures to prevent the circulation of allegedly seditious printed materials. Part 2 of this book examines the effects of these legislative changes from the perspective of staff at the Colonial Office in their engagements with anticolonial African newspapermen, on the one hand, and colonial governors, on the other hand, for their growing fear of communism, coupled with the increasing political celebrity status of particular African editors, created numerous policy tensions between Britain and the colonies, requiring careful management from London.

PART II

Case Studies from the Colonial Office

3 ∽ The View from Afar

*The Colonial Office, Imperial Government,
and Pseudonymous African Journalism*

FOR MOST of the colonial period—except for the two world wars, when newspapers in Britain and the colonies were censored to prevent the publication of militarily sensitive information and material deemed to boost enemy morale—staff at the Colonial Office were reluctant to intervene directly in the contents or management of African-owned newspapers. Even with the escalation of the Cold War and mounting pressure from governors for colonial press censorship, they remained consistent in their belief that people in Britain's overseas possessions should enjoy similar, if not the same, press freedoms as in Britain, including the freedom to write anonymously and pseudonymously and the freedom to read politically "undesirable" (but not seditious) material. Staff in Whitehall knew all too well that censorship ordinances in the colonies "would be severely criticized in the British Press, if they were known."[1]

Until the beginning of World War II, the view from London seemed to be that "on general principles, legislation interfering with the liberty of the Press is highly undesirable and provides an effective target for public criticism of the Administration."[2] "It is well known," wrote Sir Arnold Hodson in November 1934 when he took office as governor of the Gold Coast in an atmosphere of heightened sensitivity and debate about press freedoms in the region, "that overstatement and exaggeration eventually defeat their own ends and exert little influence on the great mass of public opinion" (see the first case study in this chapter).[3] By contrast, he continued, "repressive legislation evokes the sympathy

... of a section of the public and tends to encourage the leaders to regard themselves as martyrs in a good cause."[4]

Through a set of West African case studies drawn from Colonial Office files, this part of the book will examine the ways in which the largely universalist notion of the press and the public sphere held in London competed with the paternalistic ideology of pacification, protection, and civilization. That ideology was used, first, by proimperialists to promote British colonial rule globally; second, by those hoping to underpin the existence and work of the Colonial Office itself; and, third, by individual governors to suppress press freedoms in particular West African territories. Rather than encouraging the enactment of punitive laws against publications deemed to be politically offensive, staff at the Colonial Office in London spent a great deal of time acting as a buffer between liberal sections of British public opinion and colonial governments, especially in attempting to limit the public relations damage caused by overzealous governors who often took executive action and introduced newspaper ordinances that were anything but progressive. At the same time, however, staff at the Colonial Office respected the discretion of individual governors in attempting to prevent the circulation of texts that might prove inflammatory with local populations.

A host of contradictions arose from this fundamental incompatibility between liberal notions of the public sphere and the practical enactment of British imperialism. In seeking to gauge these cultural processes in the first half of the twentieth century and in focusing on continuities, shifts, and failures in West African newspaper legislation, the following case studies will attempt to convey a sense not of a binary power relationship between colonizer and colonized but of a distribution of political power among several constituencies with differential access to executive, administrative, law-making, mediating, and opinion-forming roles. Largely revolving around governors' attempts to remove the protective cloak of anonymity from local writers—and African activists' resistance to these efforts—the studies presented here assess the contradictions between imperial ideology and ideals of press freedom at local and historically immediate levels.

As mentioned earlier, the prevalent opinion at the Colonial Office was that the banning or censorship of newspapers and other printed materials could cause more damage to public relations in Britain and the colonies (and also draw more international attention to an allegedly seditious text) than the confinement of offensive materials to a zone of official silence and neglect. Even at the height of British concerns about the importation and local impact of communist and anticolonial publications in West Africa between the mid-1930s and early 1950s, the positive local effect of the official "toleration given to violent and extremist articles" was considered to outweigh the negative "effect on the minds" of "documents of a subversive nature, from which local editors are in the habit of quoting."[5] This view prevailed for forty years, but it was continuously and increasingly modified by a willingness to "leave to the Governors themselves to decide in each Colony" according to "local conditions."[6]

With ever greater difficulty as the century progressed, staff at the Colonial Office attempted to adhere to a liberal view of the press while respecting the autonomy of individual administrators in each territory. For the latter group, so-called native populations were often regarded as "backward folk of a primitive mind who . . . can be easily misled" by "irresponsible" yet "advanced" members of the local intelligentsia.[7] As one assistant secretary at the Colonial Office, John D. Higham, commented in 1949, "Conditions in a relatively primitive colony may justify more arbitrary [censorship] measures than would be deemed right in a more developed territory."[8] Even so, he added immediately, in a cynical version of the liberal attitude adopted in previous decades, if the sales and circulation of texts were low in a colony as a consequence of low local literacy rates, then the presence of "undesirable" publications would cause little moral harm to the general population.[9]

Higham's separation of literate from illiterate Africans ignored the dynamic everyday interactions between readers and nonreaders in colonial West Africa, where texts such as newspapers and posters could be rapidly mobilized across diverse sectors of the population. Many West African governors on the ground were aware of the irrelevance of such dichotomies: for them, audiences in "relatively primitive" colonies lacked the cultural and literary sophistication of metropolitan readerships and required greater official surveillance and intervention than audiences at home. In such circumstances, newspapers controlled by a foreign-educated African intelligentsia could be deemed harmful at *all* levels of colonial society. As Sir Thomas Shenton Whitelegge Thomas, governor of the Gold Coast, wrote in 1934: "It is the illiterates who are affected most, and young semi-educated men. They have the paper read to them and lap up all they hear."[10] "With the ever increasing input of unemployed semi-literates," agreed Henry

William Bamford, the Gold Coast inspector general of police, "there are more readers to accept as truth what they see in print, and the irresponsible persons who turn out such distorted accounts of events and invariably provoke hostility towards Government measures should be checked."[11] According to this view, the minds of volatile and gullible African readers were clearly vulnerable to manipulation by better-educated anticolonial agitators.

By the late 1920s, in the face of mounting official concerns about the influx of American popular movies portraying sexual promiscuity, drinking, gambling, erotic dancing, and above all "racial feeling," the governor of the Gold Coast, Sir Frederick Gordon Guggisberg, expressed concerns about the impact of "border-line" North American movies upon African audiences.[12] The governors of other British colonies agreed with Guggisberg that "films made and exhibited in America . . . are not suitable for display" elsewhere.[13] These comments came in response to a confidential circular that was sent out in January 1927 by the secretary of state for the colonies, Leo Amery, to all governors of British colonies and protectorates. In it, Amery recognized the "special character and susceptibility of the native people," as compared with British audiences, and encouraged each governor to censor films or sections of films that might "arouse undesirable racial feeling by portraying aspects of the life of any section of His Majesty's subjects which, however innocent in themselves, are liable to be misunderstood by communities with other customs and traditions."[14] These official sensitivities about the misuse of "native" leisure time in the late 1920s were overlaid directly onto concerns about the role of printed texts in anticolonial agitation between the 1930s and 1950s, when the start of the Cold War combined with an intensification of "racial feeling" in the colonies. Even so, the majority of officials in London reiterated their belief that "on the point of principle . . . any kind of censorship is alien to our ideas."[15]

Such views about the peculiar susceptibility of native readers to alien ideas were not confined to European officials in the colonies. As the last chapter indicated, old-school African newspapermen sometimes commented disapprovingly on the libelous, sensational, or politically confrontational material produced by the newly educated generation in their communities. "There have arisen among us MEN who have set themselves among simple-minded folks as LEADERS who are out to show them the better way of dealing with their Government who have been called all sorts of names," claimed one editorial in the *Sierra Leone Weekly News* in July 1939. The paper was opposed to the role allegedly played by I. T. A. Wallace-Johnson and the West African Youth League in encouraging a mutiny of seventy-three African gunners, which resulted in the imprisonment of eleven young men for up to fifteen years each.[16] The editorial ended with a demand for British intervention to "save this land of God" from the anarchy of the Youth League and, in so doing, to protect "simple-minded folks" from further propaganda from self-appointed, false leaders.[17]

Obviously, the circulation of "irresponsible" printed material to readers in colonial settings could lead directly to problems for established local elites as well as for colonial regimes. Nevertheless, as the case studies will demonstrate, London tried—albeit with increasing difficulty—to maintain its policy of broad toleration toward the West African press, in keeping with metropolitan newspaper traditions. Press freedoms were synonymous with "our way of life," as the veteran editor and Labour Party member of Parliament (MP) Fenner Brockway stated in 1950 during his protest against the banning of George Padmore's *Britain's Third Empire* in the Gold Coast and East Africa.[18] By 8 May 1950, Padmore's book had been banned in five African colonies—Kenya, Uganda, Tanganyika, Gold Coast, and the Gambia—each time under executive powers assumed by individual governors rather than centrally from London.[19]

The broad liberalism of London toward West Africa contrasted with the Colonial Office's view of other British territories. In locations such as Cyprus, India, eastern Sarawak, and Malaya, for instance, press restrictions were often considered to be fully justified in the face of organized panregional networks of resistance to British rule. Thus, the censorship and banning of particular publications in Hong Kong and the Straits Settlements were deemed to be acceptable "because of the urgent importance of dealing with subversive Chinese activities."[20] The presence of a Chinese population in Sarawak, as well as in Malaya and Hong Kong, justified more stringent press controls than in Nigeria between the mid-1930s and late 1940s; similarly, the large Indian population in East Africa was seen to justify measures to control the press from 1915 onward.[21]

By 1940, censorship was in place in seven British colonies—Bermuda, British Guiana, Palestine, the Seychelles, the Straits Settlements, Trinidad, and Hong Kong—designed "to prevent the publication of matter likely to create racial or political difficulties," justified by wartime conditions.[22] But as the secretary of state for the colonies, Malcolm MacDonald (May 1938–May 1940), hastened to explain in 1940, the restrictions adopted in these colonies did not represent "political censorship" in that they did not "operate against the expression of political opinions on the grounds that the political views expressed differ from those held by the authorities."[23] Rather, the censorship was aimed at "prevent[ing] the circulation of material which would provoke ill-feeling between the various races in the colony or matter which it is apprehended may lead to any serious form of disorder in the Colony."[24]

In contrast to these other colonies, British West Africa was not deemed by the Colonial Office to be sufficiently "disordered," ethnically mixed, geographically strategic, or politically volatile to merit such punitive measures, and for most of the 1930s, senior Colonial Office staff remained skeptical about the imposition of newspaper restrictions in West Africa. "I find it hard to believe that the position in the Gold Coast is so serious as to warrant our introducing Press legislation on the lines of that existing in Cyprus where conditions are peculiar," commented one senior civil servant in 1934.[25]

Newspapers in West Africa were not ignored by officials in London, however. From the early twentieth century onward, extensive debates took place in the Colonial Office about each press-related ordinance stemming from these territories. In numerous detailed memos, staff at the Colonial Office reflected upon the tension between establishing "fair"—that is, universally applicable—legal principles, on the one hand, and respecting local specificities and the wishes of individual governors, on the other hand. The ethos at the Colonial Office, from the 1920s until the 1940s, seems to have been to encourage as much legislative consistency as possible between colonies while simultaneously and contradictorily attempting to accommodate the different legal responses generated by local conditions.

This impossible balancing act between universally applicable principles and "local conditions" generated numerous tensions in British policy and characterized colonial press relations in West Africa for the first half of the twentieth century. The view from London was that "only a strict local censorship in each separate territory can really be effective since the interpretation of what is or is not undesirable must in each instance depend largely upon special local conditions, and what is harmless in London may well be, and often is, open to grave objection in a colony."²⁶ Yet one of the problems for officials in London was that different colonies, including near neighbors such as Nigeria, Sierra Leone, and the Gold Coast, introduced different press regulations at different moments in order to deal with editors who were members of pan-West African networks, avid readers of one another's papers, and familiar with the press regulations of neighboring territories. "As has been remarked more than once," wrote Alex Fiddian in a frustrated memo to his Whitehall colleagues, "the West African Governments make it a point of honour never, if they can help it, to find out what the other West African Governments are doing."²⁷ "Colonial Governments may find it helpful to have some information and advice about the difficult subject of Press legislation before the Bills are finally drafted," a secret Colonial Office memo tactfully suggested many years later, in 1949, before inviting local officials to seek guidance from the center in their efforts to control local newspapers in their territories.²⁸

Such a lack of uniformity allowed local African elites constantly to compare and contrast the statutes of other colonies with one another in the pages of the press and to highlight the disparities. Thus, editors in Sierra Leone and the Gold Coast reacted nervously in 1903 when legislation to prevent the publication of libelous and seditious material was introduced to the Colony of Lagos under the Ordinance for Regulating the Printing and Publishing of Newspapers.²⁹ Triggered by the constant attacks on the administration in the Lagos press and inspired by similar press laws in Trinidad, this act introduced a compulsory yet prohibitive bond of £600,³⁰ designed as a deposit to set against any future penalties that proprietors might incur for material proven in the courts to be seditious or libelous, particularly in cases where the anonymous or pseudonymous authors of articles could not be identified and brought to justice.³¹

African editors were unanimous in their opposition to the Nigerian law, fearing its rapid transportation across British West African borders. Aware of Britain's liberal tradition of press freedoms—and full of the print bias described in the last chapter—editors argued that newspapers were the sole vehicles for African political representation and therefore should not be regulated. The Lagos administration's unpopular proposals would not only ring "a death-knell to the newspapers" but also "kill public opinion in its embryo."³² In addition to public protests in Lagos and a petition to the House of Commons in London, there was opposition to the 1903 ordinance on the part of all three African members of the

Legislative Council in Lagos—Hon. C. J. George, Hon. Dr. O. Johnson, and Hon. C. A. Sapara Williams—each of whom agreed that "public opinion was just being formed under the fostering care of the newspapers."³³ To impose a registration fee on local proprietors, they argued, would inhibit the establishment of new presses and "throttle freedom of expression."³⁴ A bond of £250 was finally introduced as part of this bill.³⁵

Often part of imperial networks stretching from the West Indies to Southeast Asia, East Africa, and West Africa, British colonial governors possessed considerable experience in managing emergent print cultures in the colonies. Many governors had worked in diverse regions of the empire before being transferred to West Africa. The profile of Sir Shenton Thomas, governor of the Gold Coast from 1932 to 1934, typifies these imperialist networks and biographies: in total, he had a thirty-year career in colonial service, starting his administrative training in Kenya in 1909 and then taking up positions in Uganda, Nigeria, and the Gold Coast before his appointment as governor of Nyasaland in 1929. After two years back in the Gold Coast, he went to Malaya as governor in 1934 and served there until 1942.³⁶ When it suited officials such as Shenton Thomas—whose unpopular newspaper regulations, which will be discussed, were inspired by clauses taken from similar ordinances in Hong Kong, Cyprus, Tanzania, and Nigeria—colonized populations worldwide could be regarded as a similar type of native, as a homogeneous imperial readership in a colonial world that required legal standardization. Thus, Governor Thomas carefully consulted other colonial statute books before tabling his new antisedition laws in 1934.³⁷

In the face of such panimperial homogenizing tendencies and in the face of local editors' own networks and cross-comparisons between colonies, civil servants in London scrutinized new ordinances for their fairness in relation to other territories. In the process, the Colonial Office acted as a legislative and public relations hub, trying to extrapolate principles from the executive actions of governors who were, on occasion, more irritable than rational in their ad hoc decisions. Against this quest for parity, however, in numerous scrawled memos officials in London regularly reminded one another that local populations in the colonial world were too heterogeneous for verbatim borrowings from one another's statute books. Though they sometimes yearned for standardization across regions and certainly insisted upon uniformity in halting the circulation of communist and anticolonial publications after the mid-1930s, the impracticality and undesirability of achieving legislative coherence across the British Empire was recognized as a principle in London.

This lack of legislative uniformity between British colonies allowed the most politically challenged officials to cherry-pick freely from the diversity of ordinances enacted worldwide and to attempt to justify their most punitive measures by referring to the existence of the same ordinances, or legal precedents, in British colonies elsewhere. As Fiddian recognized in relation to this practice in the 1930s, "If you collected the most drastic clauses of the press laws of some dozen different colonies (as, for instance, Cyprus in 1930 and since), you could make out a pretty draconian code."[38]

In the colonies, as Fiddian realized, officials would cross-refer to precedents in India, Cyprus, and elsewhere, seeking legally defensible methods to prove seditious "intention." In November 1938, for example, the Gold Coast attorney general, Henry William Butler Blackall, wrote, "Owing to the similarity of local conditions in West Africa to those in India, the 'Law of Crime' by Ratanlal and Thakore is worthy of perusal."[39] Problematically and paradoxically, Blackall then used this alleged similarity with India to assert the irreducible specificity of local conditions in each and every British colony. "Attention is particularly invited to the reference to the case of Kaly Nath Roy 1920," he wrote, "in which it appears that the Privy Council laid down that—'Once it appears that the principles of the law of sedition have been rightly understood by the local tribunal, the question whether those principles have been properly applied is so much in the nature of a question of fact and depends so largely upon local conditions that it is difficult for the Board to interfere on this ground with the conclusions arrived at by the Courts in India.'"[40]

Blackall thus asserted the universality of a principal of nonintervention from London on the basis of the latter's ignorance of local conditions. The universal melted into the local in this view: irreducible and absolute cultural differences, understood only by colonial officials with local knowledge, were put forward as universal legal principles.

Though there was no doubt in London that colonial officials should not be permitted to suppress key principles of press freedom, the Colonial Office nevertheless showed sensitivity toward British administrators. This was particularly true when anticolonial editors printed politically inflammatory articles in their papers, hiding their contributors' identities behind untraceable pseudonyms while openly naming and insulting

British officials and procolonial Africans. When it came to press censorship and the banning of imported publications, they agreed with Blackall that "the decision on so delicate an issue depends to a very large extent on the particular local circumstances, which only the Governor is really in a position to assess."[41] Blackall's principle of local irreducibility gained widespread acceptance in London with the intensification of organized, international anticolonial movements, often connected in officials' minds with sponsorship and subversive literature going to the colonies through political networks stretching into the Soviet Union.

As the actions of Governor Shenton Thomas and his successor, Sir Arnold Weinholt Hodson, would demonstrate, however, seditious libel and seditious or malicious intent on the part of pseudonymous journalists were considerably more controversial with reading publics in London and the colonies, and more difficult to prove in court, than these governors hoped or imagined. West African journalists and their supporters were capable of creating significant public relations problems for the British when they brought their cases for press freedom, their arguments for the necessity of a liberal public sphere, and their insistence on preservation of the principle of pseudonymity directly to the heart of "enlightenment" in London.

THE UNMASKING OF "EFFECTIVE" IN COLONIAL GHANA

In the mid-1930s, two foreign-educated West African activists, Isaac Theophilis Akunna Wallace-Johnson of Sierra Leone (1894–1965) and Benjamin Nnamdi Azikiwe of Nigeria (1904–96), arrived in the Gold Coast and entered the country's vibrant and politically confrontational arena of journalism. Wallace-Johnson, a friend of George Padmore, was a trade union activist, journalist, contributor to the *Negro Worker*, and zealous convert to communism. He arrived in the Gold Coast in November 1933 via Hamburg, Moscow, and Nigeria to continue his career in political journalism, using his own name as well as various pseudonyms.[42] Meanwhile, Azikiwe had finished his studies at Howard University and Lincoln University in the United States and returned to West Africa in November 1934 to take up the editorship of the *African Morning Post* in Accra. According to some, this job was made available at the invitation of the *Post*'s proprietor, Alfred John Ocansey, a businessman and the owner of various presses and cinemas in the Gold Coast.[43] According to British secret service reports and Azikiwe's own account, however, Zik contacted Ocansey in person to request the position, and the *Post* was established as a new daily paper for him to edit.⁴⁴ Whatever the case, Ocansey was already under close British surveillance as the publisher of the oppositional *Gold Coast Spectator* and proprietor of the *African Morning Post*, as a recipient of copies of the communist and antiracist *Negro World*, and as a regular correspondent with the known "subversive" George Padmore.⁴⁵ The arrival of Azikiwe in Ocansey's office would have aroused immediate suspicion among officials about the two men's political intentions.

Many West African newspapermen articulated resistance to British colonialism through nation-centered as well as pan–West African and pancolonial networks in the 1930s and 1940s, but Azikiwe and Wallace-Johnson were exceptional for the manner in which they triggered legal and structural transformations in the relationship between colonial regimes and the local press. To many British officials in the Gold Coast and to Sir Philip Cunliffe-Lister, secretary of state for the colonies in London between November 1931 and June 1935, the arrival of Wallace-Johnson and Azikiwe marked the final transformation of the Gold Coast from the quietly progressive colony that Governor Guggisberg had created prior to the Great Depression into a location where the natives and the press closely resembled what one exasperated educator described as "jolly old India."⁴⁶

Singly, each of these men was a thorn in the side of the colonial regime. But when they joined forces on the *African Morning Post* at the start of 1935, writing anonymous and pseudonymous columns as well as race-conscious material under their own names, they generated considerable consternation among government officials in Accra, especially because both men worked alongside known "link subversives" in the country. Among these was William Esuman Gwira (or Kobina) Sekyi (1892–1956), who was under close secret surveillance for his anticolonial views and for his correspondence with a number of foreign anticolonialists, including George Padmore.⁴⁷ Together, these "active seditionists," as Cunliffe-Lister labeled the opponents of imperialism, used newspapers as a vehicle for political agitation, drawing readers' attention to the work of Marcus Garvey and Padmore and disseminating what Rev. Charles Kingsely Williams in Accra described in alarm as "literature from subversive Negro societies in America" and "revolutionary stuff from communist blokes."⁴⁸

Arriving in the colony a year apart, Azikiwe and Wallace-Johnson widened the gulf already opened between journalists and the government by outspoken critics of imperialism such as Sekyi and Ocansey, and they made texts and ideas available locally that further rattled British colonial self-confidence. Already, between March and December 1933, the Colonial Office had been compiling a list of "all persons known by the local authorities to be in contact with such groups as the Communist Party, the International Trade Union Committee of Negro Workers (ITUC-NW), the International League Against Imperialism, the Negro Welfare Association, and the Red International of Labour Unions (RILU) or Profintern."[49] In the Gold Coast, as Stanley Shaloff notes in his comprehensive study of Ghanaian press controls in the mid-1930s, "anyone who distributed publications which either advocated or tacitly approved of breaches of the law, or tended to encourage treasonable action" was placed under close observation.[50]

Commenting on the political atmosphere in colonial Ghana at this time, Shaloff remarks that "some administrators became almost paranoid in their fear of a communist plot behind any opposition to government policy."[51] This paranoia would have been fed, on a daily basis, by newspapers such as the *Gold Coast Leader* (1902–c. 1934), the *Gold Coast Spectator* (1927–55), the *African Morning Post* (1934–55), the *West African Times* (1931–35), and many others. All of these papers regularly carried articles that criticized administrators, condemned colonialism, embraced pan-Africanism (and sometimes also communism), attacked proimperial Africans, and criticized government policies with apparent impunity from prosecution.[52] For officials, then, the Gold Coast press had run out of control.

The arrival of Wallace-Johnson in November 1933 in the politically and economically charged environment of a colony that was still reeling from the effects of the Great Depression, with such an outspoken and volatile press, was so intolerable to the governor, Sir Shenton Thomas, that some commentators have suggested the two ordinances he tabled in January 1934 were specifically designed to silence this activist's voice and to limit the impact of his ideas upon Gold Coast society.[53] The Criminal Code (Amendment) Ordinance and its companion act, the Newspapers, Books and Printing Presses Ordinance, were inspired by and modeled upon similar legislation in Cyprus and Hong Kong. Both measures were designed to counteract what the regime regarded as deliberate misrepresentations of government policy in the press.

In fact, though, the former measure predated the arrival of Wallace-Johnson in the Gold Coast, so it cannot be attributed directly to his activities: the Sedition Bill, as it came to be known, was first proposed not by Shenton Thomas but by his chief commissioner, Harry Scott Newlands, in January 1933, ten months ahead of Wallace-Johnson's arrival in the country. In private correspondence with the Colonial Office, Newlands demanded legislation to halt what he condemned as the "constant stream of innuendo, imputations of unworthy motives, unfair criticisms and charges of breach of faith" faced by Gold Coast officials in the local newspapers.[54] In a clear example of the "paranoid" connection of political criticism with communism, Newlands also insisted that the press should be "put under reasonable control as soon as possible to suppress subversive Communist propaganda" and that the British government should act quickly to halt the development of radicalized, race-conscious elements in the colony.[55]

Governor Thomas stood in the shadow of Governor Guggisberg, whose lengthy and popular regime from 1919 to 1927 coincided with a postwar economic boom that provided Africans with opportunities for education and advancement in colonial society. Sir Shenton, by contrast, was appointed in the immediate aftermath of the Great Depression, which had devastated the economies of British West Africa and contributed to riots and disturbances in the early 1930s.[56] Appointed in November 1932, he rapidly gained a reputation with African commentators as an intransigent and racially arrogant individual, and he fed local discontent by approving frequent furloughs for European members of the administration, who continued to travel to England on full pay at a time of economic instability and retrenchment of African workers. Moreover, unlike Guggisberg, who liberally encouraged African self-expression in the press and nurtured a cadre of "civilized" Africans at Achimota School (established in 1927), Sir Shenton made no secret of his belief that, as he informed a meeting of senior officials at the Colonial Office in June 1934, "the proprietors and editors of the Gold Coast newspapers could hardly be described as civilized."[57]

In addition to modifications to the Criminal Code, Governor Thomas also wished to extend the Gold Coast's Book and Newspaper Registration Ordinance of 1897 and the Newspaper Registration Ordinance of 1894 in order to empower the courts to suspend a newspaper from publication for up to three years for material deemed seditious by the governor-in-council. As part of this process, he also wished to outlaw pseudonymous writing; to introduce a character test before allowing an editor to take charge of a newspaper; to introduce the compulsory registration of newspapers; and to prohibit any proprietor convicted of seditious publication from involvement with newspapers in the future, whether as a publisher, editor, journalist, or sponsor.[58] In keeping with other West African colonies, the governor also wished to compel newspaper proprietors to pay a bond of £200 "to secure the payment of any fine which may be imposed upon the proprietor, publisher, printer or editor" and to cover "any damages (and costs) that may be awarded in any action for libel in respect of any matter appearing in the newspaper."[59]

With this raft of measures in place, editors and proprietors would be held responsible and liable for all material published in their newspapers, including pseudonymous items where the actual author's identity could not be established.[60] "Judging by what I know of the local press, and the present behavior of some of the intelligentsia, I should think this is a very sensible provision," commented Fiddian at the Colonial Office, in a scrawled marginal note.[61] To the consternation of Fiddian and his colleagues, however, Governor Thomas took the sedition legislation several steps further than in other British colonies. For instance, he included, in the category of printed documents, "anything typewritten or roneoed," and his definition of a printing press included, in Fiddian's words, "the typewriter, Roneo and Ormig or even a dish of gelatin properly prepared for reproducing copies!"[62] Furthermore, in contrast to antisedition legislation passed in 1927 in Nigeria, he claimed powers for the governor-in-council to prohibit the importation of *any* printed materials, rather than limiting the application of his amendment only to materials deemed to be seditious by his council or the Colonial Office. He did not provide legal protection for individuals "in innocent possession of seditious literature" who, in the proposals, would face prison terms of up to seven years.[63]

The legal adviser to the Colonial Office in London, Sir Kenneth Roberts-Wray, described these penalties as "absolutely preposterous," and in a move that undermined the entire rationale behind the governor's amendment, he suggested that the possession of seditious literature should not be deemed an offense at all.[64] In this, he was overruled, perhaps because Colonial Office staff had started to express concerns about the effects of imported publications on the minds of British colonial subjects. As a result of such concerns, 1934 witnessed the first in a series of secret dispatches from the secretary of state for the colonies to all governors, containing lists of specific publications to be prohibited throughout the British colonial world. By this point, increasing quantities of supposedly seditious materials were arriving in Gold Coast ports. In June 1934, the inspector general of police reported that "in 1931 the number of copies of various publications found and destroyed was approximately 76; in 1932 it was approximately 940; and in 1933 it was 1,750, of which 1,100 copies were of the 'Negro Worker,' a communist North American journal which preached revolution against colonialism and white domination."[65]

Unsurprisingly, Gold Coast newspapers vigorously condemned Shenton Thomas's proposals. What is striking about their numerous editorials, articles, and letters on this topic is the way in which contributors made use of excessive, spectacular language, as if pseudonymous authors wished to act out or reperform the very substance of the governor's complaints against them. Capitalizing on what might be their last moments of free printed expression, pseudonymous correspondents and critics of the regime provocatively deployed a language that was at once seditious and libelous and also playfully parodic of seditious and libelous discourse. An example of this parodic approach toward official concerns about print appeared in a series of articles for the "Women's Corner" (also known as the "Ladies' Corner") of the *Times of West Africa* by "Marjorie Mensah," whose pseudonym is discussed in more detail in chapter 6:[66] "If this bill is passed, I may find myself one fine day between the unprepossessing hard-faced stern-looking, horrid men just perhaps by making a remark that His Excellency is not as attractive as before, having noticed one or two wrinkles in his rather handsome countenance. Wouldn't that be too dreadful?"[67] Marjorie comically trivialized the governor's concerns about sedition, while gently perpetuating the carnal discourse that had so infuriated the regime in recent months.

These responses reveal the way in which the techniques of satire — the art of excessive representation — were used to highlight the regime's own legislative overreaction to the problem of critical journalism. The strongly personalized, visceral caricatures of Shenton Thomas and his officials that appeared in the press seemed to play games with the limits of free speech, parodically demonstrating to the governor what was and what was not beyond the limits of acceptability. The targets of the proposed new legislation thus used satirical abuse in order to turn the governor into their own target. In acting out the governor's logic — his abhorrence of print-covered pseudonymous voices, his need to enforce visibility, his rejection of excessively critical opinions about the regime—the newspapers demonstrated their capacity to get under the governor's skin even as they simultaneously inflated that skin through caricature and abuse. The excessively carnal descriptions of the governor also demonstrated the extent to which press etiquette had changed in a colony where editors had, in previous decades, generally followed the "gentlemen's agreement" described in chapter 2, which held that to indulge in "personality" was inappropriate to printed debates about government policy.

Shenton Thomas had not sought advice from the Colonial Office before drafting his bills, and having drawn up the legislation, he left for England, preceded by a secret telegram to the Colonial Office claiming that any opposition to the measures was a "result of newspaper agitation supported by Wallace-Johnson," rather than a reflection of genuinely indigenous African concerns.[68] Lacking public relations skills, Shenton Thomas simply announced, in his *Extraordinary Gazette* of 21 February 1934, that the Criminal Code (Amendment) Ordinance was designed to "protect" Africans from malign external forces among them and would "not affect the right of the Press or of any person to make a fair criticism of the Government or any Government proposal."[69] He made no effort to liaise with local editors about his proposals, which occurred at precisely the moment when African-owned newspapers expanded in number, in readership, and in political assertiveness. Worse still, his refusal to engage in dialogue with local elites included the African "unofficial" members of his own Legislative Council, who unanimously opposed the measures. Instead, in a telegram to the secretary of state for the colonies dated 26 March 1934, the governor expressed his wish to override the African members of the Legislative Council, to rush the amendment into law, and to prohibit "certain subversive literature" with immediate effect.[70]

The governor's accusation that Wallace-Johnson was behind local newspaper agitation was inaccurate. Opposition came from the entire spectrum of the colony's political organizations and presses, including the archconservative editor of the *Gold Coast Independent*, Frederick Victor Nanka-Bruce, and the procolonial paramount chief Nana Sir Ofori Atta, both of whom were sworn enemies of the so-called seditionists. Even Akilagpa Sawyerr of the conservative Ratepayers Association in Accra—who was, like his political ally Nanka-Bruce, "a man not noted for radicalism"—opposed the need for the ordinance on the grounds that it devalued Gold Coasters' patriotic loyalty to the British

Empire.⁷¹ Of course, opposition also came from the ardent anticolonialist Kobina Sekyi and the Aborigines Rights Protection Society in Cape Coast, from J. B. Danquah and his *Times of West Africa*, and from Azikiwe and the *African Morning Post*, among many others.

With full press coverage in Britain and West Africa and with the support of British-based organizations such as the West African Students Union (WASU) and the League Against Imperialism, in July 1934 two rival delegations arrived in London to petition the secretary of state for the colonies against the new restrictions.⁷² The petitioners believed the imperial center would be more receptive to arguments for press freedom than regimes in the colonies that were, by definition, interventionist and paternalistic. In asserting an idea of shared imperial citizenship between West Africa and London—albeit from an embarrassingly divided platform—the petitioners recognized and sought to exploit the triangle of tensions between colonial governors, British public opinion, and staff at the Colonial Office.⁷³

At the Colonial Office, however, Fiddian and his colleagues remained convinced that the petitioners had no cause for concern, not least because while Shenton Thomas was in Britain, Acting Governor Geoffrey Northcote had liaised with African members of the Legislative Council and modified the Sedition Bill to bring it into line with a similar Nigerian antisedition law of 1927.⁷⁴ The modified proposals were both justified and fair, in the view of Colonial Office staff, and the secretary of state allowed the Criminal Code (Amendment) Ordinance to pass into law. Meanwhile, Sir Shenton's second proposed ordinance was quietly dropped, for when asked whether the Newspapers, Books and Printing Presses Ordinance should pass into law, the incoming governor, Sir Arnold Hodson, "expressed himself as definitely opposed to any attempt to put the Press in leading strings [i.e., walking reins] and he wanted first to see what he could effect by a 'softly, softly' policy."⁷⁵

In approving the passage of the Sedition Bill, officials in London had failed to appreciate the negative impact of Sir Shenton's leadership style on local public relations as mediated by the press. Rather, they judged the fairness and legality of the draft ordinance with the wider stability of British West Africa—and the British Empire—in view. They took for granted the need to balance freedom of expression with the paternalistic need to protect "half-educated" African readers from manipulation by foreign-trained political agitators.⁷⁶ For literate elites in the Gold Coast, by contrast, the attempted clampdown on the press soured relations with the colonial regime, even as it confirmed the success of West African newspapers as a platform for protest.

A marked hardening of official attitudes toward the native press occurred at that point. Governors became convinced that the "red peril" was spreading across the colonial world and into Africa, and increasingly, they "seemed determined to interpret the expression of any nationalist sentiment as a seditious statement."[77] At the same time, the activities of anticolonial newspapermen encapsulated a new current in colonial West Africa, in which journalists used print deliberately and provocatively to attack colonial regimes, employing pseudonyms but more and more often also their own proper names to challenge the legitimacy of British colonialism. In this climate, several West African governors took executive action in an effort to prevent a rise in politically inflammatory journalism from editors and pseudonymous correspondents who appeared to be intentionally misrepresenting government policies to native populations.

In the Gold Coast, the Sedition Bill was deployed only once, in a sensational case that demonstrates the striking incompatibility between British principles of press liberalism, on the one hand, and the imperialist need to suppress anticolonial critique, on the other hand. Sir Arnold Weinholt Hodson's arrival on the Gold Coast in October 1934 had been greeted with relief and hope in the pages of the press. Hodson had been governor of Sierra Leone and had gained a reputation in London for calmness and maturity in the government of West Africa.[78] "In my opinion," he informed Sir Philip Cunliffe-Lister in November 1934, "the present time is inopportune for introducing further legislation to control the press and regulate the printing and publication of newspapers."[79] Explicitly positioning himself against the overly reactionary legislation of his predecessor, Hodson attempted to temper the confrontational atmosphere in the Gold Coast with his "softly, softly policy." "The tone of the local press has undoubtedly left much to be desired for some time past," he wrote, "but I question whether it has been worse than in many other Colonies."[80]

This honeymoon period was terminated by the publication of a short article entitled "Has the African a God?" in the *African Morning Post* on 15 May 1936. Written under the pseudonym "Effective" and therefore, in a post–Sedition Bill context, legally the responsibility of Azikiwe as editor, the offending article "created a sensation in Accra":[81]

Personally, I believe the European has a God in whom he believes and whom he is representing in his churches all over Africa. He believes in the god whose name is spelt *deceit*. He believes in the god whose law is "Ye strong, you must weaken the weak." Ye "civilised" Europeans, you must "civilise" the "barbarous" Africans with machine guns. Ye "Christian" Europeans, you must "christianise" the "pagan" Africans with bombs, poison gases, etc.

In the colonies the Europeans believe in the god that commands: "Ye Administrators, make Sedition Bill to keep the African gagged. Make Forced Labour Bill to work the Africans as slaves. Make Deportation Ordinance to send Africans to exile whenever they dare to question your authority. Make an Ordinance to grab his money so that he cannot stand economically. Make Levy Bill to force him to pay taxes for the importation of unemployed Europeans to serve as Stool Treasurers. Send detectives to stay around the house of any African who is nationally conscious and who is agitating for national independence and if possible round him up in a "criminal frame-up" so that he could be kept behind bars.[82]

Staff at the Colonial Office believed that "the article in question . . . is not so very much worse than what the *African Morning Post* usually publishes" and, furthermore, that it "hardly amounts to what we regard as sedition."[83] Hodson and his administrators disagreed: oversensitized by the tone of Azikiwe's press, they interpreted the piece to be an overtly seditious incitement to popular discontent in the Gold Coast. Ignoring the playfulness behind the pseudonymous Effective's use of the phrase "personally, I believe" and rejecting the fact that no specific colony, European power, or actual ordinance was named in the piece, they insisted that the article was replete with seditious intentionality.[84]

The manner in which they furnished evidence of this bears some examination, for in making their case, British officials unwittingly performed the sole interpretive maneuver required by Effective to render the article seditious in intent. In order to demonstrate the local specificity behind the writer's generalized statements about European colonialism, officials mapped a recent piece of Gold Coast legislation onto each mock ordinance listed in the article. Where the article satirically misnamed a range of Gold Coast ordinances—the "Forced Labour Bill," the "Deportation Bill," the "Ordinance to grab his money"— British officials carefully translated each measure back into legislation recently introduced to the Gold Coast statute books. In so doing, they offered a lesson in practical criticism, demonstrating how to undertake a seditious reading, and they showed, at the same time, that seditious intent lies as much with the reader as with the author of such nonspecific material as Effective's article.

The case is marked by another ironic reversal. To unmask the identity of Effective, the regime performed—indeed, it had been performing for many months already—the very surveillance operations suggested by the author of the article in his reference to detectives' efforts to "stay around the house of any African who is nationally conscious" in the hope of achieving a "frame-up." Thus, less than ten days after publication, conclusive evidence of Effective's identity was discovered inside packages intercepted by colonial spies. The packages were posted by Wallace-Johnson to the League Against Imperialism and the Negro Welfare Association in London, and they contained typewritten copies of "Has the African a God?" together with duplicates of other "embargoed" materials.[85] The regime's most detested "Bolschevik" agitator was immediately charged with sedition under the Criminal Code. Indeed, Governor Hodson wasted no time in prosecuting both Wallace-Johnson, as author, and Azikiwe, as editor. Simultaneously—in a maneuver that was as politically desperate as it was politically transparent—he started to draft new legislation for the deportation of foreigners convicted of sedition in the Gold Coast.

At separate hearings, both riddled with procedural anomalies, each man was found guilty, but to the irritation of senior officials, both walked free from court, having been given the option (as was usual in such cases) to pay a £50 fine rather than to face six months' imprisonment. These guilty verdicts could not have been reached without the court having access to the two men's so-called proper names: Azikiwe and Wallace-Johnson were in the dock, not Zik and Effective. In this way, the most controversial part of Shenton Thomas's legislation—the requirement for seditious intention to be attributed to a named, unmasked person—was deployed to engineer the trial of the regime's most vocal antagonists. In particular, as Wallace-Johnson's editor and ally and as the person responsible, by proxy, for the intentions of all of his pseudonymous contributors, Azikiwe was drawn into the legal consequences of publishing material that the authorities regarded as seditious.

Some months later, in the West African Court of Appeal in March 1937, Azikiwe's lawyer, the veteran Sierra Leonean barrister Frans

Dove,[86] cleverly exploited a loophole in English law regarding the legal status of proper names in relation to pseudonyms. "The popular identification of Zik with Azikiwe and Azikiwe with the *African Morning Post*," Dove argued, might have some truth value in the public sphere, but it "meant nothing to the law."[87] Though Azikiwe was indeed the editor of the *African Morning Post*, the prosecutors had furnished no evidence to prove that he was the same person as Zik, whose name appeared as editor on the day of the appearance of "Has the African a God?" And consequently, they also could not prove beyond reasonable doubt that Azikiwe had "either authorized, elicited, or inserted Wallace-Johnson's article in the paper on that date."[88] To the frustration of the regime, Azikiwe walked free on the basis of this legal loophole, holding the refund of his £50 fine amid scenes of "hilarious uproar" in the courtroom and "singing, dancing and merrymaking" outside.[89] His proper name had been cleared: only his popular pseudonym, disembodied in print, was guilty of sedition.

Azikiwe thus escaped attribution through the loophole provided by his nickname, but the pseudonymous Effective was caught red-handed through the package intercepted by colonial secret services. Within eighteen months of Dove's coup with nomenclature, however, Wallace-Johnson's legal team would use a similar tactic to devastating and humiliating effect to outwit the colonial authorities in Sierra Leone (see the second case study later in this chapter). On this occasion, though, Wallace-Johnson failed to have his verdict overturned in the West African Court of Appeal. Remarkably, given its lack of specificity, "Has the African a God?" was found to have met both of Shenton Thomas's definitions of seditious intention: "(1) to bring into hatred or contempt or to excite disaffection against the person of His Majesty, His heirs or successors or the Government of the Colony as by law established, or (2) to bring about a change in the sovereignty of the colony."[90]

Wallace-Johnson left for London, where, supported by Sir Stafford Cripps and the National Council for Civil Liberties, he prepared a successful case requesting further leave to appeal. He lost this final appeal before the Privy Council, however, on the grounds that "the words themselves," as printed on the page, furnished irrefutable evidence of seditious intention.[91] Meanwhile, Wallace-Johnson's legal team tried to argue that "extrinsic evidence of intention," such as riots or outbreaks of anticolonial violence, was necessary in order to furnish proof of seditious intention.[92] The Privy Council rejected the introduction of contexts and held firm to its model of close reading, confirming the view of the attorney general of the Gold Coast that "the difference in tone and spirit and general drift between a writer who is trying to stir up ill will and one who is not is generally unmistakable."[93]

This British belief that authorial intentionality could be extrapolated from the "tone," "spirit," and "general drift" of a publication that, in itself, contained no explicit place-names or references carried numerous problematic assumptions about reading and interpretation, particularly in relation to a text written under a pseudonym with all the flexibility, inventiveness, playfulness, and performativity such ventriloquism implied. In proving seditious intention beyond doubt, the British legal system insisted upon reattaching the contents of the article to a named, culpable body—first to Azikiwe and then to Wallace-Johnson—but it did so, perversely, precisely in order to refute the author's explanations about the context and social effects of his article in the world beyond the printed page. Entangled in a fallacy of textual objectivity, the Privy Council in London, like the Gold Coast courts before it, preferred to assume that reading and interpretation took place in a vacuum, unaffected by factors such as their own imperial power, culture, history, and ideology. Nevertheless, as suggested previously, conclusive proof of the seditious content of this article could only be furnished through a translation of each veiled reference into a specific piece of Gold Coast legislation. Such a process, in other words, involved a deployment of similar contextual, off-page evidence to that excluded from Wallace-Johnson's defense.

In the intimate and bitter conflicts over attribution between colonial governors and African newspapermen, pseudonyms came to exemplify the incompatibility between liberal principles of freedom of expression and the imperialist desire to suppress anticolonial critique. "Has the African a God?" was interpreted by the colonial regime as evidence of an intention to destabilize the British Empire, but it was presented by Wallace-Johnson and the British civil liberties campaign as an expression of an author's "right, as a British subject of African descent, to discuss public affairs fully and freely" and under a pseudonym.[94] Although Azikiwe and Wallace-Johnson both narrowly avoided imprisonment on this occasion, the case of Effective's article illustrates the thin line between freedom of expression in the colonies and the imperialist need to control allegedly seditious journalism. This tension is dramatized even more vividly in the next case study, which examines the behavior of the

Sierra Leonean regime when faced with Wallace-Johnson—one of the most uncooperative newspapermen in West Africa—in the late 1930s.

"MR. WALLACE-JOHNSON PURE AND SIMPLE?":
REX VERSUS I. T. A. WALLACE-JOHNSON

Mr Johnson: In what capacity are you putting the question to me?

Mr Carew: As Mr Wallace-Johnson.

Mr Johnson: As Mr Wallace-Johnson pure and simple?

Capt. Callow: As Mr Wallace-Johnson[;] it may be that you are pure, but I am quite sure you are not simple.[95]

On 10 October 1938, "Mr Isaac Theophilus Akunna Wallace-Johnson of 4 Bombay Lane, Freetown," was subpoenaed to appear before a commission of inquiry into the publication of two leaked confidential dispatches between Sir Douglas James Jardine, governor of Sierra Leone, and the secretary of state for the colonies in London. Published in the *Sierra Leone Weekly News*, the secret documents conveyed the governor's concerns about the intensification of African labor agitation in Sierra Leone and the need to find means to suppress the politicization of workers by members of Wallace-Johnson's West African Youth League (established in June 1935), who were regarded as a significant communist threat to British colonial rule throughout the region. The publication of the dispatches led to mass meetings and demonstrations against the government in Freetown, protests to the secretary of state in London, questions in the House of Commons, and considerable embarrassment for Sir Douglas Jardine.[96] As Wallace-Johnson wrote in his commentary on the content of the secret dispatches, "*Truth* was actually crucified by some of the statements of the Governor" that were published in the *Weekly News* for all to see.[97]

In *Rex versus I. T. A. Wallace-Johnson*, the commissioners wished to find the defendant guilty of possession of these dispatches, which he had boldly declassified half a century ahead of time, and they wished to proceed to a criminal prosecution using his confession as evidence. They also wanted to discover how he had managed to intercept the documents and from whom this serious leakage had stemmed in the Colonial Office. Although there was no anonymity to protect in this case—indeed, the entire hearing revolved around the fact that the offending material was boldly signed "Wallace-Johnson, Organising

Secretary of the West African Youth League"—the defendant and his legal team seemed to draw inspiration and strategies from the region's long tradition of pseudonymous textual production and from precedents established in other West African court cases as they played cat and mouse with imperialist systems of naming.

Wallace-Johnson was no stranger to the colonial court system. He was known to the authorities throughout West Africa as a Soviet-trained "professional agitator."[98] Even as this case commenced, he had two other court cases under way. His appeal to the Privy Council in London against the guilty verdict for his allegedly seditious article "Has the African a God?" was in progress, and he was also awaiting trial on a charge of criminal libel brought by his archenemy, Herbert Bankole Bright, for two anonymous, satirical "Obituaries," copies of which the Youth League had posted around Freetown after the municipal elections of November 1938.[99]

The proceedings opened with a standard procedural question from the chair of the inquiry, Capt. Graham Callow. "You are the Organising Secretary of the West African Youth League?" Callow asked, following protocol. "I am not sure," came the cagey reply.[100] The defendant went on to inform his inquisitors that the subpoena "summoned [me] here in my private capacity" as Wallace-Johnson of 4 Bombay Lane.[101] Present as a "private individual" rather than as a public figure, the accused would not produce the correspondence required by the hearing, believed to contain evidence of how the organizing secretary of the Youth League had acquired the secret documents. "I am not in a position to say anything in my private capacity," he insisted again and again, and he repeatedly answered questions with vagaries such as "I am not sure," "I am not aware of anything," and "I cannot say."[102]

Wallace-Johnson would have learned about the British legal definition of a person's "capacity" in October 1933 during a police raid on his premises when he was secretary of the African Workers' Union of West Africa in Nigeria. Notebooks and correspondence were seized and confiscated during this raid, although no copies of the prohibited *Negro Worker* were discovered.[103] When Reginald Bridgeman of the League Against Imperialism wrote to the Colonial Office to protest the police intervention as "interference with the right of the African Workers to form a Trade Union," the governor of Nigeria answered that the "search warrant was not executed against Mr Wallace-Johnson in his capacity as Trade Union Secretary."[104] Rather, the search warrant was issued against Wallace-Johnson in his capacity as a person suspected to be in possession of seditious publications. Five years later, Wallace-Johnson must have relished the opportunity to use the regime's tactic against it.

From the outset, the defendant transformed the hearing into a piece of subversive absurdist theater (see appendix 1). When a second, third, and fourth commissioner took up the cross-examination, the case degenerated further into farce. "I think the name of Wallace-Johnson signed articles which were subsequently published, and the subpoena I take it was addressed to him in the name of Wallace-Johnson, so it would naturally compel him to say something?" Commissioner Carew asked cunningly, mimicking the defendant's logic, acknowledging the failure of the first-person pronoun, and attempting to catch him with his own discursive net. "I think you are only talking about what you think," came the equally cunning reply.[105]

The colonial legal system was incapable of accommodating the discursive strategies of this most agile of West African tricksters with his team of legal advisers who introduced instability into the very pronouns upon which the commissioners depended in order for the case to proceed. As the hearing progressed, the law court lost its gravitas and became, instead, the forum for a legal farce in which the juridical relationship between naming and culpability, rather than the leaked dispatches, took center stage. "Did you contribute these two articles to the *Weekly News?*" asked Mr. Carew, handing the offending newspaper to the defendant and pointing to the latter's name, clearly printed on each piece.[106] "No this is not a contribution of mine at all," Wallace-Johnson replied. "You notice your name appears?" Captain Callow interjected in support of Carew and the evidence printed before their eyes, only to be informed, in response, that "the name of the Organising Secretary of the Youth League appears there."[107]

The commissioners turned around the same obstruction for the duration of the hearing:

> Mr Beetham: Will you have a look at that signature and say if it is yours?
>
> Mr Johnson: It is the signature of the Organising Secretary of the West African Youth League.
>
> Mr Beetham: You know that?
>
> Mr Johnson: Yes, because I am connected with the League.
>
> Mr Beetham: What is your connection with the Youth League?

> **Mr Johnson:** I am the Organising Secretary of the West African Youth League.
>
> **Mr Beetham:** Did you write that? (Shown Exhibit No. 21 signed "Wallace-Johnson.")
>
> **Mr Johnson:** I do not know.
>
> **Mr Beetham:** You do not know?
>
> **Mr Johnson:** I do not know because I am not here to say whether I know.[108]

Aware of the seminal status of naming as a starting point for legal processes in the British judicial system, Wallace-Johnson and his large team of sixteen lawyers parodied and resisted the commissioners' insistence that he confess to *being* himself in court.[109] At all costs, the defendant had to avoid any admission that he was the source of the published material. Knowing that self-identification combined with confession to form the basis for the determination of guilt in British law, he simply refused to allow his body to be identified with his pen in the fixed, singular manner required by the system.[110] As with pseudonymous writers, an avoidance of attribution would secure his escape from retribution. Moreover, the presence of his legal team at the hearing—sixteen lawyers speaking on behalf of their client, creating his performance, intervening and conferring with one another on legal details—would have further complicated the system's demand for sincerity from the colonial subject standing before the commissioners with his unsure, slippery "I." Indeed, the fact that Wallace-Johnson "did not go into the witness box" at all or speak to the commissioners except through these sixteen lawyers added a further layer of complexity to the evasive "I" recorded in the transcripts.[111]

Wallace-Johnson carefully remained within the limits of colonial law throughout the hearing, toeing the boundary between legality and contempt in his refusal to be named, while exploiting, in justification, the very dichotomy between public and private that underpinned bourgeois British social values. The concept of privacy—and its ideological-cum-spatial accompaniment, the private sphere—dominated British domestic and legal ideologies and informed many of the assumptions about civilization and progress that legitimized imperial expansion.[112] Similarly, in order to avoid repercussions, the private "I" that Wallace-Johnson presented in court was carefully segregated from any form of public or print-mediated subjectivity.

This deployment of the public-versus-private divide was clearly a form of parodic mockery, driven by contempt for British colonial rule.[113] Interestingly, however, at no point in the cross-examination did any of the commissioners question the defendant's exploitation of this seminal dichotomy. Thus, when Captain Callow finally accepted that Wallace-Johnson would not yield his public "self," he attempted instead to encourage the "private individual" to express personal emotions about the case, including feelings of betrayal and trust:

Mr Johnson: . . . in the capacity I am here I am not in a position to say anything.

Capt. Callow: Do you feel if you did it would be a betrayal of trust?

Mr Johnson: I do not feel anything, but I have not anything to say as far as that is concerned, it is not a matter of feeling.[114]

When Wallace-Johnson was appealed to as a man of empathy and sincerity, his legal team immediately recognized the ruse. In responses such as this, the lawyers who represented the name Wallace-Johnson inserted their client not as an empathetic person but as a function of the colonial court system.

"I do not feel anything" is the polar opposite of liberal historians' desire for colonial subjectivity to be represented through interiority and pain in order to secure recognition within a humanist framework. Wallace-Johnson disavowed his identity as a man with thoughts, feelings, or personality. "Feeling," with its implications of continuous subjectivity and its expression of intention, is not accepted as a bridge to connect the private and the public selves. If parody is a parasitic form of discourse that echoes and acknowledges the targets from which it borrows its resources, always verging upon complicity, Wallace-Johnson evaded complicity with the system that he parodied by acting as a discursive function, rather than as a human subject.

In addition to its subversive exposure of British legal processes, "Rex versus Wallace-Johnson" contained a more respectful and less destructive form of borrowing or quotation. As a legal performance, the exchange between the leader of the West African Youth League and the representatives of the British regime resonated with a biblical legal precedent. In the trial of Jesus by Pilate, narrated in the book of John, the first question asked of Jesus by the Roman governor is, "Art thou the King of the Jews?"[115] Jesus's evasive reply problematizes the questioner's assumptions about identity: "Sayest thou this thing of thyself, or did others tell it thee of me?"[116] In an attempt to avoid the self-incriminating labels upon which the interrogation depends, the defendant explains, "My kingdom is not of this world . . . now is my kingdom not from hence":

> Pilate therefore said unto him, Art thou a king then?
>
> Jesus answered, Thou sayest that I am a king. To this end was I born, and for this cause came I into the world, that I should bear witness unto the truth. Every one that is of the truth heareth my voice.
>
> Pilate saith unto him, What is truth?[117]

This refusal to be named in a way that entraps one in a hostile legal system illustrates a similar process of oppositional resistance to that enacted by Wallace-Johnson in Freetown. In both cases, the powerless individual cunningly escapes from being named or interpolated by the state or ruling institution, and in both cases, the other side's legal rhetoric is contrasted with "truth" as a value upheld by the accused, extrinsic to the legal process. Legalistic modes of naming as a form of entrapment are thus set against morally absolute supralegal values.[118]

As with Malcolm X two decades later, Wallace-Johnson confronted the regime's system with its own naming practices and refused to collaborate with its strategies for entrapment. This individual, whose name carried so much celebrity status in public life and whose signed articles and ardent speeches found large publics in Sierre Leone, had clearly learned many lessons from pseudonymous contributors to the West African press. A master of evasion and parody, he politicized these lessons into a resistant anticolonial discourse that, discursively at least, defeated the colonial system at its own legal game.

"Fail at your peril," the summons had warned.[119] Any failure and imperilment, however, occurred on the colonial side in this case. After the closure of the hearing, when the transcripts were examined by the police magistrate, E. S. Beoku-Betts, no grounds could be found for a perjury charge, much to the commissioners' frustration. "Answers may not be full and satisfactory to the Commissioners," Beoku-Betts found, "but unless in addition they are proved not to be answered to the best of the knowledge and belief of the witness no criminal proceedings can succeed."[120] At no point did the witness make any statement that he "knew to be false" or statements that he did not "believe to be true."[121] Hoist with its own petard, the administration decided against issuing a further subpoena to Wallace-Johnson—in any capacity—in relation to this case. Fully aware of the publicity and celebrity that another such spectacle would generate for the very man who refused to be identified by their system, the legal adviser decided against a follow-up to the hearing; nor was the inquiry's report ever made public, a fact that Wallace-Johnson highlighted and ridiculed several months later in the *African Standard*.[122]

If Wallace-Johnson resisted the colonial legal insistence upon the acknowledgment of proper names and produced an exquisite piece of theater in the process, one less comedic consequence of the case was the further souring of the sensitive relations between rival factions of the Sierra Leonean press. When approached by the irate governor about the source of the leaked dispatches, the editor of the *Sierra Leone Weekly News* did not defend his correspondent but instead allegedly "directed Government to certain Ordinances which made provisions for such [court] action." He even went so far as to remind the governor of the option to imprison Wallace-Johnson for noncompliance if he did not disclose his own sources.[123] If true, such a betrayal of trust demonstrated the extremity of the rivalries between members of the Sierra Leonean press by the late 1930s.

Wallace-Johnson's court performance can be understood through several overlapping frameworks. His legal team combined the cunning of a West African folktale trickster with the obstructionism of a legal pedant, allowing their client to silently perform his anticolonial ideology without attracting either attribution or retribution from the court. Above all, the legal team exploited the region's long tradition of flexible naming practices that, when set against the rigidity of colonial legal processes, exposed the impotence of the British system. Even though the publications in question were anything but pseudonymous, the legal team's responses mocked the idea that an individual in colonial society should or could possess a singular proper name. In the manner of a person using multiple pseudonyms, the legal team injected Wallace-Johnson's given name with numerous alternative subject positions or "capacities," ranging from the public to the private, from the political leader to the ordinary citizen. In other words, they treated his printed name as if it were as mobile as a pseudonym. As they did this, they took West African traditions of flexible, multiple naming to new heights of political provocation and anticolonial resistance. Free to continue his political activities, for the time being at least, Wallace-Johnson went back into the city and continued to circulate his views freely for several years, "a matter [causing] . . . some apprehension to those who are responsible for the defences of the Colony."[124]

THE RISE OF CELEBRITY JOURNALISM

Azikiwe's and Wallace-Johnson's acts of naming in print were gestures of a new kind of political leadership. Unlike most earlier newspapermen, they adopted populist and charismatic styles, literally *pressing* their leadership claims into the colonial public sphere, disregarding notions of the neutrality of journalism as a fourth estate. Claiming celebrity status in the process, both men used print as well as public lectures to disseminate their radical views as widely as possible.

Celebrity—or rather, notoriety—became inextricable from the two men's political leadership claims, self-presentation, and public reception. Unlike the anonymous and pseudonymous newspaper contributors of earlier decades, they had a confrontational political style centered on the naming and shaming of antagonists, on the one hand, and the praising of named cultural heroes—including George Padmore and Marcus Garvey—on the other hand. On occasion, the latter process was undertaken through an inscription of themselves into the roll call of African heroes. Wallace-Johnson adopted a particularly self-aggrandizing rhetoric in his journalism, attributing praise names to himself such as "the Political Leopard of West Africa" and hailing his own political principles in an inflated language: "My life has been dedicated to the cause of Justice. With this as my Vanguard, I press towards the high calling for 'Liberty or death.'"[125] Both men thus benefited from continuities with established African praise-naming traditions in the performance of their power as political leaders.

The popular response to these individuals was overwhelming. "Azikiwe has undoubtedly won the admiration of the people of Nigeria for championing their cause," the Nigerian superintendent of police reported to the Colonial Office in 1941. Indeed, he continued, "they regard him almost as their 'idol.'"[126] Wallace-Johnson was also regarded as an "Inspirer and Hero" locally.[127] Under his "magic wand," venues such as Wilberforce Hall in Freetown were "transformed into a soothing well-spring where a thirsty community . . . eagerly assembled."[128]

Old-style African newspaper editors did not welcome the two men's apparent egotism or their vehement critiques of colonial rule. Frederick Victor Nanka-Bruce's *Gold Coast Independent* published numerous articles condemning Wallace-Johnson's outspoken politics in the mid-1930s, including the injunction to "Shut Up or Get Out" in 1934 if he continued to oppose decisions made by the Gold Coast Legislative Council.[129] In so doing, Nanka-Bruce asserted an older tradition of newspaper authorship in which personality was absent and self-naming was subdued.[130]

Elite Africans' resistance to Wallace-Johnson's populist political views was not confined to the Gold Coast. Successive editors of the *Sierra Leone Weekly News* railed against the misuse of newsprint by unnamed but easily identified antagonists. As one editorial put it: "ORGANISATIONS have been formed wherein inflammatory Lectures have been delivered week by week for the purpose of convincing people Educated and Uneducated that their condition of Oppression by wicked Oppressors could not be matched any where on the Face of the Globe; and that it behoves them—men and women, to rise up as one man and to use the Big Stick against their Government for the purpose of securing what they call their RIGHTS."[131] Anticipating local support for the Youth League and appealing for "calm" newspaper reading, the editorial continued, "Any one who may be in doubt as to the truthfulness of this Statement has simply got to sit down and calmly read through certain Journals amongst us."[132]

Part of the problem was that sales of the two men's publications outstripped that of established newspapers, marking the popularization of the West African press with politically conscious new readerships. Circulation of the *West African Pilot* "quickly surpassed that of its contemporaries," with an estimated paying readership of twenty thousand by 1941.[133] The overt interest of Zik in publishing "the grievances of native employees" attracted new readerships.[134]

For established newspapermen as well as for colonial officials, the arrival of Azikiwe and Wallace-Johnson on the scene of West African journalism thus marked a challenge to the traditional content and style of newspapers. "Certain educated Africans of the old school . . . are perturbed by the tone of the *West African Pilot*," reported the governor of Nigeria, Sir Bernard Bourdillon, in a secret letter to the secretary of state for the colonies in November 1941. These informers, he added, have "gone so far as to express the opinion that Mr Azikiwe is a fifth columnist."[135] For the governor and old-school Africans alike, part of the problem lay with the popularity of Zik's newspapers and his ability to connect with new constituencies of reader, particularly "the poorer workers," considered to be more vulnerable than established elites to communist propaganda.[136] In response, in 1942 Sir Bernard attempted to introduce press laws specifically aimed at limiting the inflammatory publications on race and racial prejudice in Azikiwe's *West African Pilot*.[137]

Wallace-Johnson and Azikiwe forced a renewal of debates about print and news content. "There is no doubt that with the advent of the *West African Pilot* under his management, a new race consciousness began to dawn on the people of Nigeria," read a secret British surveillance report in 1941 entitled "Benjamin Nnamdi Azikiwe alias 'Zik.'"[138] Popular, outspoken, and innovative with technology, with literary forms, and with journalistic styles, the *West African Pilot* and the other newspapers owned by Zik Press compelled fellow editors to question half a century of West African journalistic etiquette and thereby to confront the possibility that personalities and scandal might be introduced to the printed page.

Older West African newspapers faced considerable competition, especially from Zik's expanding media enterprises, which helped to inaugurate a new culture of celebrity in the West African press. As a form of naming, celebrity was not new to West Africa, of course: Wallace-Johnson's and Zik's production of celebrity had roots in oral praise traditions and a long textual history in books and articles about African role models containing tableaux of "great men of affairs" and "West African celebrities."[139] Azikiwe, in particular, perfected celebrity as a mode of public naming, using populist journalistic techniques including photographs, biographical portraits, and gossip about local personalities. In this, he came into conflict with the old guard on the Lagos newspapers, particularly H. C. M. Bates and other managers of the *Nigerian Daily Times*, who saw in Zik's press a deterioration of agreed journalistic standards in West Africa.[140]

Zik and Wallace-Johnson should not, however, be regarded simply as examples of assertive, self-naming African agitators who used newsprint freely to produce themselves as political leaders. Though concepts such as individual agency and the freedom of the subject are vital to an understanding of their bold disruptions of British imperial ideology, their personal agency was situated within, inextricable from, and articulated through the framework of colonial jurisprudence. As shown in the case studies in this chapter, these antagonists of colonialism were enmeshed in legal frameworks where proper names were crucial to the exercise of British colonial authority. Their names recur in British secret surveillance files. As a consequence, their journalistic work and pseudonymous writings should be read through imperial eyes as well as through the eyes of the Africans they wished to empower.

If the Colonial Office's reluctance to approve measures to suppress or control African newspapers and other publications in the 1930s stemmed from a tradition of press freedom in Britain, it also, perversely, enabled the surveillance of political agitators within the colonies, allowing officials to track the impact of suspected fifth columnists on local populations. If the government's secret surveillance operations were designed to fathom Zik's and Wallace-Johnson's political intentions behind the scenes, the newspaper articles these alleged agitators produced under their own names, archived in Colonial Office files alongside secret service reports, contain the articulation of those intentions, translated into political ideology for the whole colonial world to read.[141] Their signed articles were seized upon by officials, cut out of the public sphere, marked up in blue pencil, and sent to London to be placed in classified files as evidence of their subversive and seditious intentions.

Even though their use of proper names and nicknames implied a confident reconnection of body and voice, both Wallace-Johnson and Zik had to strive to avoid implication and complicity—what Louis Althusser described as interpellation—in the system of colonialism.[142] British colonialism was exercised through both the production and the enforcement of laws of identity. In response to official efforts to limit activities undertaken in their names, these well-known celebrities were forced to develop ways to resist being "hailed" by colonial power. In the process, they revealed that nothing about proper names was natural or fixed in colonial West Africa and that their public presence was constituted in large part by an ideology that depended upon the legal enforcement of particular naming practices.

PART III

Case Studies from West African Newspapers

4 ✑ Trickster Tactics and the Question of Authorship in Newspaper Folktales

COMMENTING ON a newsletter produced from 1959 onward by the Association of Indigenous Senior Officers of the Nigerian Railway Corporation, Tokunbo A. Ayoola expresses puzzlement about the appearance of a regular folktale column entitled "Gentleman Tortoise."[1] Immensely popular with readers, this "strange" and "difficult to surmise" column, with no apparent author, contained "critical commentaries on unfolding developments in the corporation" and included satirical poems targeted at specific European officials who were seen to be abusing their positions of authority.[2]

Ayoola's confusion about the column is unwarranted, however, for he immediately and persuasively explains that Tortoise, the trickster-hero of Yoruba and other West African folktales, is a "small and very weak" creature, marginalized within the jungle hierarchy.[3] Instinctively antisocial and rebellious as a consequence of this exclusion from power, Tortoise brilliantly outwits his enemies and subversively asserts his own moral agenda. A more appropriate metaphor would be difficult to find for Nigerian railway workers in the period of transition from colonial to postcolonial rule, when European managers appeared slow to indigenize the corporation and African labor unions were increasingly vocal in expressing discontent.[4] The inclusion of such a column is only "difficult to surmise" if one is immersed in a tradition of historical scholarship in which genres such as fiction and poetry are excluded from platforms of political analysis and self-articulation. By contrast, as numerous studies of African oral cultures have demonstrated, the use of popular art forms to articulate dissent—including poetry, song, dance, and folk story—have long histories throughout the continent.[5]

Numerous named African authors have made use of folktales, mythology, and folklore in their creative writing, and some, in the manner of the Brothers Grimm, have published collections of local tales, often aimed at young readers.[6] In different ways, writers such as Chinua Achebe, Ngugi wa Thiong'o, Bessie Head, Wole Soyinka, Ken Saro-Wiwa, and Amos Tutuola have all been inspired by the oral archives of their cultures, incorporating references to folktales and local mythologies into their work and experimenting with the (im)possibilities of transcription and translation into English print. Efua Sutherland's play *The Marriage of Anansewa* is a particularly successful example of this literary inspiration by oral genres.[7] Written to be performed, filled with song and dance, the play revels in the antisocial behavior and cunning of the Akan folktale trickster Kweku Ananse as he manipulates four wealthy chiefs who wish to marry his daughter and sets them against one another to his own material advantage. Through the trickster, Sutherland humorously exposes the faults in the marriage payment system, while simultaneously showing how the wily and greedy Ananse enriches himself by exploiting the trust of others.

Sutherland achieves two ends through her use of folktale, both of which are fundamental to the discussion of newsprint folktales in this chapter. First, in a manner similar to that of oral narrators, she reiterates a familiar public narrative and fills it with her own creativity, politics, individuality, and innovations. Second, also in the manner of oral storytellers, she imbues the familiar tale with a social or moral agenda: in this case, a gently comic critique of patriarchal marriage practices, especially the ostentatious competition between powerful men on the marriage market in Ghana. Sutherland thus uses "traditional" art forms for the dissemination of a moral that resists customary prescriptions about marriage. Her use of age-old templates to legitimate a break with the past is a common feature of the folktales discussed in this chapter, necessitating a reappraisal of conventional models of oral genres as complicit in and central to the "invention of tradition."[8]

This chapter tentatively suggests that some of the features of trickster tales—particularly the trickster's use of cunning, masking, and disguise but also, more generally, the storyteller's strategies of reiteration and critique—can be used to describe the tactics adopted by many of the authors of folktales in colonial West African newspapers. One must be cautious, however, not to reproduce what Bob W. White identifies as the reductive and romanticized tendency of cultural critics to "apply" the dehistoricized figure of the trickster across cultures in a uniform way.[9] In the words of Kwawesi Tekpetey, Ananse is an intensely "problematic figure," being "a combination of trickster and culture-hero" who creates disorder wherever he goes and exceeds moral containment.[10] In many stories, he is deceptive, greedy, disloyal, antisocial, and selfish; in others, he is cunning, wise, comic, witty, lovable, and heroic.[11] Indeed, part of the pleasure of Ananse tales is for audiences to guess whether a particular narrator will portray the amoral Akan trickster in a positive or a negative light. Here, therefore, is a figure so ambiguous that he *requires* the storyteller's moral or interpretative commentary, attached like scaffolding around the contents of the tale.

Unsurprisingly given African creative writers' long-standing fascination with orality, there is a large body of scholarship about the deployment of oral discourses, especially in postcolonial African literatures. For Edward Sackey, "African traditional oral poetics [are] . . . at the center of the on-going experiments and innovations in modern African literature."[12] Similarly, for Abiola Irele, an "aesthetic traditionalism" can be found at the heart of printed African literatures.[13] Other analyses of orality range from Pietro Deandrea's discussion of "folktale realism" in postcolonial West African literatures and Ato Quayson's discussion of oral genres in magical realist writing through to Brenda Cooper's controversial feminist critique of folktale conservatism in West African fiction.[14] Taken together, these scholars—and the creative writers who fuel their ideas—demonstrate the dynamic status of oral genres as culturally pervasive forms and the ways in which narrative traditions, as well as particular storylines, can simultaneously be familiar to readers and also be mobile and reapplicable, rooted in the past but not fixed to it. To this extent, one could say that folk stories are always already modern but that they also dissolve the very dichotomy that positions tradition as the counter-discourse of modernity.

Focusing in particular upon the *Gold Coast Nation*, mouthpiece for the colony's chiefs and "natural rulers," this chapter discusses the mobilization of oral genres within the colonial press and the ways in which African-owned newspapers mediated, complicated, and anticipated the types of relationships with oral discourses evidenced by Sutherland, Ngugi, Achebe, and other postcolonial African authors. Significant numbers of folktales were printed in the anglophone West

African newspapers, sometimes in African languages but most often in English-language columns inspired by vernacular proverbs and storylines. Particularly between the 1880s and the late 1920s, newspapers regularly carried "folk" material: stories of the trickster and his greed as well as people's efforts to outwit him, stories of the strange gentleman who seduces a beautiful girl into the forest before mutating into a monstrous snake,[15] stories of female spirit-children who transform into fish or alligators when their secrets are betrayed, and so on. In addition, the newspapers featured folklore columns explaining how particular customs or place-names came into being.

One common feature unites this plethora of stories in the newspapers, setting them apart both from oral discourses in the colonial period and from postcolonial African literatures: their anonymity. Of course, folktales have no authors as such, being collectively owned by narrators and by the culture groups within which they circulate. But in oral discourses in the early twentieth century, each folktale would be reiterated by *particular* performers or groups who—even if masked—were present to, interacting with, and often known by the audience. In colonial Africa, performers were visible and located in relation to their audiences, albeit concealed behind costumes and masks. As Osumaka Likaka points out in his study of African naming practices in colonial Congo, a narrator's "facial expressions and pitch of voice" were important to convey "an unspoken message" that "reinforced . . . [a] common theme."[16] Similarly, Kwesi Yankah writes of Akan oral cultures that "the spoken word and face-to-face communication rely on multisensory experience for the encoding and decoding of meaning."[17] No matter how familiar a tale might be to an audience, the narrator's physical, multisensory presence is vital to the reception and interpretation of each story.[18]

As with other types of contributions to the press, folktale authors seem to relish the ambiguous subjectivity and free speech conferred on them by print. In contrast to the mobilization of folk discourses by postcolonial authors and contrasting with the embodied art of oral folktale narration, newsprint authors seem to invest in the idea that print itself—through its uniform appearance—confers anonymity, invisibility, and publicness on the individual. The specialist narrating body of the storyteller, or griot, is erased, and in the process, the tales are given over to the public sphere of print.

What distinguishes the majority of folktales from other types of writing in the colonial West African press is the absence of *any* kind of naming. In the majority of tales, the author's identity is simply not accessible from behind the public stamp of newsprint. Writers seem to donate their stories to the public sphere rather than claiming them as personal literary achievements. Torn away from expert performers, the printed folktale becomes a form of what Kwesi Yankah calls "clandestine discourse" or "veiled speech," filled with the memories (and mnemonic devices) of bygone tales, ready for applications in new contexts.[19] Made available to ordinary people through the anonymizing medium of print, folktales thus become one of the rhetorical forms identified by Yankah as taking "the form of indirection, metaphor, proverb, allegory, circumlocution, [and] innuendo."[20] Such a public discourse is positively asking to be reactivated as political critique.

By and large, however, the anonymously authored columns contain folk stories with generally applicable, politically unspecific morals relating to human greed, fate, and social and marital behavior. Perhaps surprisingly, the political reactivation of this material occurs most often when folktales are relinked to the speaking subject using the authors' initials or proper names. Though moral politics cannot simply be separated off from party politics and placed into a private or domestic realm, two distinct modes of folktale narration can be identified in the press. Columns by anonymous authors are delinked from current affairs, whereas columns by named or nearly named authors are filled with contemporary social and political references, and they often contain innuendo about or direct criticism of local personalities.

This runs contrary to what one might expect, particularly if anonymity is regarded as a mask behind which an individual safely hides in order to criticize or abuse powerful individuals and institutions. Yet when named authors renarrate folktales in the West African press, many subversive possibilities become available. Authorial *presence*, not anonymity, transforms the folktale into a political tactic. When pseudonymous or initialized writers make use of the traditional archive, the folktale is reactivated as a tactic for the expression of critical—and sometimes potentially libelous or seditious—commentaries about colonialism, local personalities, and current affairs.

In *The Practice of Everyday Life*, Michel de Certeau suggests that ordinary people are intelligent and tactical users of official discourses, with the capacity to appropriate and subvert institutional practices and representations.[21] Applied to West African print cultures, de Certeau's definition of tactical consumption is useful for the way in which it helps one to acknowledge the hegemony of colonial power and the resilience of African oral discourses, alongside the techniques employed by ordinary people to navigate through these dominant local orders, appropriating modes of representation along the way. In this, de Certeau anticipates postcolonial theorizations of colonial agency, particularly Homi Bhabha's work on the ambivalence of mimicry and his theorization of local engagements with colonial stereotypes.

Both Bhabha and de Certeau have been criticized for defining resistance as an individualistic, sometimes unconscious set of responses to hegemony on the part of otherwise passive consumers.[22] In supplementing de Certeau's notion of tactical consumption with the figure of the trickster, this chapter draws attention to agency and deliberation on the part of folktale narrators without losing sight of the evasive, identity-blurring effects of anonymous and pseudonymous authorship in colonial contexts.[23] As indicated earlier, two different types of trickster tactics are at play in the African-owned newspapers: first, in the wholly anonymous tales, the folktale itself functions tactically, borrowing its form from tradition in order to communicate moral messages to present-day readerships. Such a maneuver echoes and illustrates de Certeau's notion of the tactic. Mischievous and cunning like the folktale trickster, the anonymous authors appropriate, "consume," and offer readings of recognizable discourses. Second are the initialized tales and those by named authors, the majority of which are themselves trickster tales about Kweku Ananse; these are the most politically critical and personally abusive folk stories to be found in the Ghanaian press.

The medium of the newspaper helps to makes such insubordination possible. Authors often play with readers' local knowledge about who they might be, without fully disclosing their identities. One folktale author from the 1880s signs his story "Cudjoe" in the *Gold Coast Echo*, inviting the assumption that he is Cudjoe Coomah, author of occasional articles in the *Echo* on topics such as female education and polygamy. Another author, writing for the *Gold Coast Nation* in 1915, signs a folktale "S. S.": this is possibly S. Sacoom, president of the Axim branch of the Aborigines Rights Protection Society, the organization for which the *Nation* was the official organ.

The Ananse tale by S. S., entitled "A Modern Anansi Story: A Gold Coast Fable for the Times," provides an excellent example of the utilization of folktales for the criticism of public figures by writers playing with masks of anonymity. This tale describes how, while Ananse and his chiefs are fighting a great war, his queen, Abakuma Sikafu,[24] helps to organize a fund for the protection of the community; however, Ntsikuma, "one of the chief sons" of the royal couple, decides to raise a fund independently from his brothers.[25] Ananse interprets the two separate funds as signs that Abakuma cannot manage to control her family and household. As a result, the elders and sages of the community are "exceeding sorrowful" about Ntsikuma's divisive behavior.[26]

Readers will guess immediately that, without directly naming its target or translating its message into an "application" at the end of the tale, this Ananse story represents a coded warning to J. E. Casely-Hayford, the prominent politician and soon-to-be leader of the ARPS's rival organization, the National Congress of British West Africa (NCBWA, established in 1920). In January 1915, as World War I escalated, Casely-Hayford was seen by the ARPS leadership to be giving Ananse (Britain) the impression of disunity in the Gold Coast by disrespecting the "natural rulers." To vocal disapproval in the *Gold Coast Nation*, Casely-Hayford had organized a "war fund" separate from the Society's "official" fund, using the columns of the *Nation*'s rival paper, the *Gold Coast Leader*, to advertise his scheme.[27] In naming him after Ananse's most intelligent son, the folktale acknowledges Casely-Hayford's intellectual prowess and good intentions toward the Gold Coast in the war and invites him to reenter the political fold, while simultaneously reprimanding his impudent independence from the chiefs and their representatives.

S. S. insists on near attribution rather than full anonymity for his targeted personal criticism of Casely-Hayford in the folktale, and his message gains weight and impact as a consequence. If this *is* Sacoom, as the initials and context imply, the author is no "small boy" hiding behind a pseudonym to criticize an emergent political heavyweight in the region but a "big man," full of authority and presence as president of the Axim branch of the ARPS. Naming is vital to the effectiveness of the critique, revealing the close connection between naming and leadership in West Africa, a theme that was examined in more detail in chapter 3.

Nevertheless, S. S.'s use of initials cleverly evades colonial libel legislation with its hunger for proper names. As it happened, this critical folktale marked the beginning of the permanent rift between Casely-Hayford's camp and the ARPS, which by the late 1920s led to open hostilities in the Legislative Council and frequent libel suits between the rival sides. S. S.'s avoidance of printed identification in his "fable for the times" is an early example of African playfulness with British legal concepts of naming. Although the target of criticism is African in this case, the authorship of the piece is framed by British legal definitions of identity and defamation, a theme taken up in the last chapter's analysis of the confrontational, law-baiting strategies of I. T. A. Wallace-Johnson.

The anonymous folktales generally offer moral advice to readers and contain material that *could* be politicized but is not explicitly positioned for the critique of local power elites. By contrast, the pseudonymous, initialized, and fully named authors are concerned not with intimate relations or morality but with public behavior. These writers have explicit targets: they aim sharp barbs of criticism at local men of influence and make no secret of the status of their tales as extended metaphors, or allegories, for specific contemporary situations. In so doing, they assert their own leadership claims through their political deployment of folktales.

One fully named folktale author, who wrote a regular column for the *Gold Coast Nation* in 1912, was called "Atu Penyin of Anumabu." Compared to the anonymous and pseudonymous material surrounding his column, Atu Penyin of Anumabu as a signifier is overabundant with information about the author's family, ethnicity, and coastal location.[28] Many of Atu Penyin's folktales take the form of political critiques of colonialism.[29] In fact, the author's politics are disclosed not in the narratives but in the "moral" section that concludes each tale, for Atu Penyin often adopts a historical approach to well-known folktales and presents his stories as examples of local spiritual beliefs and practices. For example, one of his Ananse tales from 1912, entitled "Asentrafi (The Night-Jar)," describes a fetish priestess, Asentrafi, who, "according to the superstitious rites of the time," builds a barn to prevent the theft of her crops by the "shameless liar," Ananse.[30] Rather than offering a generic moral comment about human greed or the need to be wary of liars at the end, the moral of this tale turns on a strikingly different pivot: "If the English people have come to the Gold Coast with a view to trading, they must go on; but if it is their intention to take advantage of our being weaponless to deprive us of our means of livelihood and of our ancient privileges, then they must tell us so frankly. We have no misgivings but hope that Members of Parliament will see that our rights are inviolably preserved."[31]

As with the tale in which Casely-Hayford is criticized, this tale's moral demands to be situated and read through contemporary political events. Given that a second deputation of Gold Coast leaders had recently traveled to Downing Street to protest against the Forestry Bill, which threatened customary land rights, this agricultural tale about past customs and beliefs thus cleverly becomes the assertion of a *precedent*, through which established, inviolable customary "privileges" are claimed. In the process, the Ananse tale is transformed into a political allegory that comments explicitly on current affairs.[32] The tricksterlike cunning of Atu Penyin involves the attachment of a supposedly timeless moral tale about Ananse to political and social specificities in the colonial public sphere. Newsprint plays a vital role in severing the tale from the authorial body: sheltering under the collective public opinion of the folktale morality of anonymous tales published in the *Gold Coast Nation*, Atu Penyin uses the tale as a mediating device to refuse to accept the legitimacy of current colonial legislation.

Another one of Atu Penyin's folktales is worth focusing upon for its lengthy moral. First, there is a short tale describing how the children of Mother Tortoise are captured by a hunter but have to be liberated because the hunter's people see it as an "abominable crime . . . infringing the laws of mankind" to incarcerate and consume such creatures. Following that, the moral reads: "The application of the story is, that if all the white men in the Colony or Protectorate will join the German fast boat to England . . . on account of the Forestry Bill, there is one person in the name of His Majesty King George V who will show that white men on the Gold Coast are not justified in claiming from the natives their rights with impracticable Bills."[33] The structure of this story illustrates how the authority of folktale narrators in the newspapers lies in the reiteration of a familiar tale, which is attached, magnetlike, to present circumstances.

As with the other folktale authors, Atu Penyin is not attempting to reify tradition in the manner of cultural nationalist constructions of a usable past to set against European cultural incursions. Rather, this is an effort to produce new versions of familiar material for the consumption of current readerships. Reversing the history-making processes famously identified by Eric Hobsbawm and Terence Ranger, whereby colonized subjects undertake an "invention of tradition" to legitimate present actions, these newsprint folktales celebrate the *currency* of age-old characters and plots and refute the historicity of folktale heroes by inserting them into contemporary settings.[34]

Trickster tales are perfectly suited to the power dynamic between colonizer and colonized in the public sphere. In his study of oral poetics in West African fiction, Edward Sackey observes that "the trick is always hatched by the weaker or the disadvantaged person because an open confrontation is not in their interest."[35] The tricksterlike cunning of African authors—the weaker party in relation to the state—involves the attachment of familiar moral tales to political and social specificities. Contrasting fully anonymous tales, authors such Atu Penyin and S. S. rapidly transform so-called traditional tales into parables and allegories. Atu Penyin's folktales, published week after week in the years leading up to World War I, are recognizable for this combination of political specificity and emblematic characterization. His column cleverly *trains* readers to extrapolate historically informed, oppositional political interpretations from common folktales. Readers are not allowed simply to "apply" a story morally or allegorically to current political situations. Combining the familiarity of the folktale with the visibility of his authorial name, Atu Penyin transforms each tale into a vehicle that, first, narrates African history (through examples of cultural precedents or embedded references to slavery, as in the Mother Tortoise tale); second, comments explicitly upon current events; and third, implicitly contrasts British colonialism with alternative local governmental processes.

Not all nearly named authors are as confrontational as Atu Penyin and S. S.; other named authors transform folktales into parables in less politically resistant ways. Thus, a popular Ananse story, reiterated by Ebenezer J. Anderson, a teacher at Mfantsipim School in Cape Coast, describes the way in which Ananse outwits Tiger by making him jump a second time into the pit from which Little Rat has saved him. The story concludes by explaining that the Tiger is Satan and that Ananse represents "our Blessed Saviour." "Now let us try to guess the moral," Anderson writes: "Jesus Christ has delivered us from the hands of Satan."[36] Similarly, a story entitled "The Pilgrim," by "Abue," indicates the political evasiveness of some authors. "In a magnificent castle, there once dwelt a rich Knight," the tale opens; this knight refuses hospitality to a pilgrim until the latter persuades him that he is merely the caretaker of his mansion for succeeding generations.[37] Resisting the obvious moral—a critique of Britain's occupation and "care" of the colony's "castle"—the author seems to get cold feet and recites a ditty instead of suggesting an application at the end of the tale: "Wealth and treasure pass away / Goodness enjoys an endless day."[38]

Readers schooled in Atu Penyin's methods will easily read this parable as a critique of colonialism. Abue, however, refuses to risk such an explicit interpretation. In a similar vein, the nonpolitical "Folklore" column written regularly by Kobina Kwaansa, a frequent contributor to the *Gold Coast Times* in the late 1920s and early 1930s, often builds stories around Fante proverbs, translating and embellishing them with folktale story lines. Quotations from Shakespeare, English poetry, Greek classics, the Bible, and other Fante proverbs are absorbed into these tales, which generally have flat morals like "Such has always been the way of the world!"[39]

NEWSPRINT AND LITERARY REALISM

Whether newspaper folktales are anonymous, pseudonymous, or signed by named authors, one of their striking aspects is their use of realism as a literary technique. As with oral narrators, who often embed material in familiar settings, newsprint authors incorporate realistic details to locate events and characters in the immediate vicinity of the readership. In one early rendition of the famous tale "Ananse's (the Spider's) Pretended Death," published in the *Gold Coast Echo* in 1888, the anonymous author makes use of intricate psychological detail to narrate Ananse's rise and fall. In this comic story, the artful protagonist feigns death in order to gorge upon the yams and vegetables his family has labored for months to grow.[40] The rich psychological details in this story add to its comedy: Ananse is portrayed like any ordinary man: we learn that after a "nice dinner," he filled his pipe, "struck a light, and went and sat at a place where the wind was blowing softly. He was indeed a happy man."[41] This cunning and manipulative hero is firmly situated within his local community, and a great deal of local vigilance is required for his tricks to be discovered. By the end, the narrator leads us through the details of Ananse's "mental agony" as he is outwitted and publicly punished by his own family. "He who seeks the ruin of others in nine cases out of ten comes to disgrace himself," reads the moral.[42]

In tales such as that of Ananse's pretended death, realism is not used with the goal of achieving mimetic representation—resemblance to or imitation of the "real"—so much as to catapult readers into a moral realm of exemplary and errant human behavior. Readers are explicitly requested by narrators at the end of these tales to condemn or endorse particular modes of behavior or to accept the unalterable nature of fate, and they are encouraged, in the process, to participate in the production of moral lessons from the story. Realism serves to enhance this moral engagement by situating folk material in recognizable contemporary settings. In this manner, realist narrative techniques are used to help readers draw lessons from ostensibly nonrealist tales.

Such a separation of realism from nonrealism is not particularly useful to describe colonial West African print cultures, however: in particular, it risks introducing a false dichotomy between fact and fiction and between reality and the moral realm. These concepts may not require separation in West African newspaper cultures. In his study of print in precapitalist Europe, Lennard Davis suggests that prior to the rise of bourgeois society, readers "could not routinely assume, as modern critics have done, that the works they were reading were fictions."[43] The division between "true" and "false" narratives is a relatively recent categorical imposition, Davis argues, arising with the European bourgeoisie in the eighteenth century and attaching to particular genres. Prior to that, printed and oral narratives offered insights and guidance on ethical behavior. Readers would know that a story was neither original nor real, but they would nevertheless regard it as a "factual fiction" if it contained a core of moral knowledge that could be extracted and applied to the world.[44] Often, such "truths" were set like gems in a bed of contemporary references and allusions, details that strengthened the reader's reality experience of a fantastic tale.[45] Davis suggests that history was not segregated from fiction as a category in precapitalist Europe: the two genres enveloped one another without contradiction. With his European material in mind, he retrieves the pre-Enlightenment word *newes* to describe the ways in which readers responded to printed texts. *Newes* designates a type of narrative—such as "Jack the Giant Killer" or "Robin Hood"—that was fictional in its characterization and setting yet was interpreted and debated by readers in the knowledge that it contained newslike and morally engaging and therefore "true" material.[46]

Many folktales in the West African press adhere to a similar aesthetic to that described by Davis. In presupposing that readers will morally engage with the debates that are staged through the story, authors seem to take a particular aesthetic standpoint for granted, according to which readers participate in the text, judge characters, and involve themselves in discussions of dilemmas. In the words of Marjorie Mensah, the pseudonymous and immensely popular author of the "Women's Corner" in the *Times of West Africa*, characters in fictional stories are people "that we meet in the streets every day."[47] But as Marjorie points out, they are also "purely fictitious and the incidents, although [they] may be true, are not specially designed against any member of the community whatsoever and should not cause discomfiture to any person. I think such notice is absolutely necessary to prevent misapprehension and safeguard *the beauty of a moral* from being lost."[48] In Marjorie's weekly column, morally evaluative writing takes precedence over hard-news stories and descriptive journalism. The column thus produces "newes": sentimental fictions are developed from real-life anecdotes, instilled with a combination of realism and the exaggerated prose of the popular romance, and readers are invited to participate in ethical discussions deriving from what they have read.

Narrators such as Marjorie Mensah relish the publicness of their stories, the depersonalization that occurs to "real" characters when they enter the public sphere through the medium of print and become "newes." These stories play with the anonymizing potential of print and demonstrate readers' overwhelming requirement not for fiction or creative writing but for real-life moral material from which they can extrapolate lessons for themselves. Such a technique of connecting fictional models with social realities has a clear ancestry in African oral narratives, where storytellers are expected to embellish familiar texts and to apply socially relevant morals at the end and where readers debate and learn from the dilemmas contained in a tale.[49] The authors of newspaper folktales seem to insist that readers adopt the receptive mode that characterizes folktale audiences: that is, an aesthetic of active audience participation in the interpretation of texts, extrapolating and applying the moral of the story while being led by narrators who address them at the end with suggestions for real-life applications.

UNLETTERED AFRICANS AND READER RECEPTION

Printed reception is, however, not the *same as* oral receptive modes. In his study of the history of Revivalism in East Africa, the cultural historian Derek Peterson discusses the ways in which proverbs and riddles from oral discourses were turned into print by Gikuyu Christians in the 1930s and 1940s. On the printed page, he writes, oral discourses were "enumerated, standardized, and circulated to a wider audience," and in the process, transcribers became authors, writing under "an obligation to create useable knowledge."[50] In the course of being transcribed, Gikuyu proverbs were recast "as moral admonitions or practical wisdom," which could guide conduct and shape culture.[51] According to Peterson, by putting oral discourse into print literate Christians created a form of knowledge that was designed to uplift and educate readers, as well as to render "the past accessible," relevant, and exploitable.[52]

One might wish to regard the regular folktale columns in the newspapers as a gesture of inclusiveness toward nonliterate communities, as bridges between readers and nonreaders, making use of what one anonymous poet referred to in 1897 as the "unlettered archives / Of men, that in rude moulds are cast."[53] West African editors were certainly aware that readers translated columns aloud to friends and family members. In this way, readers reoralized the printed material, reinserted it into the "unlettered archives," and disseminated press opinions for debate in the wider community.

Perhaps with these unlettered audiences in mind, in 1912 the editor of the *Gold Coast Nation* announced a "Prize Essay and Story Competition" for readers. Rather than seeking original fiction from contributors, he invited them to submit "A Story illustrating the sagacity and wit of Anansi (The Spider)."[54] This competition reflected the status of Ananse tales as moral and aesthetic vectors that were nevertheless open to innovation. The competition also implicitly demonstrated the distrust among literate West African elites of the effects of novels on the minds of readers. In 1902, for example, the *Gold Coast Aborigines* carried an article by "A Youngman" that declared, "Above all things, never let your son touch a novel or romance . . . they teach the youthful mind to sigh after beauty that never existed; to despise the little good that Fortune has mixed in our cup, by expecting more than she ever gave."[55] The prescriptive remit of the *Nation*'s folktale competition, by contrast, demonstrated the manner in which printed folktales were expected to contain recognizable schema for readers—evidence of Ananse's sagacity and wit narrated through familiar structures of anticipation.

Such an explicit absorption of Ananse tales into elite literary culture illustrated the delight of elites in folktales, but the competition also revealed a bias against oral modes of narration, for entries were only permitted from literate elites in the community—people "holding at least Seventh Standard Certificates" (that is, primary school leavers).[56] On the matter of naming, the editor declared that "the Winner's name will be published" but copyright of all contributions "will be in the Editor of the 'Nation.'"[57]

Peterson's key point, applicable to the folktales appearing in West African newspapers, is that the Christian transcribers of oral discourses lifted proverbs and riddles away from specialist interpretive communities and sought, instead, to make their "meanings generalizeable."[58] Moreover, "they were not simply scribes," for the democratic gesture of general public dissemination was accompanied by moral interventions, as the Christian transcribers "cleaned up the past, scrubbing out embarrassing customs and substituting creditable practices in their place."[59] Evidence from West Africa confirms a similar "scrubbing out" process, for lewd and sexually explicit material was excised when missionaries and Christian African elites rendered oral material into print. As Robert Sutherland Rattray, head of the colonial Anthropology Department of Asante in the mid-1920s, commented disapprovingly in his study of Asante folktales, when "literate natives" write stories down, "their long training in the mission or other schools [causes them to] . . . write in a curious uniform standard of unidiomatic expression which is not the language in which these tales were originally told."[60] Moreover, bawdy and scatological material was also excised in the supposed transcriptions.[61] The activities of these vested scribes illustrate the impossibility of ignoring the textuality of the supposed orality in African print cultures. English literacy and African orthographies were far from neutral acquisitions, and little orality remains in the printed folktale.

FOLKLORE AND HISTORICAL REFLECTION

In discussing the relationship between folk narratives and newsprint, it is necessary to draw a generic distinction between folktales and folklore in the African-owned press. Whereas printed folktales erase the historicity of heroes and plotlines by allowing them to transmute into metaphors and allegories for contemporary situations, the folklore columns adhere to a different temporal logic in which the past and past cultures are clearly distinguished from the present.

West African newspapers contain numerous examples of folklore as a mode of narrating and reflecting upon social history. Particularly in the first decades of large-scale newspaper production in the 1880s and 1890s, columns such as "Fanti Tales" in the *Gold Coast Echo* and "Folklore" in the *Western Echo* printed African legends and myths in order to offer explanations for place-names, family names, behaviors, taboos, customs, prescriptions, and beliefs. Folklore functioned as the anthropological arm of cultural nationalist endeavors in this period. Among many others, John Mensah Sarbah in the Gold Coast and Edward Wilmot Blyden in Liberia and Sierra Leone transcribed customary laws and legal procedures into lengthy tomes in order to assert the existence of definitive, legally rigorous precedents in the face of colonial interventions in local institutions. In the newspapers, anonymously authored folklore columns established the rationale and antecedents for particular local beliefs and behaviors.[62] Even as African elites assiduously wrote books containing customary legal knowledge, their newspapers produced ethnographic and cultural knowledge through the narration of folklore.

Many instances of this process can be found in newspapers from the 1880s and 1890s. In January 1886, the *Western Echo* of Cape Coast carried in its "Folklore" column a story entitled "Fabulous Origin of the Towns of Asaybu and Mouree (Moree)."[63] The founders of these towns, "it is traditionally reported," were two giants who emerged from the sea with their followers, observed by "a certain huntsman [who] . . . is said to have clapped his hands and exclaimed, 'how numerous!'"[64] Ground clearing at the seaside town of Mouree (Moree) was completed after six days, "probably on Monday," and the people rested the next day, from "which seems to have originated the observance of that day as a day of rest among our fishermen."[65] Meanwhile, in the inland agricultural community of Asaybu (Asebu), Friday became the day of rest, a custom that the settlement's giant "is said to have instituted" so that he could visit his friend on the coast each week.[66] In spite of its anachronistic translation of an ancient Fante calendar into the terms of a Christian seven-day week, this story seeks to explain the historical reasons for peculiar social patterns in the two towns and to understand different day-of-rest practices between local communities.

Another folklore column in the *Western Echo* described the "fabulous origin of a certain family living in Chama, known by the name of the descendants of Boneta or Boneta family; in the vernacular, Safur Nannam."[67] Published in three installments, this story told how a fisherman fell in love with a strange woman, who was in reality a transformed fish from the ocean. He was harpooned by his comrades while visiting her family underwater, and when, many years later, the secret harpoon was discovered hidden in his thatched roof and his other wife confronted her rival, the fish-woman melted back into the sea, leaving the man to grieve for his true love. "The descendants of Boneta are very many in Chama," the story concluded, "and they still go by the same fabulous name, of Safur Nannam on account of their supposed origin. None of them ever eat Boneta or Safur" (see fig. 5).[68]

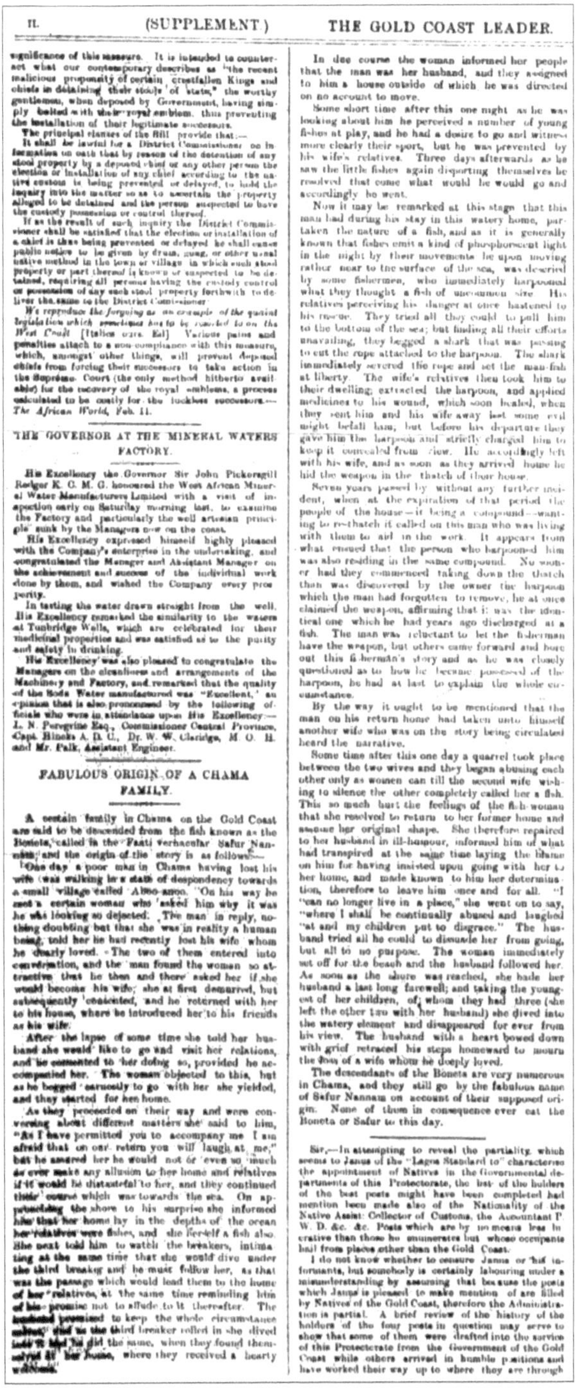

II. (SUPPLEMENT.) THE GOLD COAST LEADER.

significance of this measure. It is intended to counteract what our contemporary describes as "the recent malicious propensity of certain crestfallen Kings and chiefs in detaining their stools of state," the worthy gentlemen, when deposed by Government, having simply bolted with their royal emblem, thus preventing the installation of their legitimate successors.

The principal clauses of the Bill provide that:—

It shall be lawful for a District Commissioner on information on oath that by reason of the detention of any stool property by a deposed chief or any other person the election or installation of any chief according to the native custom is being prevented or delayed, to hold the inquiry into the matter so as to ascertain the property alleged to be detained and the person suspected to have the custody possession or control thereof.

If as the result of such inquiry the District Commissioner shall be satisfied that the election or installation of a chief is thus being prevented or delayed he shall cause public notice to be given by drum, gong, or other usual native method in the town or village in which such stool property or part thereof is known or suspected to be detained, requiring all persons having the custody control or possession of any such stool property forthwith to deliver the same to the District Commissioner.

We reproduce the forgoing as an example of the quaint legislation which sometimes has to be resorted to on the West Coast [Italics ours. Ed] Various pains and penalties attach to a non-compliance with this measure, which, amongst other things, will prevent deposed chiefs from forcing their successors to take action in the Supreme Court (the only method hitherto available) for the recovery of the royal emblems, a process calculated to be costly for the luckless successors.—*The African World, Feb. 11.*

THE GOVERNOR AT THE MINERAL WATERS FACTORY.

His Excellency the Governor Sir John Pickersgill Rodger K. C. M. G. honoured the West African Mineral Water Manufacturers Limited with a visit of inspection early on Saturday morning last, to examine the Factory and particularly the well artesian principle sunk by the Managers now on the coast.

His Excellency expressed himself highly pleased with the Company's enterprise in the undertaking, and congratulated the Manager and Assistant Manager on the achievement and success of the individual work done by them, and wished the Company every prosperity.

In tasting the water drawn straight from the well, His Excellency remarked the similarity to the waters at Tunbridge Wells, which are celebrated for their medicinal properties and was satisfied as to the purity and safety in drinking.

His Excellency was also pleased to congratulate the Managers on the cleanliness and arrangements of the Machinery and Factory, and remarked that the quality of the Soda Water manufactured was "Excellent," an opinion that is also pronounced by the following officials who were in attendance upon His Excellency:—L. N. Peregrine Esq., Commissioner Central Province, Capt. Blinks A. D. C., Dr. W. W. Claridge, M. O. H. and Mr. Falk, Assistant Engineer.

FABULOUS ORIGIN OF A CHAMA FAMILY.

A certain family in Chama on the Gold Coast are said to be descended from the fish known as the Boneta, called in the Fanti vernacular Safur Nannam; and the origin of the story is as follows:—

One day a poor man in Chama having lost his wife was walking in a state of despondency towards a small village called Abbo-anoo. On his way he met a certain woman who asked him why it was he was looking so dejected. The man in reply, nothing doubting but that she was in reality a human being, told her he had recently lost his wife whom he dearly loved. The two of them entered into conversation, and the man found the woman so attractive that he then and there asked her if she would become his wife; she at first demurred, but subsequently consented, and he returned with her to his house, where he introduced her to his friends as his wife.

After the lapse of some time she told her husband she would like to go and visit her relations, and he consented to her doing so, provided he accompanied her. The woman objected to this, but as he begged earnestly to go with her she yielded, and they started for her home.

As they proceeded on their way and were conversing about different matters she said to him, "As I have permitted you to accompany me I am afraid that on our return you will laugh at me," but he assured her he would not or even so much as ever make any allusion to her home and relatives if it would be distasteful to her, and they continued their course which was towards the sea. On approaching the shore to his surprise she informed him that her home lay in the depths of the ocean her relatives were fishes, and she herself a fish also. She next told him to watch the breakers, intimating at the same time that she would dive under the third breaker and he must follow her, as that was the passage which would lead them to the home of her relatives, at the same time reminding him of his promise not to allude to it thereafter. The husband promised to keep the whole circumstance secret, and as the third breaker rolled in she dived into it and he did the same, when they found themselves at her home, where they received a hearty welcome.

In due course the woman informed her people that the man was her husband, and they assigned to him a house outside of which he was directed on no account to move.

Some short time after this one night as he was looking about him he perceived a number of young fishes at play, and he had a desire to go and witness more clearly their sport, but he was prevented by his wife's relatives. Three days afterwards as he saw the little fishes again disporting themselves he resolved that come what would he would go and accordingly he went.

Now it may be remarked at this stage that this man had during his stay in this watery home, partaken the nature of a fish, and as it is generally known that fishes emit a kind of phosphorescent light in the night by their movements he upon moving rather near to the surface of the sea, was descried by some fishermen, who immediately harpooned what they thought a fish of uncommon size. His relatives perceiving his danger at once hastened to his rescue. They tried all they could to pull him to the bottom of the sea; but finding all their efforts unavailing, they begged a shark that was passing to cut the rope attached to the harpoon. The shark immediately severed the rope and set the man-fish at liberty. The wife's relatives then took him to their dwelling, extracted the harpoon, and applied medicines to his wound, which soon healed, when they sent him and his wife away lest some evil might befall him; but before his departure they gave him the harpoon and strictly charged him to keep it concealed from view. He accordingly left with his wife, and as soon as they arrived home he hid the weapon in the thatch of their house.

Seven years passed by without any further incident, when at the expiration of that period the people of the house—it being a compound—wanting to re-thatch it called on this man who was living with them to aid in the work. It appears from what ensued that the person who harpooned him was also residing in the same compound. No sooner had they commenced taking down the thatch than was discovered by the owner the harpoon which the man had forgotten to remove, he at once claimed the weapon, affirming that it was the identical one which he had years ago discharged at a fish. The man was reluctant to let the fisherman have the weapon, but others came forward and bore out this fisherman's story and as he was closely questioned as to how he became possessed of the harpoon, he had at last to explain the whole circumstance.

By the way it ought to be mentioned that the man on his return home had taken unto himself another wife who was on the story being circulated heard the narrative.

Some time after this one day a quarrel took place between the two wives and they began abusing each other only as women can till the second wife wishing to silence the other completely called her a fish. This so much hurt the feelings of the fish-woman that she resolved to return to her former home and assume her original shape. She therefore repaired to her husband in ill-humour, informed him of what had transpired at the same time laying the blame on him for having insisted upon going with her to her home, and made known to him her determination, therefore to leave him once and for all. "I can no longer live in a place," she went on to say, "where I shall be continually abused and laughed at and my children put to disgrace." The husband tried all he could to dissuade her from going, but all to no purpose. The woman immediately set off for the beach and the husband followed her. As soon as the shore was reached, she bade her husband a last long farewell; and taking the youngest of her children, of whom they had three (she left the other two with her husband) she dived into the watery element and disappeared for ever from his view. The husband with a heart bowed down with grief retraced his steps homeward to mourn the loss of a wife whom he deeply loved.

The descendants of the Boneta are very numerous in Chama, and they still go by the fabulous name of Safur Nannam on account of their supposed origin. None of them in consequence ever eat the Boneta or Safur to this day.

Sir,—In attempting to reveal the partiality which seems to Janus of the "Lagos Standard to" characterise the appointment of Natives in the Governmental departments of this Protectorate, the list of the holders of the best posts might have been completed had mention been made also of the Nationality of the Native Assist: Collector of Customs, the Accountant P. W. D. &c. &c. Posts which are by no means less lucrative than those he enumerates but whose occupants hail from places other than the Gold Coast.

I do not know whether to censure Janus or his informants, but somebody is certainly labouring under a misunderstanding by assuming that because the posts which Janus is pleased to make mention of are filled by Natives of the Gold Coast, therefore the Administration is partial. A brief review of the history of the holders of the four posts in question may serve to show that some of them were drafted into the service of this Protectorate from the Government of the Gold Coast while others arrived in humble positions and have worked their way up to where they are through

FIG. 5. "Fabulous Origin of a Chama Family," from the *Gold Coast Leader*, 11 March 1905, Supplement 2

Negotiating between the demands of realism and fabulous narration, stories such as these produce a form of "newes" for readers. There is no obvious disjuncture, in the tales, between the mythical and the mundane. Narrators domesticate the fabulous details—giants leading crowds of people out of the sea or women mutating into fish—with heavy doses of realism in order to explain the reasons for the emergence of particular traditions. This is helped by the figure of the onlooker situated within the tale, as with the huntsman in the story of Asaybu and Mouree, who witnesses events from the margins of the story. Through these columns, different days of rest or dietary rules in different kinship groups are shown to arise from practical causes rather than from inexplicable or irrational behavior; furthermore, the logic of a custom is shown not to be hidden from the communities who continue to observe it.

In a revealing commentary published in place of a story in the "Folklore" column in April 1886, the editor of the *Western Echo*, James Hutton Brew, explains his reasons for including "articles under this caption" in each issue of the paper. "By means of Folk Lore, and its publication in our columns," he writes, "we establish a claim to recognition as part and portion of the human race."[69] He continues, defensively: "Now there are some who think that intellectually the black man is much below the ordinary run of creatures," but this is erroneous, for the African "obtains facts, traces their analogies and secures the conclusions deducible from a collection of them."[70] Characterized by the ability to reason, just like any other member of the human race, Africans are capable of "retaining facts" and, moreover, "of perceiving and tracing their various analogies and relations."[71]

African folklore columns take on an intensely political character in the light of Brew's analysis. Anything but quaint or archaic, folktales and folklore are positioned as a vital part of the continent's intellectual history. Rejecting any notion that traditions are blindly adopted and emphasizing the deliberative capacity of past generations, Brew insists that "the black man submits every thing he obtains through a process of investigation and enquiry to the same test and scrutiny as do others of the white skin, prior to deducing any conclusions therefrom."[72] To demonstrate the analogous development of African and European civilizations, the "Fanti Mythology" column in the *Western Echo* two months later establishes explicit parallels between the Fante genesis story and the biblical Garden of Eden story. In this column, a creator places a man and a woman on earth, who swear to follow his prescriptions for the preparation of food; while he is away, a third person enters, seduces the woman, and tempts her to break the creator's injunctions.[73] One culture's myth is thus rendered inextricable from the other: Fante mythology is Christianized, Christianity is Fante-ized, and each story is passed through the other's logic in a manner that defies assumptions of superiority by either tradition.

Brew indicates that a form of cultural knowledge is contained in African folklore: through these stories, the reasons and principles behind particular customs and values can be explained in a rational manner. In the process of storing narratives in which the origin of family names, place-names, customary practices, and prohibitions are explained, local communities are shown to have long traditions of deliberative behavior. Seen in this way, the folklore columns demonstrate how reactions that might seem "irrational" to external viewers—people's fear of particular creatures or their respect for taboos and unseen forces—are always harnessed to a set of events to which local communities have applied a careful logic.

The completely anonymous authorship of folklore columns adds to the anthropological credibility of the material. Unlike the folktale in later decades, which was sometimes signed by an individual storyteller wishing to assert eloquence or leadership, folklore is only ever presented in the press as collective, as the reaction of communities to events. It is not, however, presented as an empirically reliable account of the past, furnished by the oral archive. As Brew's comments demonstrate, folklore columns offer a reflective metanarrative through which "traditional" processes of decision making can be understood by contemporary readerships. If the content of particular myths and beliefs appears to be illogical, these columns reveal how, in the past, people acted pragmatically and collectively in the face of a (magical) situation, extracting principles to ward off a recurrence of problems. To this extent, the folklore columns produce historicity and metahistory—an understanding, first, of people's understanding of events and, second, of the reasons why specific practices have come into force—rather than history per se as a series of recorded events.

By the mid-1930s, reiterations of well-known folktales had lessened in the press and folklore seems to have disappeared altogether as a genre, with the increasing publication of original short stories and serializations of fiction, especially in racy, high-tech journals such as Azikiwe's

African Morning Post and in Duse Mohamed Ali's journal, the *Comet*. Some newspapers, however, such as the *Gold Coast Leader* (1902–29) and the *Sierra Leone Weekly News* (1884–1951), never showed any interest in folk material, preferring from the outset to showcase new poetry and to serialize new fiction and works of history. The material in this chapter does not, therefore, furnish evidence for theories of a linear evolution or emergence of modern African fiction out of folk-inspired roots in a teleological model of literary history whereby the folktale makes space for later developments in fiction.

༄

Oral genres—especially folktales—continue to be mobilized in printed texts, reworked by authors for political and moral ends. In addition to the renarration of familiar stories, many authors adopt what might be termed orality effects and folktale styles to narrate new stories and to produce new morals. In numerous serializations of fiction during the colonial period—and in large numbers of locally published novels and self-help pamphlets since then—authors strive for orality effects in which, rather than following an aesthetic of cathartic consumption, readers are expected to think about the relevance of stories to their societies. For example, at the height of his political opposition to the postcolonial regime of Daniel Arap Moi in Kenya, Ngugi wa Thiong'o made use of characters such as the *marimu* (ogre) from Gikuyu folktales in order to satirize and cast negative judgments on postcolonial Kenyan politicians and businessmen.[74] Other authors, including the Nigerian Amos Tutuola and his Booker Prize–winning protégé, Ben Okri, play with popular, shared folktale templates, utilizing familiar figures in playful ways that work against the moral framework of the oral tales from which they are borrowed.[75]

In the introduction to *The Marriage of Anansewa*, Sutherland writes that the Akan storyteller has "a conventional right to know everything" and "a right to be personally involved in the action."[76] Such personal involvement in the story and its action does not come to West African authors in a form that is unmediated by print, directly from oral sources; nor does personal involvement necessarily take the form of involvement by named persons. The newspaper folktales and the examples of folklore examined in this chapter certainly drew from oral tradition, but they also helped to create a public engagement with print and to generate attitudes toward print and literary interpretation among readers. Although the authors of folktales and folklore may have adopted some of the narrative strategies used by oral narrators, they pressed tradition into the service of print; they mobilized familiar tales for particular moral or political ends; and in the fully anonymous material, they shifted agency onto the tale in the name of public opinion. As a consequence, newsprint itself, rather than authors, often carried the weight of any uncomfortable truths conveyed by the tale. Through folk narratives in colonial newspapers, we therefore seem to be confronted with a "death of the author" and a birth, in its place, of a radical notion of print as existing beyond the subject, conveying a public voice and public opinion, rather than the personal bias of an individual storyteller.

5 ⁓ Printing Women
The Gendering of Literacy

IN JUNE 1918, Lady Clifford, wife of the Gold Coast governor, Sir Hugh Charles Clifford, and a novelist in her own right as Mrs. Henry de la Pasture, published details in the *Gold Coast Leader* of a writing competition for Africans, with the proceeds of the resulting publication to be donated to the Red Cross.[1] In addition to the main competition — six hundred words on "A Day of My Life," open to anybody — Lady Clifford created two further competitions. The first was aimed specifically at African schoolgirls, inviting them to write letters on the topic of "why educated girls ought to be able to keep house, clean and cook, better than uneducated girls."[2] The second competition invited boys under sixteen to write letters on "what work do I wish to do in the world when I am a man, and why" (see fig. 6).[3] To ensure the anonymity of each submission, competitors were instructed to write under pseudonyms and to place their real names and addresses inside sealed envelopes with their noms de plume written on the front; further, teachers were required to authenticate the schoolchildren's letters. Such procedures were designed to guard against fraudulent or illegitimate entries: boys would not easily be able to ventriloquize as girls, for example, nor Europeans as Africans nor adults as children.[4]

The splitting of Lady Clifford's competition along gender lines provides a vital insight into the way in which writing for public consumption, or public writing, was gendered in colonial West Africa, and explains why gender-neutral language has not been adopted in this book so far, with its emphases on pressmen and newspapermen in colonial

FIG. 6. "Lady Clifford's Prize Competitions in Aid of the Red Cross, 1918," from the *Gold Coast Leader*, 29 June 1918, 8.

West Africa.⁵ At the same time, her choice of themes illustrates that women as well as men can manifest gender conservatism, that not all women write from the same ideological position simply because they are women, and that "patriarchy" is a system through which women as well as men can exercise power. With these issues in view, this chapter and the final chapter debate the ways in which the gender of an author *matters* to our appreciation of literary content, in a social and material as well as in a perspectival sense. How useful or necessary is the scholarly—particularly the feminist—desire to ascertain the gender and biography of pseudonymous writers, especially in historical and cultural contexts where gender as a social construct was hotly contested and rendered unstable by disagreements between different power groups about how to describe its supposed essence?

Such an obvious gendering of literacy as found in the topics Lady Clifford chose for each sex demonstrates the ideological biases with which literacy, particularly literacy in English, was imbued in the early twentieth century.⁶ Revealingly, in her efforts to encourage young writers and to lay the foundations for African literary expression, Lady Clifford presupposed and attempted to actively reinforce absolute differences between male and female literacies.⁷ Given the bias of the topic for discussion, it is not surprising that the winner of the first prize among the girls, Nellie Ampiah of the Catholic Girls' School, Cape Coast, described how literacy endows girls with manifest superiority over their uneducated sisters:

> Educated girls know also that we are in this world to serve God. . . . They know they are bound to be subject to their husbands, and to do all they can to make him happy. . . . An uneducated girls [*sic*] never heard of these things. . . . Educated girls know also that clothes last much longer when they are properly washed and ironed. . . . Uneducated girls do not know this, they keep their clothes until they are dirty then they put them aside until they have a lot together and one day they go to wash them. The clothes are so dirty that they cannot get the dirt out easily, then they rub and scrub until the stuff is torn, then mix the blue and put in so much that no one would know what colour the article was in the beginning.⁸

Each of the girls' essays published in Lady Clifford's volume takes for granted this moral assumption that literate girls ought to outperform their uneducated sisters in the domestic tasks expected of all women. If cleanliness is next to godliness in this Christian-inflected view of African femininity, then literacy is the glue used to fix African girls' good habits in place.[9]

Lady Clifford held regular essay and story competitions for newly literate Africans during her time in the Gold Coast in an effort to harness people's literacy to morally worthy ends. Her first competition, in May 1914, called for essays by women on the theme "House-Keeping on the Gold Coast" (see fig. 7).[10] A silver tea service was the first prize, a silver coffeepot was offered as second prize, and the third prize was

> **HOUSE KEEPING ON THE GOLD COAST.**
>
> Lady Clifford is offering a Prize for the most practical Essay written by a Lady on "House-keeping on the Gold Coast."
>
> The first prize will be a Silver Tea Service, the second a Silver Coffee-pot, and the third a Silver Salver.
>
> Any European or Native West African Lady at present domiciled on the Gold Coast, or one who has lived there for not less than an aggregate of 2 years since January 1904, may compete.
>
> Essays must reach Lady Clifford at Government House, Accra, on or before 31st December, 1914.
>
> Essays must be written on one side of the paper only; the sheets must be fastened together, numbered, and signed with a pseudonym.
>
> A sealed envelope with the same pseudonym inscribed clearly *on the outside*, must be sent with each essay. This envelope must contain the real name and address of the sender coupled with a repetition of the pseudonym.
>
> The sealed envelope will be opened by Lady Clifford in the presence of the Judges as soon as the Winning Essays have been selected.
>
> Lady Clifford will invite 3 British, 1 German and 2 Native Gentlemen to act as Judges; to include, if possible, a District Commissioner, a Medical Officer, a Barrister, a Merchant, and a Missionary, in order that the Judges may be as representative as possible of each community concerned with such house-keeping.
>
> Competitors may seek advice or help from non-competitors of either sex who have personal experience of Life on the Gold Coast, but Lady Clifford requests that competitors will honourably refrain from making use of hand-books or other printed information in writing the Essays.
>
> As it is recognised that some of the competitors may be hampered by difficulties of language, the style of writing and perfection of English will not be taken into consideration, but extra marks may be obtained by clearness, simplicity, and brevity.
>
> Competitors are requested to keep a copy of the Essay sent.
>
> Competitors are advised to deal only with those points on which they possess or can obtain first hand knowledge, as the quality and not the quantity of the information given will count. Thus more marks may be gained by dealing sincerely, sensibly and from evident personal experience, with half the subjects named, than less thoroughly with all.

FIG. 7. "House Keeping on the Gold Coast," from the *Gold Coast Leader*, 16 May 1914, 6 a silver salver. Clearly, she was committed to the goal of grafting European middle-class modes of consumption and feminine behavior onto African women (and men) through the medium of their literacy.

Lady Clifford did not assume that cleanliness came naturally to girls simply because of their gender. In segregating masculine themes from feminine ones and, furthermore, in attaching the former to the public sphere and the latter to the domestic sphere, she reiterated an established Victorian gender stereotype in which masculinity was expected to be enacted through one's work and worldliness and femininity through one's household and conjugal duties. As in Britain, schoolgirls and schoolboys across the colonial world were exposed to the gender-biased syllabus produced by such bourgeois Christian assumptions. In no small part, schooling represented an education in femininity for girls and in masculinity for boys.[11]

If African girls required conversion to the cult of domesticity, Lady Clifford did not invest exclusively in this ideal for other social classes and ethnic groups. Her own novels often focused on the unfulfilled lives of well-educated, upper-middle-class English women trapped in drudgery and domestic servitude by egotistical husbands and sons who were out and about, working in the world as men. Preoccupied with women's emotions and experiences, her books were immensely successful with women readers in Britain and the United States, frequently reprinted as cheap popular editions by publishers such as Nelsons. Several of her novels—including *Peter's Mother* (1906) and *The Lonely Lady of Grosvenor Square* (1907)—were made into stage plays and silent movies in the 1910s and 1920s.

The British gendering of literacy was by no means an exclusively colonial process, but it did have particularly strong ramifications in the colonies. As a consequence of the dissonance between local and imperial notions of gender and sexuality, British colonial societies witnessed frequent and very public airings of disagreements about gender. As Ann Laura Stoler and other "new imperial historians" have shown, gender was one of the vehicles for the expression of tensions between local and imperial codes and values in the colonial period.[12] These tensions were almost exclusively centered upon women's bodies, particularly concerning their victimhood at the hands of local men.[13] Support for the "civilizing mission" often revolved around the protective surveillance of so-called native women, especially those who were regarded as abused. An early piece of legislation in Lagos, for instance, was the Slander of Women Ordinance (No. 12) of 1900. From across the denominational spectrum, British missionaries and philanthropists morally condemned the exploitation of women arising from polygyny, bride-price, arranged marriage practices, and the treatment of widows. Often with the support of local Christianized elites, British governmental interventions in established domestic arrangements included the prohibition of "bride-burning," or sati, in India. Throughout the colonial world, British administrations introduced legislation to monitor arranged marriage practices to ensure female consent and to secure women's divorce and inheritance rights.[14]

Whether or not local women knew it, their dirty linen in the colonies was fully on display to the imperial gaze. In British West Africa at least, the bourgeois domain of the private sphere—which in England was supposed to contain and conceal intimate conjugal behavior—was in fact regularly described and debated in the public sphere, to the extent that the colonies followed the trajectory described by Michel Foucault in *The History of Sexuality*.[15] In other words, the discourse through which sexuality was privatized, assigned, labeled, regulated, and patrolled was openly performed in the public domains of newspapers, legislative councils, law courts, schools, textbooks, mission stations, church pulpits, and the clubs and societies frequented by native and European elites.[16] The "private" was thus first and foremost a "public" discourse about the private sphere. The difference in West Africa—and the source of this intense public debate—was that competing notions of sexuality and marriage circulated in the colonial public sphere, for the bourgeois dichotomy between gendered public and private domains did not achieve hegemony in the region, even among Christianized, educated African elites.

Some of the first major legislative items on the agendas of the new administrations in British West Africa after the "scramble for Africa" in the late nineteenth century were marriage ordinances for each territory. In 1884, for example, the Gold Coast and Lagos passed laws to determine where and how marriages could be contracted.[17] These ordinances reified the division between Christian monogamy and so-called traditional, or polygynous, marriage customs, setting up a two-tier system that attempted to make it impossible for a polygynous man to marry a woman in the church or the civil court without first dispensing with his current non-"ordinance" wives. Although this legislation was unenforceable in practical terms, by the late 1920s women who married according to the colonial ordinances had accrued additional divorce, inheritance, and property rights that were legally recognized by colonial courts, over and against the distributive practices of customary systems overseen by traditional courts, which often favored male members of the husband's patri- or matrilineage.[18]

Lady Clifford's competition can be viewed in relation to these legislative interventions as part of the expansion of British imperialism into local people's social lives and relationships. The visible, secular projects of colonial expansion—the barracks, roads, railways, schools, hospitals, and water and sanitation facilities—were often justified by the British with reference to a civilizing mission that involved intrusion into these intimate and domestic spaces in people's lives and the judgment of local people's morality according to Victorian Christian codes of cleanliness and sexual restraint.[19]

Given the British obsession with native intimacies throughout the sprawling empire, the preoccupation with female sexual behavior in the fiction that appeared in African-owned newspapers from the 1880s onward is hardly surprising. If an entrenched public-versus-private dichotomy had emerged in Britain by the end of the nineteenth century, physically separating an ideal of masculinity from an ideal of femininity (as argued by Michael S. Kimmel, Jeff Hearn, and others), British overseas territories contained a multitude of competing local discourses about sexuality and marriage, particularly in relation to women, few of which replicated the monogamous conjugal model promoted in Europe. Countless West African editors and journalists wrote fiction and drama in the colonial period, including from the Gold Coast alone J. E. Casely-Hayford, Rev. Solomon Attoh-Ahuma, W. E. G. (Kobina) Sekyi, Mabel Dove-Danquah, and J. B. Danquah. Beginning in the mid-1930s, increasing numbers of nonelite journalists joined the ranks of these elite authors, producing popular novels with racy titles such as *Matrimonial Tragedy*, *The Illicit Gin Mystery*, and *The Dangerous Four*.[20] In these narratives, authors employed the discursive styles of newspaper editorials and articles, combining social realism with dilemma situations to encourage readers to debate and judge characters' behavior and marital situations and thereby helping to influence the formation of postcolonial reading cultures in the region.

West African fiction in the colonial period was dominated by the theme of marriage, and it was underwritten by the topic of female sexuality to the point of near obsession.[21] Similarly, newspaper editors monitored colonial marriage legislation closely, serializing governors' speeches and portions of bills; offering commentaries; and in the case of particularly controversial ordinances, publishing petitions and open letters to governors. Throughout British West Africa during the decades of colonial rule, African-owned newspapers carried countless articles debating the merits of polygyny compared to monogamy, commentaries on female morality, and articles proposing appropriate topics for the syllabi of local girls' schools. Print and literacy were thus bound into local elites' responses to colonial gender ideologies.

Printed, male-authored texts containing marital advice have a long history in West Africa. Whether they engaged with the colonial marriage ordinances of the 1880s, with the controversies over polygyny in different denominations of the Christian church, or with questions of how to know if a young woman was seeking a suitor's wealth or his undying love,[22] male authors returned repeatedly to a similar set of themes. Large numbers of these morally discursive texts were reproduced in colonial West African newspapers. Taking the form of Christian sermons, folktales, dilemma tales, and proverbs, the texts would often be packed with advice to women on how to conduct themselves, especially in marriage. Physical and emotional intimacies were rarely touched upon in printed texts, however: until the emergence of locally published marriage guidance pamphlets in the late 1980s, sexually explicit information and physically intimate advice for girls seem largely to have been transmitted and controlled by women in the visible community, rather than by the Christianized male elites who ran the region's printing presses.

Set beside journalistic articles and editorials, fiction as a genre offered a rich and rather different set of possibilities, allowing journalists to embellish editorials and debates from the press and to engage in the specificities of colonial ordinances from an intimate, subjective, biased perspective, without overtly commenting on or condemning colonial government and politics. Through fiction, the journalist could honor the second part of the editorial commitment "not only to record events as they transpire, but also to call attention to what he considers public dangers, misconceptions or abuses."[23] As the pseudonymous Marjorie Mensah wrote in 1933, the stories in her daily column were "purely fictitious and the incidents, although [they] may be true, are not specially designed against any member of the community whatsoever and should not cause discomfiture to any person. I think such notice is absolutely necessary to prevent misapprehension and safeguard the beauty of a moral from being lost."[24] Through fiction, the consequences of particular pieces of legislation and social debates could therefore be imagined and dramatized—often made scandalous—without the risk of libel.

Authors of the earliest West African novels shared a preoccupation with the theme of monogamous Christian marriage. One of the earliest serialized novels—*Marita; or The Folly of Love*, by "A Native," published in the *Western Echo* (Cape Coast) between 1886 and 1888—told the story of the near-disastrous ordinance marriage of Mr. Quaibu and Miss Wissah.[25] Written by an author referred to by the editor as "a native gentleman," this unfinished story exposed the sexual hypocrisy and corruption of the Methodist Church for its imposition of the rule of monogamy on its members while simultaneously encouraging unsupervised, mixed-sex prayer meetings in the evenings between laymen and unchaperoned married women. At the domestic level, monogamous marriage transformed the docile, cloth-wearing Miss Wissah into the henpecking, frock-wearing Mrs. Quaibu. With the taming of the termagant and the couple's "complete reconciliation" came two key promises, both representing an effort to reassert masculine authority within a Christian conjugal arrangement: the wife "promis[ed] lawful obedience to him, and, he promis[ed] her protection, and free scope to worship her Maker any where but at that place which had been a bone of contention between them which very nigh led to a separation."[26] In addition to this main story of feminine obedience and masculine protection, the narrative was spliced with numerous didactic story fragments, each of which offered "wholesome lessons and valuable advice" about marriage, prayerfulness, and the need for masculine authority in the household.[27]

African-owned newspapers are packed with similar examples of didactic original fiction by pseudonymous authors. This material deserves considerable further attention for the manner in which it contributes to the cultural history of the region, producing aesthetic and interpretive models that influenced the approaches and themes of subsequent generations of West African authors. Another lengthy serialization—*Adelaide of Adelaide Street; or Train Up a Child in the Way She Should Go*, by the Sierra Leonean writer "J. C."—presents one of the earliest and most detailed explorations of colonial mimicry in the context of conjugal relations.[28]

The stereotypical character of the mimic came to dominate representations of the anglicized native well into the postindependence era. The mimic was a pancolonial literary figure, providing a vehicle for colonial elites to satirize men and women belonging to the group they regarded as socially illegitimate and culturally alienated—that is, semieducated locals who aspired to emulate Englishness in dress, language, and etiquette without having properly internalized or understood the complexities of English culture.[29] The male incarnation of such upstarts, as the narrator of *Adelaide of Adelaide Street* makes clear in a biting social commentary, is a "small boy with little education and less common sense" who expects status and public recognition simply because he has "some quids in his pocket and some account in his favour at the Bank" as a result of his African trading activities.[30] Similarly, the female incarnation of the colonial mimic and the protagonist of J. C.'s story possesses a "false view of ladyship . . . obtained from the white woman" in which "ladyship was regarded as both synonymous with and utterly equivalent to dressing in gay fashion (an improvement on the simple style of the white woman), talking the English language in an affected style, walking in foreign fashion, getting a piano, *and doing no homely work.*"[31]

Published in the *Sierra Leone Weekly News* throughout 1911, *Adelaide of Adelaide Street* charts the morally disastrous consequences when parents "spoil" a daughter by transforming her from a Christian Mende girl into a colonial mimic who has "been taught to look upon the common drudgeries of home life as supremely beneath the attention of a young and beautiful girl who had attended school at the Grove."[32] Though no details can be found of a school called the Grove, the action of the story is located in real streets in Freetown, in the type of spacious modern house inhabited by coasters (traders in international products who frequently worked for the large European firms in West Africa), traders, and other aspiring members of the emerging bourgeoisie. As with the story of Ṣẹgilọla, discussd in detail later in this chapter, the realist narrative style of *Adelaide of Adelaide Street* places the story sufficiently close to readers for its moral warnings to cause discomfort among those whose class is described. The social realism is, however, infused with parabolic layers reminiscent of John Bunyan's *The Pilgrim's Progress*, including the appearance of didactic characters with names such as Selina Talktative, Mrs Busybee, and Nellie Virtue.[33]

In numerous pseudonymous and locally published narratives in the colonial period, the focal point is the same as in *Marita; or The Folly of Love* and *Adelaide of Adelaide Street*: the misbehavior of a disobedient, badly trained woman who exploits her position as mistress of a Christian monogamous household to reject her husband's authority and to run riot socially. The moral responsibility of the husband, this newspaper fiction shows, is to rein in the termagant and reestablish male superiority. The authors' preoccupation with feminine behavior can thus be regarded as part of the public moral discourse hosted by newspapers concerning civic virtue, family morality, and personal reputation.[34] In the case of *Adelaide of Adelaide Street*, J. C. depicts the results of the protagonist's poor moral training stage by stage, from the girl's infancy through to her marriage to a decent coaster named Teddy Envers who mistakenly regards her as a virtuous Christian woman keen to enter conjugal domesticity. The final sentence of this unfinished novel reads, "Poor Envers, boy, youth, inexperienced, was in blissful ignorance."[35] One can only imagine the moral disasters planned by the author for the subsequent, unpublished installments of this story.

Many other texts might be added to those discussed here, but one nonpseudonymous novel merits mention for its difference from these narratives. *Guanya Pau: A Story of an African Princess* was written by the American-educated Liberian author Joseph J. Walters. First published as a book in 1891 in Ohio, this important "rights of women" novel was later serialized for African audiences in the *Liberia Recorder* between 1905 and 1906.[36] Like the works of A Native and J. C., *Guanya Pau* addresses women's rights and roles in marriage from a Christian point of view, dramatizing the tensions between Christian and customary marriage practices and also exploring the consequences of the marital culture clash between colonialism and tradition on African couples' domestic power relations. Unlike the newspaper novels discussed earlier, however, Walters's novel unambiguously endorses a Eurocentric Christian discourse and anticipates a key theme in popular Nigerian "market literature" in the 1950s and 1960s: an African girl's resistance to her arranged marriage to a repulsive but wealthy old polygynist. In *Guanya Pau*, the African princess escapes from the old man's clutches, only to witness the pervasive victimization of African women through the length and breadth of the country.[37] Anything but cultural nationalist in its rejection of tradition, Walters's tragic novel is Christian and paternalistic in a similar manner to colonial discourses about native women's rights. In this, *Guanya Pau* exemplifies the manner in which local Christianized elites asserted their own political leadership and modernity through a rejection of traditional African masculinities and through a protective discourse about female victimhood and the personal tragedies it engenders.

In the fiction of the pseudonymous A Native, the untraceable J. C., and the well-biographized Joseph J. Walters, we encounter some of the most recurrent character types to appear in West African fiction in subsequent decades: the henpecked and gullible husband; the colonial mimic; and the modern "frock lady" and her counterpart, the "cloth woman," who transmuted, after the 1920s, into the "prostitute" and her morally respectable alter ego, the "loyal wife." These popular fictional characters appeared in newspaper serials, pamphlets, and paperbacks throughout the colonial period, as well as in emerging popular dramatic forms such as the Ghanaian concert party and the Yoruba traveling theater after the 1940s.[38] Persisting well into the twentieth century, they changed with the times but always served to present strong authorial opinions and to inspire debates among readers about the morality or immorality of particular gendered behaviors in African settings.

From a sociological standpoint, each of these female character types can be seen to reflect upon the social changes to gender relations that came in the wake of the colonial encounter, especially the expansion of commerce and trade in African cities. In particular, the colonial city offered educational opportunities that facilitated women's emergence into the white-collar workforce as teachers, secretaries, and shop assistants, so that by the 1930s and 1940s, the mobility and independence of Western-educated African women was greater than in the early colonial period.[39] Yet as vehicles for opinion and debate, the protagonists and themes discussed previously were far more than social reflectors of the colonial encounter. The story lines inhabited by characters such as Miss Wissah, Adelaide, and the African princess were imbued with African responses to imperialist representations of native cultures and relationships.

Given the attention to women's behavior in each of these narratives, how important is it to discover the identity—especially the gender identity—of authors such as A Native and J. C.? In the majority of pseudonymous contributions to West African newspapers, the identities and biographies of authors are hidden from history: they cannot simply be retrieved from the archive. To what extent, however, would readers' interpretative processes be affected or altered by the knowledge that the creator of Adelaide and of Miss Wissah was a man or a woman?

The quest for authorial gender identity brings with it a borderline essentialism in which gender as a set of discourses, debates, and social constructs is posited as fundamental to the production of people's realities, essential to their interpersonal and interpretative experiences. Similarly, the world of print loses its supposed neutrality if one supposes that gender or other sociological categories such as ethnicity or class come before and determine textual meaning. Such assumptions risk putting the cart before the horse, attributing masculinity to texts for which there is a suggestion of male authorship and femininity—or feminism—to supposedly or self-confessedly female-authored texts. More problematic still is the temptation to attribute particular types of content to the literary productions of each sex.

Actually, all is not as gender balanced as it seems. By inscribing women's voices into the moral core of their narratives, these early authors stage ideological interventions in debates about the negative effects of British marriage laws on the gendered balance of power in the colonies. Through fiction, they closely monitor the behavior of monogamous newly weds, but as with the colonial patrolling of intimacy, their focus is upon the female body as an errant or abused entity, requiring men's intervention or protection. Above all, in these textual displays of exemplary and unreasonable marital behavior the moral catalyst each time is the figure of the wife. Through the characters of Miss Wissah, Adelaide, and Guanya Pau, each author contrasts and interrogates polygynous and monogamous marriages for their positive or negative effects on masculine authority over women in the household. Husbands and fathers are placed under scrutiny for encouraging or allowing their women's misbehavior, but the moral critique is precipitated, each time, by the behavior of a woman. Though the primary perspective is feminine, therefore, the positionality and bias of each story remain masculine.

These concerns about the gender of authors were resolved or at least rendered irrelevant by West African newspaper readers themselves. In their responses to the issues raised by particular stories, readers generally demonstrated no desire to source original fiction to particular individuals in the community.[40] Literary texts were regarded as works of social critique, rather than as self-contained artistic creations available for literary criticism. The originality of the work of oral storytellers often arises from the brilliance of a personality-in-performance or from a bard's charismatic self-presentation,[41] but the originality of printed stories, for West African readers, lay in the vivid fictional characters and (im)moral scenarios made possible by authors' withdrawal of self or personality from the public sphere.

The Sierra Leonean author "Erne's Friend" exemplifies this process. At the start of "His First and Only Love," a story published in the *Sierra Leone Weekly News* in three installments in 1894, the author explains that he or she writes fiction in order to "fully dissect" some of the "burning question[s] of the day."[42] Erne's Friend states that he or she has already produced three other narratives, entitled "Cruelly Treated," "Loving and Liking," and "Municipality," the content of which was designed to stimulate public debate. The author continues:

> For reasons best known to me, however, I have not as yet published the [latter two]. In the tale "Loving and Liking," I endeavoured to prove that though we are only "Black Englishmen" we have correct ideas of the meanings of the two words, to love and to like . . .
>
> In the other story, "Municipality," I endeavoured to have this burning question of the day fully dissected in a discussion between some very principal factors, although that tale was also a love story.[43]

Erne's Friend takes for granted the belief that the value of creative writing lies in the ethical debates that stories will stimulate among readers, without the interventions or presence of an identifiable author. Akin to parables, stories thus function as didactic and discursive tools, created by authors to lever open and expose the moral core of "burning" social issues such as marriage by ordinance, romantic love in Africa, the creation of a colonial municipality, or the education of women. Perhaps this is why readers rarely commented directly on stories or expressed curiosity about the identities of authors. The preference of readers to debate the moral issues raised by the story, rather than to comment on the content and form of individual narratives, indicates the existence of a literary culture in which the publicness of literature was conferred by the avoidance of attribution. A search for "real" authors seems misplaced in such a context, and as a sign of its futility, such searches frequently lead the researcher further into a labyrinthine paper trail of pseudonyms: a hunt for the author of Erne's Friend, for example, runs dry at "The Czar," author of "Cruelly Treated" in 1889.[44]

Bearing in mind that women as well as men can express patriarchal views, the three early works of fiction discussed in this chapter illustrate a dilemma common to feminist literary scholarship: although the desire to discover an author's gender is problematically essentialist, there are many reasons—integral to the texts and extraneous to each story—to suppose that *Marita; or The Folly of Love*, *Adelaide of Adelaide Street*, and *Guanya Pau: A Story of an African Princess* were indeed all written by men. Internal evidence includes the masculine positionality of each narrative. Extraneous evidence includes the author's name, as in Joseph Walters's case, or information about the author, such as the editor of the *Western Echo*'s reference to the "native gentleman" author of *Marita; or The Folly of Love*.[45]

Lady Clifford's choice of the genre of the letter for her gender-divided schoolchildren's competition reflects the outward-oriented, proselytizing character of literacy in Britain's colonies—the need for a full "correspondence" between writers and readers. One could argue that the printed material discussed in this section—for and about African women—contributed to the production of the very differences in theme and preoccupation that caused women's writing to be neglected and labeled irrelevant in subsequent decades.[46] As with Lady Clifford's writing competition, however, the African-authored texts examined earlier reveal the extent to which gender was produced and monitored in colonial societies through writing per se and, conversely, how writing contributed to the production of the social realities it described.[47] Lady Clifford's conservative and essentialist gendering of literacy seems unpalatable today for its imposition of distinctive feminine themes and roles upon women, but West African women's contributions to journalism in the colonial period—pseudonymous or otherwise—existed in the shadow of these European ideals and prejudices about gender and literacy.

Such ideals and prejudices influenced authors' choices of pseudonyms. The next section asks about the degree to which male writers' textual attempts to "pass" as women facilitate the vocalization of opinions considered off limits to men *as* men, allowing them to employ literary genres and themes not considered to be properly masculine. With different degrees of success, two male editors, I. B. Thomas and J. V. Clinton, cross into the separate sphere designated for women's discourses and activities, "dragging" their masculine authorial articulations into the social world of women. Thomas, in particular, uses the figure of a prostitute to impart didactic, sensational material about the supposed misuses of urban female sexuality outside of marriage.

FEMININE FICTIONS:
WRITING ACROSS GENDER BY NIGERIAN NEWSPAPER EDITORS

Unlike A Native, Tired, and the other writers who adopted generic pseudonyms in the West African press, the two journalists examined in this section did not slough off all signs of social status and identity in favor of an emancipated, free-playing subjectivity. They adopted other identities. In the case of Isaac Babalola Thomas (c. 1888–1963), the persona chosen is that of "Ṣẹgilọla," an ex-prostitute living in a state of extreme moral and physical affliction in late 1920s Lagos who submits weekly installments of her life story for publication in *Akede Eko*, the Yoruba-language newspaper edited by Thomas between 1929 and 1953.[48] Ṣẹgilọla's testimonial, or confession, is offered to readers as a true account, occurring in the reader's present world, rather than as a work of the creative imagination: indeed, so insistent is Thomas on Ṣẹgilọla's nonfictional status that an impressive battery of narrative strategies is deployed to demonstrate her physical presence and contemporaneity with Yoruba readers. "No one has put a rope around Ṣẹgilọla's neck to make her confess," he insists: "We never asked this elderly lady to write her life-story for the paper for all the world to read."[49]

The second case study is rather different. In the 1960s, James Vivian Clinton (c. 1898–1973), freelance journalist, civil servant, and veteran editor of the *Nigerian Eastern Mail* (Calabar, 1935–51), enthusiastically and decisively embraced the gender- and culture-crossing potentialities of creative writing.[50] Ṣẹgilọla's insistence on female authenticity was replaced in Clinton's pseudonymous fiction with the discovery that literary markets, rather than individuals, help to produce an author's name, gender, and mode of expression. A romantic story for a UK magazine such as *Woman's Weekly* by an author with an African man's name would, Clinton realized, probably fail to attract white women readers; likewise, stories written for male-oriented magazines such as *Spear* and *Drum* should be "about some aspect of the sexual situation from the male point of view."[51] With these principles in mind and having struggled to make ends meet since the bankruptcy of the *Mail* in the early 1950s, Clinton embarked on a detailed study of the art of writing popular fiction in the 1960s. He produced a voluminous stream of romances and detective stories under female, male, African, and European pseudonyms for submission to Nigerian, British, and North American magazines.

Despite the fact that Thomas and Clinton were born within approximately a decade of one other at the end of the nineteenth century, a historical gulf separates the production of the story of Ṣẹgilọla from Clinton's popular romances and detective stories. In the intervening thirty years, secondary and higher education expanded in Nigeria; the country gained political independence from Britain; local publishers flourished in the educational market; and Heinemann's African Writers Series, established in 1962, brought international attention to Nigerian writers through novels such as *Things Fall Apart*,[52] *Efuru*,[53] and *The Concubine*.[54] These powerful political and cultural currents helped to give shape to Nigerian literature in the 1960s, influencing local authors' choices of themes and styles in a manner that some recent commentators have regarded as potentially self-limiting but others have welcomed as marking West African literature's coming of age.[55] Literary genres—especially the novel—flourished in the years that followed independence. In particular, the market for school reading books expanded rapidly as publishers sought African-authored material for the postcolonial syllabus.[56] In the literary culture inhabited by Clinton, therefore, the polygeneric newspapers that he and Thomas edited in the 1920s and 1930s must have seemed like remote crucibles for literary expression and experimentation compared with the modern presses producing newspapers, fiction, and pamphlets in postcolonial Nigerian towns and cities.

Given the extent of these differences, my justification for connecting both newspapermen across the decades in this chapter is not simply that they were of the same generation and occupation. Important as these factors were, the two men shared another characteristic. Unlike the majority of West African journalists who produced fiction in the colonial period, Thomas and Clinton adopted feminine pseudonyms and used print to attempt, more or less successfully, to mask their masculinity by taking up feminine points of view.[57] Stemming from the same era of Nigerian newspaper production in the 1920s and 1930s, their different approaches to pseudonymous authorship demonstrated the dynamism and social responsiveness of Nigerian print cultures to political and social transformations, as well as the adaptability of these two individuals to new technologies and markets. Furthermore, the similarities and differences between their gender-crossing literary practices revealed the plurality of ways in which male authors engaged with debates about women's social roles and positions through the production of literature in West African communities.

In adopting feminine pseudonyms, perhaps Thomas and Clinton were embarrassed to publish intimate or domestic material under male names for fear that it would undermine their authority as commentators on political and legislative matters. For several reasons, however, such a blatant public (masculine) versus private (feminine) opposition is not feasible in this case. In spite of the efforts of Lady Clifford and the European colonial educators discussed in the previous section, gender politics in colonial settings did not simply mirror Victorian and Edwardian spatial and discursive dichotomies. Unlike the domestic ideology that inspired the civilizing mission in the metropolis, in the vast territory that made up Nigeria many women engaged in diverse "own-account" activities involving independent travel and trade.[58] Feminist historians of West Africa have produced numerous studies of women in positions of political influence. As "market queens," as titleholders in local chieftaincies, as "female husbands" within gender-dynamic households, as votaries of deities, and as ordinary traders, farmers, mothers, wives, and cowives, large numbers of African women would have failed to recognize the private sphere as a designated zone for female occupation and activity.[59]

In spite of their status as members of the literate elite, closely implicated in the civilizing mission as its products and ambivalent mouthpieces, Thomas and Clinton could not have ignored the irrelevance in society at large of gendered oppositions between the public and private spheres.[60] As the remainder of this chapter will suggest, rather than simply reproducing Christianized and anglicized gender rules their decisions to adopt feminine personae related to a different cluster of cultural codes involving complex relationships between genre, print, masking, gender, and power.

A "WOMAN OF LETTERS" IN 1920S LAGOS: THE STORY OF "SẸGILỌLA OF THE FASCINATING EYES"

In July 1929, Isaac B. Thomas, prolific journalist and editor-proprietor of the new Yoruba-language newspaper *Akede Eko* (Lagos Herald, 1929–53), published a strongly worded letter from a woman using the pseudonym "Sẹgilọla of the Fascinating Eyes." This name, as the narrator points out repeatedly in her correspondence over the coming months, has been adopted for the purpose of "preserv[ing] secrecy."[61] "No one under this sky [must] . . . hear my given name pass your lips," she instructs the editor again and again, or else she "will turn . . . into a fugitive and vagabond in this city of Lagos in which I was born."[62]

The pseudonymous writer's relationship with the editor of *Akede Eko* is thus established from the outset in the form of a contract and a threat. Only with regular reassurances of editorial confidentiality will Ṣẹgilọla continue to submit her letters, each of which promises to disclose further details about her sexually scandalous life as a prostitute in Lagos. The contributor expresses trust and vulnerability, and the editor shows protectiveness and integrity, earning showers of praise from Ṣẹgilọla in subsequent letters for his discretion, professionalism, wisdom, and intelligence. Indeed, the only man in Lagos praised unconditionally in this serial is the editor himself: "You, editor, are one of the most insightful and wise people anywhere in the world," she repeats.[63]

This interaction between Ṣẹgilọla and the editor typifies, in dramatic form, the correspondent-editor relationship until the mid-1930s, when the tightening of colonial sedition laws against pseudonymous writers and the emergence of celebrity-oriented journalism signaled the beginning of a new era in the West African press (see chapter 3). Appearing each week between July 1929 and March 1930, "The Life Story of Me, 'Ṣẹgilọla of the Fascinating Eyes,' She Who Had a Thousand Lovers in Her Life" tantalized and captivated the literate elites of Lagos, stimulating commentaries, songs, correspondence, occasional poems, and a great deal of curiosity about the identity of this fallen Yoruba woman. "Ever since we began publishing it," the editor comments at the start of the seventh installment, "reports have been pouring in from all sides, at home and abroad. . . . Countless friends at home or away have been seeking us out, or writing to us, to plead with us to tell them her real name, or the name of the neighbourhood where 'Ṣẹgilọla of the Fascinating Eyes' lived in this city of Lagos."[64]

Ṣẹgilọla is coterminous with her readers, sharing the same public sphere as them, reading her own letters in *Akede Eko* each week, and commenting on readers' reactions and correspondence in subsequent installments of the serial. The fact that she shelters under a screen of strictly enforced editorial secrecy about her true identity simply reinforces her *presence* at large in her beloved hometown of Lagos.

"I will be grateful to you for the rest of my days," Ṣẹgilọla writes in the opening installment, for "space every week" to tell "my life-story for the whole world to read in your newspaper *Akede Eko*."[65] As Karin Barber points out in her substantial introduction to her new edition of the story, this comment seems designed to give local consumers a sense of connectivity, through print, with global networks of newspaper readers, particularly "friends away" in the Yoruba diaspora.[66] Though *Akede Eko* would not have circulated around the "whole world," even if it had been published in English, this is a comment on the potentiality of print to reach beyond borders into the "imagined community" described by Benedict Anderson as distinguishing print capitalism from other modes of communication.[67] The seemingly exaggerated notion of a global readership to be found in Ṣẹgilọla's letters communicates a perception of print widely held among West African readers—that a life story, when published, would leave the confines of the personal and take on its own separate existence within a potentially global, morally influential realm of circulation. One reader put this succinctly in a letter dated 29 September 1930, praising Thomas's newspaper: "[Akede Eko is] not only the Lagos Herald but the World Herald, because it reveals important matters to the world."[68] The entry of Ṣẹgilọla's story into the whole world, therefore, does not so much assert a global readership for Akede Eko as highlight the existence of "important matters," put into print, that the world should read in the pages of this newspaper.

Relishing his role as Ṣẹgilọla's mouthpiece and shield, at no point in his responses to correspondents did Thomas reveal that he was in fact the author of the letters. The mask of femininity stuck for several months after the end of the serial, at least until its publication in pamphlet form. Indeed, so popular was Ṣẹgilọla as a contributor to Akede Eko that the absence of an installment one week caused readers to contact the editor in consternation, fearing that the protagonist had succumbed to her extreme and deteriorating physical condition and died before completing her confession.[69] One pseudonymous reader, "Jumôkê," claiming to be an ex-prostitute herself, even posted a ten shilling note to the offices of Akede Eko for the editor to give to his unhappy contributor.[70]

Knowing all along that Thomas was the author prevents one from appreciating the startling effects that Ṣẹgilọla's "confession" must have had on those readers who believed in the protagonist's reality. Many of the "very exclusive, distinguished gentlemen" and "the top lawyers in Lagos society" referred to in this story must have read the pages of Akede Eko with trepidation each week as the narrator all but named her wealthy, married lovers around town and gave details of the material goods she had extracted from them over the years. Ṣẹgilọla did not, however, exploit her pseudonymity to "name and shame" her local lovers, for she was well aware of the negative legal consequences of naming a person in print. In one submission referring to the stern warnings she received from Thomas against disclosure of the identities of her ex-lovers on grounds of colonial libel laws, she wrote: "I'm afraid the editor of *Akede Eko* has warned me that it would be an offence against the law to name people in this context in the newspaper, whether they're alive or dead."[71] She continued: "If it were not for the editor's warning to me Ṣẹgilọla, I would have named many famous and distinguished men of the Lagos area, some of whom have since died, but a few of whom are still alive today, to whom I Ṣẹgilọla of the Fascinating Eyes was once an irresistible attraction, when my beauty was as radiant as the rainbow."[72]

Women were not exempt from these threats of exposure, for she noted that "if it were not for the power of this law, I Ṣẹgilọla would likewise expose the names of many of my female age-mates with whom I associated in Lagos for purposes of promiscuity and debauchery."[73] In this manner, Thomas played cat and mouse with those readers who had guilty consciences, reminding them of the protection afforded by colonial libel laws but, in so doing, making veiled threats about information in his possession and its potential future disclosure.

Thomas seemed to relish the tension between the narrator's pseudonymity, on the one hand, and his power to threaten to name elite men in the community, on the other hand. The fact that Ṣẹgilọla was not real and that her pseudonym masked nobody suggests that the references to libel laws were part of a moral strategy on the part of the author, designed to make "guilty" readers squirm uncomfortably for fear of exposure. As an example of West African print subjectivity, the story can thus be seen as an illustration of a productive confrontation between the anonymous status conferred on a person by print and that other hallowed principle of West African journalism in the early twentieth century, the avoidance of "personality" (see chapter 2). Nearly naming, nearly shaming, Thomas played provocatively with the minds of powerful men in Lagos society and thereby showed them that the editor was all knowing, the most powerful man of all.

With its abject, well-educated narrator who dangled titillating cliff-hangers in front of her readers each week, the story aroused great curiosity about the identity of the author. Incarnating a type of behavior and its moral consequences for the individual, Ṣẹgilọla was not allowed *not* to be real by many of her readers. Who was this fallen woman whose idiomatic Yoruba and intricate knowledge of the streets and elites of Lagos gave an air of intimacy and familiarity to the narrative? Thomas was happy to publish readers' responses in *Akede Eko* and to have Ṣẹgilọla herself comment on readers' letters: as in other West African newspapers at the time, such active audience involvement stimulated debate about public issues and generated new and desperately needed subscribers to the newspaper. In one especially clever editorial maneuver to recruit paying readers to *Akede Eko*, Thomas had Ṣẹgilọla launch an appeal after she read his column detailing the "unfortunate difficulties or money-troubles which threaten to impede you in this important work you are doing for the progress of our town." She declared, "As God is my witness, if I were in a position to help with money, I wouldn't think twice about donating generously to help you in that work."[74]

Two months after the serial was republished as a booklet, a leader in *Akede Eko*'s rival, the English-language *Nigerian Daily Times* (Lagos, 1926–present), described the story as a "collection of filth" and a "series of muck" written in a "degraded" vernacular that the government should act to censor.[75] In response, Thomas threw a flurry of insults at the editor of the *Times*,[76] calling him, among other things, "an errand-boy or labourer, a mere hired hand" and informing him that the government had more important things to consider than such trivial matters as Ṣẹgilọla's story.[77] But Thomas also inadvertently or casually confessed to the authorship of the story. As Barber observes, in boasting about the praiseworthy and publishable standard of his Yoruba and in using this to defend the quality of the story against accusations of poor style, Thomas implicitly claimed the work as his own.[78] Nobody seemed to notice or mind the discrepancy between this and earlier assertions that Ṣẹgilọla "came to our office of her own accord one Saturday evening with a proposal that we publish [her story]; and we felt very sorry for her that evening."[79]

Thomas's pretense of having met the writer in person was, of course, also a comic truth, for he did indeed know the author of the story. This double-masking maneuver can be regarded as part of a game to expose and exploit readers' desires for confessionals to stem from authentic sources. In constructing a double layer of pseudonymity, Thomas satirized the genre of life writing itself, particularly those pseudonymous texts, typical in European literature, in which narrators are sensitive and "self"-conscious about the necessity for protection by their masks.[80] If one does not know the identity of its author, the life story of Ṣẹgilọla offers an exemplary instance of that form of anonymity prevalent in eighteenth- and nineteenth-century European literature, in which authors of politically or morally controversial material kept their "true" names hidden under the cloak of a pseudonym, fearful of exposure and carefully avoiding giving any clues about themselves yet conscious of their power to expose others through scandals and tidbits of verifiable information.[81] In a manner similar to that of eighteenth-century satirists such as Jonathan Swift, Sẹgilọla's author seemed secretly to relish all the irony that was made possible by the absolute anonymity provided by print.

Once one knows that Thomas was the author, every sentence in the confession seems to resist, contradict, complicate, and play with the notion of pseudonymity as a "sincere" form of masked self-expression. In particular, if Sẹgilọla feared a loss of reputation or name through the community's discovery of her actual identity, her mask was so carefully positioned and contextualized that it became just as real as the biography of an actual person. The confession was filled with such intricate, realistic details about contemporary Lagos, alongside Yoruba songs, hymns, historical references, and well-known maxims, that the physical environment seemed full of the narrator's presence.[82] The narrative contained a multitude of strategies designed to produce and demonstrate Sẹgilọla's geographic proximity to readers. Thus, she described how she "was a child of excellent family in this city of Lagos": "I was born at Bamgbose Street on September 9, 1882, I am the 6th child of my parents, my elders had all died in their infancy; according to the account given me by my parents, I am the last born by my parents in their old age."[83] She gave precise details of her education, detailing how she "went up to Standard V in the Alapako School" and "went along to the girls' high school with the others."[84]

A more subtle authentication device in the narrative was Sẹgilọla's continuous appeal for her own death in preference to the humiliation of having her "name," or reputation, smeared: "Death is better than mockery," she repeated, "but though I Sẹgilọla beg for death, death refuses to kill me to obliterate my shame and degradation."[85] Such self-abnegation had the reverse effect, reinforcing readers' belief in her presence somewhere in Lagos, waiting remorsefully to be released into the next life. During one especially vehement spate of self-reproaching comments, she even instructed the editor to publish her name and photograph immediately after her demise.[86] The cumulative effect of these excessive truth claims over the duration of the serial was to assert that the narrator was anything but a fictional character. Readers were drawn into the magnetic field of her reality. Unlike Dick Carnis, A Native, and others whose pseudonyms playfully prevented the attribution of authorship, the vociferous, repetitive "I," "Me" and "my" of Ṣẹgilọla's confession inserted her as a carnal presence in the reader's own world.

So vehement was this narrator about her physical actuality that she even provided readers with the history of how she came to be called Ṣẹgilọla: "I was a young girl whose eyes were large and lustrous, which caused the wives of the house to give me the nickname or praise-epithet 'One with the Fascinating Eyes.' 'Ṣẹgilọla' was the name that my mother's mother called me by when I was a child—my mother told me that it was my neck which glowed darkly when they put *segi* beads around it which caused my mother's mother to call me 'Ṣẹgilọla.'"[87] The pseudonym was thus presented as a praise name or nickname, explained with such conviction that its "pseudo" status was discarded. If her name was an *alibi*, designed to hide, rather than a nickname or praise name designed to pass comment on aspects of a person's character and appearance, Ṣẹgilọla should not have required such a detailed sociohistorical explanation as was provided here.

At least one reader was taken in by these literary techniques. In an open letter to Ṣẹgilọla, "D. A. L." wrote: "When your story first began to appear, I thought that the editor of the *Akede Eko* newspaper was just joking . . . but when I began to pay attention to the names, neighbourhoods, times and all kinds of other things, this banished all my doubts, and I became convinced that all of it is true, and that the story of your life is full of lessons."[88] D. A. L.'s letter, which ended with a polite request to meet Ṣẹgilọla in person, revealed important details about interpretive currents among Yoruba readers in the 1920s and 1930s. Ṣẹgilọla's confession was not simply an instance of editorial playfulness and parody. Thomas had a serious moral purpose in composing this text, one that required readers to sense this woman's physical presence and to look for her on the streets of Lagos. He could have written a column containing marital advice to women, just as he did in *Eleti Ọfẹ* in 1924 under the pseudonym Awoluje,[89] but instead he required the reality effect of a female author. His narrative contained no playful or flirtatious hints about the author's actual identity, and it seems that the majority of readers either wanted this story to be true or did not care whether the narrator was a real person or not.

Thus far, this chapter has been dominated by a preoccupation with when and whether the true identity of the author was disclosed

Printing Women: The Gendering of Literacy ⁓ 145

to readers. Such an interest could, however, be seen to introduce a false dichotomy between fact and fiction or between realism and reality. These concepts may not have required separation in the literary culture inhabited by Sẹgilọla. Sẹgilọla's confession adhered to an aesthetic similar to that described by Lennard Davis, discussed in detail in chapter 4. As Barber points out in her introduction to the text, Sẹgilọla was far more than a pseudonym designed to disguise fiction as history: her name was a mode of moral personification that, masklike, incarnated a story of extreme debauchery and promiscuity.[90] Evidence of this moral process can be found in *Akede Eko* in July 1930, when a regular correspondent and firm Sẹgilọla loyalist, Balogun Dodondawa, wrote a column in which the figure of Sẹgilọla was invoked not simply to repeat and apply her story to society but also to construct a new version of the tale.[91] Just as Thomas used reality effects such as place-names and family details, Dodondawa built up the prostitute's physical presence using "evidence" that did not appear in the original text. Presented as if personally witnessed, this version of Sẹgilọla inherited the literary techniques to be found in the original story. "Dainty-footed as a bride," Dodondawa wrote, introducing as much realism as possible, "with neck as shapely as a spiral snail shell, teeth as white as egrets, you felt you ought to wash your hands before you shook hands with her. And what about her walk, how she strolled, how she strutted, how she swayed from side to side; her hair was like silk."[92] Having established the prostitute's physicality, Dodondawa launched his moral crusade: "Prostitution or harlotry never profited any woman, and it never will till the end of the world. If it benefits them today, it's only for a short while. At any moment, a fate worse than Sẹgilọla's may overtake them, unless they sincerely repent and forswear harlotry before it is too late."[93]

In presupposing that readers would morally engage with the debates that were staged through the story of Sẹgilọla, Dodondawa took for granted a particular aesthetic standpoint in which readers participated in the text, judged characters, and involved themselves in discussions of dilemmas. The epistolary form of the confession reinforced this assumption of readerly involvement. Like the sermon and other didactic literary genres, epistolarity assumes and demands the presence of an addressee or recipient, albeit a fictionally constructed reader used to legitimate the publication of scandalous, intimate, "private" material. From Cicero onward, pedagogues have used the epistolary form to convey ethical advice and warnings about immoral behavior.[94] By definition, letters have addressees, who are positioned to be engaged with, educated by, and persuaded by the correspondents' descriptions.[95]

Far more than playing with the anonymizing potential of print, therefore, Thomas's narrative revealed information about how print itself was regarded in the Yoruba press and how readers responded to particular modes of writing. The ancillary texts published by Barber demonstrate readers' overwhelming requirement not for fiction or "creative writing" but for real-life moral material from which they could extrapolate lessons, what Davis labels "newes." In all of its printed manifestations, the Ṣẹgilọla "myth" strove to transform realism into reality. This technique of connecting fictional models with social realities has a clear ancestry in African oral narratives, where the storyteller is expected to embellish familiar texts and to apply a socially relevant moral at the end and where readers debate and learn from the dilemmas contained in the story. As with Dodondawa's version of Ṣẹgilọla, a good storyteller will update and improvise his or her material, taking well-known tales and characters and adding new details in order to engage listeners and to encourage them to identify, situate, and apply the lesson.[96]

The story of Ṣẹgilọla was not unique for this orality effect. In numerous West African newspaper serials during the colonial period—and in large numbers of locally published novels and self-help pamphlets since then—one finds descriptions of a relationship between writers and readers in which, rather than following an aesthetic of cathartic consumption or entertainment, both parties are expected to think about the relevance of stories to their own lives. Ṣẹgilọla's story, as her editor was frequently at pains to point out, was intended to "serve as an example and a warning [for] our young boys and girls just starting out in life, and also, importantly, for our elders, male and female, who revel in promiscuity, lewdness and lasciviousness."[97]

Such an instruction echoed verbatim through locally published Nigerian literature in subsequent decades and infused the African-owned press of the 1930s.[98] In the words of Marjorie Mensah, the pseudonymous and immensely popular author of the "Women's Corner" (also called the "Ladies' Corner") in the *Times of West Africa*, characters in newspaper articles were "characters that we meet in the streets every day," but they were *also* "purely fictitious and the incidents, although [they] may be true, are not specially designed against any member of the community whatsoever and should not cause discomfiture to any person. I think such notice is absolutely necessary to prevent misapprehension and safeguard the beauty of a moral from being lost."[99]

In Marjorie's weekly column, the "fictitious," as she called it, took precedence over hard-news stories, and descriptive journalism took second place to morally evaluative writing. Sentimental stories were developed from real-life anecdotes, instilled with the exaggerated prose of the popular romance, and readers were invited to participate in ethical discussions deriving from what they had read.

Sẹgilọla's push for reality also illustrated the ways in which print-mediated subjects in colonial West African newspapers took on exemplary moral status as a consequence of print: "How good it would be," she remarked, "if a lot of people learnt from my example and desisted from promiscuous ways before it is too late for remedy."[100] This narrator relished the printedness and thus the publicness of her story, which circulated—promiscuously—around Lagos society, and she frequently referred to letters she received from readers, to commentaries on her story published in Akede Eko, and to her own act of writing each week.

In his attempt to incarnate the female subject as a feeling subject, Thomas more or less stealthily used the mask of a prostitute to reintroduce the morality and behavioral comments of male-dominated, Christian advice-giving genres. As suggested earlier, newspaper fiction by West African men from the 1880s onward showed a preoccupation bordering on obsession with the "problem" of modern women, especially those who wished to marry according to colonial legislation. From Marita; or The Folly of Love in 1886–88 through to Sẹgilọla's audacious insistence on an "ordinance" marriage rather than a polygynous union, locally published fiction returned repeatedly to the challenges to men's household authority posed by women married according to the colonial ordinances discussed in the previous chapter. As Sẹgilọla commented after she finally achieved her goal of a monogamous marriage in court: "I began to show my mother-in-law, and my husband too, quite plainly that I was an ordinance wife with a wedding ring, and no common-or-garden wife, and therefore I would not accept any bossing about, whether from my mother-in-law or from my husband himself."[101] Many readers of Akede Eko would themselves have been in ordinance marriages, and it is tempting to speculate about whether there was a separation between male and female readers or at least a different distribution of empathy on this topic of the heroine's marriage mode. None of them, however, could possibly have supported Sẹgilọla's subsequent act of driving her mother-in-law out of the house, a moment in which a masculinist marriage discourse stifled any debate there might have been about Ṣẹgilọla's conjugal rights and sealed her into the mold of "baddie."

The story of Ṣẹgilọla and the correspondence it inspired exemplified the manner in which newspaper fiction facilitated the expression of readers' opinions and stimulated discussions about sexual morality. As with *Marita; or The Folly of Love* in colonial Ghana forty years earlier as well as the popular literature that would circulate around postcolonial Nigeria in subsequent decades, this story invoked a realm that might be labeled the "intimately political," revealing the extent to which marriage and gender relationships were part of the political structures of colonial Nigeria, absorbing and affected by government legislation.

The combination of Ṣẹgilọla's anonymity, her proximity, and her excessive physicality helps to explain the proliferation of correspondence that poured into the offices of *Akede Eko*. Perhaps, for readers, her disappearance from the printed page at the end of the serial marked her retrieval of true anonymity as a person on the streets of Lagos, moving in readers' midst as part of a Yoruba public, released from print yet also "one of us." As shown earlier, however, in Ṣẹgilọla's case there was nobody hiding behind the pseudonym. An escapee from "real" identity, she personified the "fugitive and vagabond" nature of pseudonymity. Destitute of identity, rootless, itinerant, without material possessions, Ṣẹgilọla was a "person" who was coterminous with and as short-lived as her text. Unlike the uncovering-of-identity model that characterizes studies of European pseudonymous literature, her form of anonymity manifested a particular relationship with print in which the author exploited the uniformity of a typeface to withdraw as an individual and to emerge as a moral commentator instead. Ṣẹgilọla took up what Michael Warner, in his study of eighteenth-century American pamphlets, labels negative subjectivity—that is, a form of subjectivity drained of personhood and available only through print.[102]

At least in part, Thomas's feminine persona stemmed from local readers' expectations that particular authorial bodies should be the representatives of and the agents for particular types of discourse. This is not to say that readers expected a female voice to stem from a woman's body in Nigeria; rather, they expected that a convincing mask would be worn for the duration of the gendered performance. Such a tradition of "authentic masking" plays havoc with Western theorizations of authorship, which often reductively require a connection between body and voice (see the conclusion). Though the next case study continues and develops this theme of masking, key differences emerge in authors' modes of gender cross-vocalization, for the gender of *readers* is the determining factor in the next author's choice of pseudonyms and subject matter.

EUNICE, AKPAN, VIVIAN, AND ANWAN:
J. V. CLINTON AND THE ENGLISH "TRIPE MARKET"

For much of his long life, James Vivian Clinton, OBE (c. 1898–1973) was a prolific and energetic writer. As editor in chief of the *Nigerian Eastern Mail* (1935–51), a politically moderate weekly newspaper owned by his father and published in Calabar, he provided an arena for discussions of colonial government and society, and he worked at the heart of the public sphere generated by African-owned printing presses.[103] Alongside other prominent editors in the 1930s and 1940s, including men such as Nnamdi Azikiwe and Duse Mohamed Ali, Clinton offered the reading public access to the comings and goings of local and West African celebrities; in addition, he provided news about campaigns for municipal and legislative reforms in Nigeria, as well as details of international civil rights and anticolonial movements that, in turn, fed into debates about racial inequalities in the African colonies. As with companion newspapers in eastern Nigeria, the *Mail* also carried items of local interest to readers in the east and works of poetry and prose by aspiring local creative writers.

In common with numerous other West African editors and journalists, Clinton was part of a mobile, diasporic, loosely affiliated group of Africans who traveled between Britain, the United States, and the different territories in British West Africa. His father was Charles William Clinton, a Ghanaian lawyer of Caribbean ancestry, and his mother was English, Muriel Eunice McCarthy. His childhood and youth followed a trajectory that marked him out as a member of the upper echelons of this elite grouping. As a small child, he was sent to preparatory school in Taunton, England, and then a private school in East Sussex before progressing to Downing College, Cambridge, and thence to Lincoln's Inn, London, where he was called to the bar in 1924.[104]

As this brief profile reveals, Clinton's background was more uppercrust than most: indeed, his mother was the daughter of the chief justice of the Gold Coast, and his paternal grandfather, James Clark Clinton, was a prominent, wealthy mahogany merchant in the Gold Coast in the mid-nineteenth century. Poor health prevented Clinton from succeeding in his intended career as a barrister, however, and after long periods of medical treatment in Britain, followed by a three-year stint as a journalist on the *Sierra Leone Daily Mail* from 1932 to 1935, he settled in Calabar, where his father set up the *Nigerian Eastern Mail* and gave him the editor's chair.

In contrast to the charismatic, politically radical editors who dominated the Nigerian press around him in the 1930s and 1940s, Clinton did not use his newspaper to launch vehement critiques of British colonialism or to promote anticolonial initiatives such as partnerships with African American businesses.[105] This moderate stance earned him British praise for what was regarded as the balanced objectivity of the *Mail*, and in 1949 he was made an officer of the Order of the British Empire for "services to Nigeria in the field of journalism."[106] Yet despite such paternalism from the government and despite the longevity of the *Mail*, Clinton struggled to keep the paper afloat over the two decades of its existence. When he sold the *Mail* to the Eastern Press Syndicate in 1951, he retained a substantial share and attempted to transform the paper into a daily, the *Nigerian Daily Record* (Enugu), but a lack of capital forced the closure of the enterprise just five months later. As a result, Clinton lost all of his assets.[107]

This well-born gentleman was left with nothing as a consequence of keeping the *Mail* in print for sixteen years. He entered employment in the colonial civil service, taking up senior administrative posts in the Nigerian Information Division, and as an old man in the late 1960s, he worked as a book agent in Nigerian schools, promoting the Modern Reading for Modern Times series published by Blackie and Son.[108] A lifetime of journalism was not put on the shelf, however, for while at the Information Division, he was given responsibility for editing the biweekly official publication *News from Nigeria* and for writing daily news cables to information officers worldwide.[109] Throughout the 1950s and 1960s, Clinton continued to write articles, opinion pieces, and political and historical essays on topics as diverse as "King Eyo Honesty II of Creek Town"[110] and "The Ibo Rebels."[111] A keen observer of the opposite sex, he also produced numerous commentaries on women's behavior for Nigerian women's magazines, including several articles on "The Female Leg," expressing strong disapproval of miniskirts,[112] and many profeminist pieces supporting sex before marriage, the education of women, and "Women in Men's Jobs."[113] As a freelance writer, he sent material to a variety of publications, from the *Nigerian Drum* to *Edgar Wallace's Mystery Magazine*. But the area in which he became increasingly prolific in the 1960s—the area that forms the focal point for the remainder of this section—was popular fiction for international women's magazines.

Having been bankrupted by his press, Clinton had just one remaining asset: his literacy. He was so keen to earn an income as a professional creative writer that, in the decade before his death in 1973, this highly educated newspaperman and experienced columnist enrolled in a correspondence course with a company called the British Institute of Fiction Writing Science Limited, based in Wendover, Buckinghamshire. Little is known about this organization. The proprietor, Scott Johnson, probably advertised for clients in the West African press alongside British vanity publishers such as Arthur Stockwell. Numerous letters, annotated manuscripts, and creative writing exercises have survived from the long-distance encounter between Clinton and Johnson that began in the early 1960s and continued into the early 1970s, including a large number of pseudonymous, unpublished romances.[114] Rediscovered recently by David Pratten in boxes in the National Archives of Nigeria at Ibadan, this unusual collection offers unique glimpses into an elite but "very very broke" West African newspaperman's forays into international magazine markets, particularly popular magazines for women.[115]

Under Johnson's guidance, Clinton carefully studied stories and advertisements in a range of magazines, such as *Woman's Weekly*, *Argosy*, *Ellery Queen's Mystery Magazine*, *Spear*, and *Drum*. Too poor to travel to Britain, he depended on his tutor for answers to sociological questions about British women's habits and lifestyles, as well as for a sporadic supply of popular British magazines. In one letter, for example, he wrote: "In my last letter I asked you whether the class of people who read *Woman's Weekly* can afford the expensive furniture, recipes, etc., mentioned in articles and ads in that paper. I am really interested. They certainly couldn't when I was in England in the twenties."[116] "By studying the advertisements," Johnson replied, "you should be able to visualise the kind of life led by the readers and to understand the nature of the reader-group which buys the publication, particularly its predominant economic level."[117] This information was vital to Clinton's attempts to create believable "local" characters and settings for his British romances.

Where Ṣẹgilọla's "reality" was achieved through her positioning within a Christian confessional discourse of sin and repentance, Clinton's realism was mediated by this discourse of advertising and consumption. His stories were sprinkled with references to symbolic consumer items, including diamond rings and MG sports cars. But stylistically, his approach to the romance was often too matter-of-fact for the genre. For instance, one story written under the pseudonym Anwan Eyen Efik ended with: "Any how, they were soon married and that was that."[118] The romantic hero in another story declared his love by saying to the heroine, "I think you and I are just average people and should get on very well together."[119] "Better ending needed here," Johnson commented on a host of similarly pragmatic denouements.[120]

With the help of literally hundreds of "tutorials" and "lectures" over a ten-year period, Clinton separated story after story into component parts and listed the elements according to a grid provided by Johnson. He worked hard to develop an understanding of formulaic fiction—the function of "angle-characters," the importance of point of view, the types of turning points in successful plots, and the best techniques to bring a short story to a conclusion—and he wrote his own stories in the styles of those he had studied. One is struck by the humility of the elderly man's letters to his tutor and by his willingness to learn from Johnson's feedback. "I cannot, at this stage, even attempt to write a story as smart as this," he stated in one commentary on a story published in the men's magazine *Esquire*.[121]

There was an uncomfortable balance of power in the two men's exchanges: question-packed letters were sent by Clinton, accompanied by reams of sample material; clipped or delayed replies were sent by Johnson, with occasional covering letters. "I find letters written to you are usually unanswered," Clinton stated in one exasperated letter, "while notes like this, on any specific lesson or exercise are attended to."[122] When feedback was given on the student's manuscripts and synopses, it often took the form of scrawled comments such as: "Similar conflict to previous" or "Try the story in local markets."[123] By and large, the romance synopses were described as "not soundly constructed. I do not recommend a write-up," although at least one romance was said to come "nearer the requirements of the tripe market" than the others.[124]

In spite of this unconstructive feedback, Clinton remained a committed student throughout the 1960s, relishing his discoveries about the gender differences between types of popular writing and sharing them with his tutor: "I have, at last, been able to see that in most of the Women's Magazines, the whole story is told in *oratio oblique*," he exclaimed in 1962, after analyzing a rip-roaring, masculine *oratio directa* tale entitled "Love and Pesetas," published in the American men's magazine *Argosy*. Yet since he was such an experienced newspaperman, he must have been discouraged by the large number of rejection letters he received from international publishers and by Johnson's negative comments.[125]

Clinton's studies of British and American magazines and his creation of romantic scenarios were textual or print-mediated in one significant way that set him apart from his peers. From 1924, when he was in his twenties, Clinton was stone-deaf as a result of an ear infection. He was a fluent lip-reader and taught his friends and colleagues to communicate by sign language; he also gave public lectures and radio broadcasts well into the 1950s. One unfortunate consequence of this long-term deafness, however, was that, in spite of his experience as a professional journalist, his fictional characters often struggled to communicate in fluent, persuasive dialogue. Though "I've had the very deuce of a job looking for you" might be regarded as a way to establish the "English" authorial voice of "Eunice Vivian," Clinton's persona for *Woman's Weekly*, other sections of dialogue in the Eunice Vivian romances were unrealistic and wooden in a less obviously middle-class way.[126] One character asked, "What does a poor deserted wife do, when her only source of aid and succour has departed for Truro?"[127] Other characters pleaded, "I do most humbly beg your pardon," rather than simply saying, "Sorry."[128]

Perhaps uniquely among the pseudonymous print subjects covered in this book, Clinton had a relationship with writing that was not mediated by people's voices. As a consequence, his romantic stories in English settings for English readers, depicting what should have been the most passionate of human encounters, have a decidedly textual quality about them. His feminine ventriloquism as Eunice Vivian is grammatically correct but appears overly written in its stiffness. A typical dialogue from one of these "English" stories runs:

> "Pa and Ma both go to work and they won't be back till after six."
> "My parents are also both out," Madge volunteered. "Mother has gone to town for a day's shopping and won't be back till about six, round about the time Dad comes back from work. Anyhow, I'd better see to that ankle and try to make you more comfortable. It

seems we're condemned to each others' company till your parents and mine get home."

"Do you find the prospect so terrible?" he asked her.[129]

Clearly unaware of Clinton's disability, Johnson criticized the "stilted" dialogue in these narratives, and he instructed his student to "listen to the conversation around you."[130] But Clinton continuously struggled to re-create the timbre of English people's conversations, and this was not helped by having romantic couples with formulaic names—at least for his creative writing exercises—such as John and Joan from St John's Wood.[131] Although the archive contains a record of his productivity and dedication, it also illustrates his failure to perform femininity for the international market. Unlike the voluble Ṣẹgilọla, who invoked the noisy urban world of Lagos and interspersed her confession with songs and loud cries of "oh oh oh oh!" Clinton's dialogues represented the Edwardian print language of somebody who had not been able to hear English conversation for several decades.

Clinton's pseudonyms were mobile and international. He changed names to suit his perception of the tastes of different global constituencies of reader. Authors' names, he realized, were vital elements in the positioning of literary commodities in relation to consumers and genres, part and parcel of the content of stories and essential to their sales. "I must begin to make some money now or the Lord knows what will happen," he informed his tutor in 1965.[132] For a man desperate for paid freelance work, nothing could be more strategic than the adoption of Western-inflected female names in order to access the massive women's magazine market in the West. With no apparent investment in identity, ethnicity, or authenticity, Clinton changed his pseudonyms to suit each projected market. Writing as "Eunice Vivian" and the gender-ambiguous "Vivian James" and "Vivian Warner" for British and American women readers and as "Anwan Eyen Efik" (meaning "Efik Girl") and "Akpan James" for Nigerian readerships, he aimed for cultural and sexual representativeness rather than authorial distinctiveness. In a sense, his choice of pseudonyms represents a reversal of the colonial and postcolonial exoticism identified by Graham Huggan, in which an author's cultural otherness is produced as a marketable commodity in the "otherness industry" of Western publishing.[133] Clinton chose pseudonyms that asserted *similitude* with readers and identity with genres, rather than cultural differences.

Typical or representative names such as Akpan James did not, however, necessarily indicate an everyday or standard type of femininity. In contrast to the fixed, gendered physicality of Sẹgilọla, several of Clinton's pseudonyms played with the gender ambiguity, or doubleness, of names: the English name Vivian, for example, may be given to boys as well as girls. Clinton's choice of the Efik forename Akpan for his unpublished Nigerian crime thriller, *Murderous Love* by Akpan James, is particularly significant. As Onyile Bassey Onyile comments in his article on the ways in which the Efik Abang dance engages with local ideals of femininity and gender flexibility, Akpan represents the senior wife of Akimanyom, whose jealousy toward her detested junior rival, Abang, is demonstrated in a dance involving flamboyant costume and bodily decoration. He writes: "Akpan in [the] Efik worldview is full of tricks and will not hesitate pulling tricks on the new wife to disorient her. Driven by jealousy, and rage, all her actions are meant to forewarn the new wife (Abang), that it will not be an easy ride in their matrimonial home, while affirming her status as the senior wife."[134]

Significantly, Akpan is distinguished by her facial mask, for "as part of her costume she wears a two-faced mask, meant to confuse her adversary. One face depicts a male face, while the other depicts a female's face."[135] According to Onyile, such gender flexibility typifies Efik cultures in which biological women can take up socially masculine roles and where gender is regarded locally as a socially oriented, relational category rather than an ontological category.[136] The mask thus exemplifies the disconnection and room for maneuver between socially constructed gender roles and biologically determined sexual differences.

When Clinton wrote about women under his own name, as in his column "How to Survive Matrimony," he emphasized the impossibility of ever achieving cross-gender empathy. "I'm not a girl and never was, so I don't know how I'd feel," he stated in a section entitled "Advice to Wives," in which he considered the effects of loveless marriages upon women.[137] His choice of pseudonyms highlighted the ways in which print can facilitate forms of cross-dressing similar to the masked Abang performance. The names Vivian and Akpan suggest that Clinton's cross-vocalization as a woman was more than an economically motivated effort to penetrate the popular and potentially lucrative magazine market. As with Thomas's Sẹgilọla, Clinton's female pseudonyms were also masks designed to enable themes and points of view that were not easily vocalized under a male name. The frequent failure of Clinton's

English mask to attach to the romance genre was just as revealing, in its own way, as the success of Ṣẹgilọla in becoming a believable female subject to many of her readers. Clinton's lack of success as an English romance author demonstrated that female pseudonyms had to be accompanied by a convincing, culturally believable performance of femininity, an ability to "know how I'd feel" in situations experienced by women.

Ironically, given Clinton's hard work for international markets with the British Institute of Fiction Writing Science Limited, his only significant achievement in the field of creative writing was a racy detective thriller set in Nigeria, written under his own name and published for a local market, together with several detective stories and romances for Nigerian newspapers and local women's magazines. Influenced by the James Bond stories and featuring the hypermasculine hero Charlie Okpu, *The Rescue of Charlie Kalu* was published in 1971 by Heinemann Educational Books as part of a series designed to develop secondary-level African students' English-language skills. With no popular romantic elements, this novel focused on a topic that had fascinated Clinton for decades—the infamous man-leopard murders that occurred on home territory, in Annang and Ibibio communities in the coastal southeast of Nigeria, between 1945 and 1948.[138] Though Clinton never made a living wage from creative writing, his ambition to have a novel accepted for publication was at least fulfilled by the appearance of this short detective thriller.

MASKING (AS) WOMEN

Both Thomas and Clinton deployed female subjects and feminine subjectivity to construct relationship scenarios and moral debates about women's sexuality. For Thomas, Ṣẹgilọla was a mouthpiece for the promotion of Christian monogamy and adherence to the Ten Commandments; by contrast, Clinton's popular romances, though complying with the sexual liberalism of the "swinging sixties," generally failed to perform the intimate subjectivity required by the genre. Nevertheless, the narratives that both men realized by writing as women were concerned with the intimacies of sexuality as well as domesticity and marriage. Both authors also wrote about marriage and romantic love under male names, including their own, but their female pseudonyms lent veracity to stories in which current and popular conceptions of feminine behavior were presented as experiences or inner feelings. Thomas ventriloquized as a woman in order to drive home moral messages about promiscuity and monogamy, in stories in which readers would condemn women for wearing "dresses that don't reach their knees, sleeveless, [and] low-necked to 'show breast.'"[139] Clinton, thirty years later, was also unable to accept the miniskirt as morally appropriate for African women.[140] Unlike Thomas, however, he used his female pseudonyms to express sexually liberal and atheist views in which sex outside marriage and a degree of promiscuity were practices to be encouraged before the "happily ever after" scenario demanded by the formulas of romantic fiction.

In adopting feminine personae, both Thomas and Clinton mobilized West African traditions of masked articulation. Feminine stereotypes were not simply performed without challenge in their work. If we regard their texts as masked performances, the apparent tension between masculine identity and feminine voice appears less stark than it might otherwise have seemed, for in the manner of African masked performances, both men took up and took on—and in Thomas's case, "took off" in a parodic sense—the interiority of the names they adopted. Successful or not, their narratives demonstrated the ways in which West African masking traditions could attach to print technologies and help to produce feminine printed bodies. Indeed, in the wake of Sẹgilọla, the prostitute and "good-time girl" became central figures in West African popular literature.[141] Thomas donned a mask of femininity in order to perform and to incarnate in print particular moral viewpoints about women.

Paradoxically, both men performed the flexibility of the very gender categories they implicitly reinforced by deciding to write *as* women. Both men's pseudonyms were also ethnicized in order to suggest—albeit playfully—a real authorial body behind the narratives and a location for the writers of their texts. Though Thomas's Yoruba mask was a great deal more detailed (and perhaps therefore more believable) in its self-expression than Clinton's international feminine personae, the "women of letters" produced by these men demonstrated how the mask of pseudonymity could be used to play with fixed ideas of gender as well as the fiction of a carnal body. Nevertheless, both men reinscribed the boundaries of acceptable feminine expression and behavior at the very moment of authorial gender-crossing. Albeit often stereotyped and constraining to women, however, the content of their texts and the reader responses they generated superseded essentialist notions about genre and authorial identity.

6 ✑ Nominal Ladies and "Real" Women Writers

Female Pseudonyms and the Problem of Authorial Identity in the Cases of "Rosa" and "Marjorie Mensah"

In spite of the hazards described in chapter 5, the retrieval of hitherto unrecognized women writers from behind the scenes of centuries of male-dominated canonical writing and the piecing together of these women's hidden histories have been common objectives of feminist scholarship, in Africa and elsewhere.[1] Often focusing on ephemeral writings outside official archives—including diaries, letters, journalism, unpublished manuscripts, and similar material with no recognized literary value—feminist scholars make the point that such texts form a vital and separate, if historically trivialized, part of each country's literary culture.[2]

As argued in relation to *Marita; or The Folly of Love* and *Adelaide of Adelaide Street*, however, the "gynocritical" project to retrieve and biographize women writers exists in a degree of tension with the positive valuation of anonymity as a practice that enables playfulness and experiments with identity. With its focus on women writers, this chapter will address the consequences of this contradiction, for if the adoption of a pseudonym helps an author to break away from essentialist sociological categories such as gender and ethnicity in colonial settings, then the feminist desire to identify women writers and to reinscribe them into history suggests a political necessity to acknowledge the existence of cultural and experiential differences between men and women—including newspapermen and newspaperwomen—particularly in their access to economic power and cultural capital. Yet this chapter also asks a key question: if female pseudonyms are adopted by men for the expression of particular "feminine" themes, should we not also situate female correspondents in an equally performative space when they adopt female pseudonyms to articulate ideas about femininity?

In "Women's Engagement with Gold Coast Print Culture: From 1857 to 1957," Audrey Gadzekpo describes the significant involvement of African women in a century of Ghanaian journalism.[3] Using interviews, family histories, and women's diaries, together with material published in African-owned newspapers, she painstakingly pieces together evidence of women's participation in the Gold Coast press and discovers the identities of several previously unknown pseudonymous writers. In particular, she finds evidence of the ways in which two elite women were involved in the African-owned newspapers: Mercy Quartey Papafio (later Mercy Ffoulkes-Crabbe), who wrote under the pseudonym "Gloria" in the *Gold Coast Times* between 1936 and 1940, and her sister Ruby Quartey Papafio, a teacher at the Accra Government Girls' School who wrote several articles in the early 1930s for the "Ladies' Corner" of the *West African Times*.[4]

In addition to studying the Quartey-Papafio sisters, Gadzekpo examines the lively columns of the celebrated and prolific journalist Mabel Dove (also known as Dove-Danquah), who wrote daily articles for the press under a number of pseudonyms, including "Marjorie Mensah" in the "Ladies' Corner" of the *Times of West Africa* from 1931 to 1934, "Dama Dumas" in the *African Morning Post* between 1935 and 1940, "Ebun Alakija" in the *Nigerian Daily Times* between 1936 and 1937, and "Akosuah Dzatsui" in the *Accra Evening News* in the 1950s and 1960s.[5] Though Dove was probably the most prominent of West African women journalists and political figures in the period before independence and is certainly the most visible in recent feminist historical scholarship, many other women's names can be added to the roll call of African women journalists. This list would include the prolific poet and literary reviewer Gladys May Casely-Hayford, who sometimes wrote under the pseudonym "Aquah Laluah" but generally used her own name in the numerous poems and essays she contributed to her father's newspaper, the *Gold Coast Leader*.[6]

With the exception of Gladys May Casely-Hayford's publications in the 1920s and some of Mabel Dove's political journalism in the 1950s and 1960s, correspondents writing under female names concentrated almost exclusively on topics concerning women. From this platform of femininity, their contributions covered a wide range of issues and attitudes: girls' education and access to secondary schooling; gender disparities in the urban workforce; recipes, cleanliness, mothering, and child care; the need for fairness in women's voting and inheritance rights; European fashion trends for African women; unmarried women's promiscuity; the activities of women's amateur dramatics and literary societies; conjugal relations and romantic love; and the immoral behavior of young men and women in West African towns and cities. Taken together over a period of more than fifty years, these newspaper contributors produced positive and negative images of the "modern girl" as an educated, Western-dressed, marriageable, Christian, English-speaking, and urban person whose behavior ranged from the scandalously liberated to the healthily independent.[7]

Unsurprisingly, given the topics just described, contributions signed with female names were usually published in the designated women's pages of newspapers, rather than in the surrounding columns. Without the type of meticulous biographical research undertaken by Gadzekpo, however, considerable problems arise in any scholarly quest to attach "real" women's voices to the content of articles written under female pseudonyms. As early as 1884 in the "Ladies Column" of the *Sierra Leone Weekly News*, a correspondent named "Rosa" illustrated the difficulties surrounding any attempt to extrapolate the gender of an author from the contents of a text. In a letter dated 25 September 1884, Rosa criticized local young men for their audacity in proposing marriage to "foreign educated ladies" such as herself.[8] The latter group, she insisted, were a class apart in "social status and literary qualifications" from those she labeled "locals"; as such, foreign-educated women would never "condescend to marry men who are far below us in spite of riches."[9] Nor, she added provocatively, "will we condescend to marry those who are fairly educated, but whose live-stock consists of a dozen crockeryware [sic], and a few provisions."[10]

Rosa exemplifies the problems that arise with assumptions about the gender identity of untraceable authors. Such assumptions can profoundly affect the way in which a text is interpreted, influencing whether it is seen as insulting or empathetic in tone, as parodic or authentic in style. For example, if we choose to confer authenticity and sincerity upon the female voice of Rosa, the letter can be read as a disclosure of the frustrations experienced by an elite, marriageable woman living in Freetown and the expectations of educated "been-to" girls seeking husbands who will provide the intellectual stimulation and material comforts to which women in the upper echelons of African elites were accustomed. By contrast, if the letter is regarded as male-authored, it can be read as a satirical exposure of the arrogance and superiority of "foreign educated ladies" like the letter writer herself.[11] Few men in Freetown—foreign educated or otherwise—would have promoted the notion that an educated man who was poorly endowed with material goods should be rejected as a husband by foreign-educated African women.

As might be expected, the letter generated considerable heated debate in the *Sierra Leone Weekly News*, but on no occasion did readers question the authenticity of the correspondent's identity. Thus, readers solved—by ignoring as irrelevant—the questionable articulation of Rosa's gender, preferring instead to treat the letter as a publication deliberately designed to stimulate discussion. Under a variety of male and female pseudonyms, respondents immediately condemned the arrogance of the colony's foreign-educated African women.[12] One regular contributor to the "Ladies Column," "Cleopatra (A Local)," described Rosa as a member of a "sect of termagants"; another correspondent, "Dan," suggested that locally educated women were in fact superior to women of Rosa's ilk; similarly, "Tyrtaeus" attacked "the class she represents" for its "false superiority complex."[13] But as the debate developed and spread across West Africa to reach readers of the *Weekly News* in Cape Coast, readers identifying as women became considerably more supportive of Rosa, whereas those identifying as men, including an émigré from Freetown called "An Exile," became more adamant in their condemnations of her class of women.[14] Rosa's readers were thus less concerned with the physical identity of the author than with their own gender issues, stimulated and contested or reinforced by the voice in the text.

If Rosa's audience was unconcerned about gender authenticity and authorial attribution, West African readers' attitudes toward female pseudonymity showed a noticeable shift in the 1920s, as evidenced by the strikingly visceral desire among Yoruba readers of *Akede Eko* for the prostitute Ṣẹgilọla to make herself known to the public (see chapter 5). By 1931, when the remarkable Marjorie Mensah made her debut in the "Ladies' Corner" of the *Times of West Africa*,[15] readers were gender sensitized about authorship to the extent that they reacted with considerable curiosity about the identity of this new lady correspondent.

The tone of Marjorie's daily column varied enormously in the first eighteen months of its existence, for reasons that will be explained later, but many readers suspected the presence of a solo male hoaxer. "I have been following closely the many interesting letters under the pen of Miss Marjorie Mensah since your paper made its first appearance in the journalistic arena," wrote Mr. Asuana Quartey shortly after the launch of the *Times*:

> The nature of the letters, the diction, the firm grip of the writer, tend to arouse my suspicions, and probably those of many readers; and confirm me in the conviction as to the identity of the writer being a man. I mean no offence to "your lady" correspondent, but it is very unusual that West African Ladies (even those with a superior European education) could be induced to take an intelligent interest in the affairs of the country in the same breath as your lady correspondent is doing. This is a new feature in West African journalism, for which please accept my heartiest congratulations.[16]

Noticeably, Quartey did not feel betrayed by the suspected gender deception; instead, he offered his "heartiest congratulations" to the editor for this amusing ruse, perhaps seeing in it a model for an as yet unrealized ideal of African femininity.

Between 1931 and the exposure of Marjorie's identity in 1934, countless male correspondents wrote similar letters to the editor of the *West African Times* and to Marjorie herself, repeatedly questioning whether African women had the mental capacities to produce such politically astute analyses and high-quality English prose as the column contained. In response, Marjorie teased these skeptical, overly curious individuals with replies that often overflowed with a flirtatious feminine language, which she combined with intelligent commentary on the "affairs of the country." She thus asserted her womanhood through a feminization of the very "intelligent" political discourse that, for her detractors, placed her gender in question. "I don't think you are serious when you give as your explanation of my being a man the fact of my being able to contribute daily to the *West African Times* and express a few ideas in English," she teased one skeptical correspondent, Mr. Des Bordes: "You, and a good many others like you, have the most peculiar notions of women—especially Gold Coast women—that I have ever heard of! . . . Do you really think that none of us is capable of writing up a column in a newspaper?"[17] Similarly, in response to Governor Shenton Thomas's unpopular Sedition Bill in March 1934, she playfully personalized the governor's comments about the need to protect Africans from politically inflammatory literature: "I cannot imagine that his Excellency really means to shut me up one way or the other. After all, he is an attractive gentleman. If wrinkles appear would that be sedition?"[18] "I just love the Governor, he is a dear sweet man, he has absolutely come and educated us all about sedition," she wrote again in June 1934 in an article marking the announcement of the governor's departure from the Gold Coast for the Straits Settlements: "Not satisfied with that," she continued, "he has given us a refresher course in bonds and treaties, things that were more or less fading from our minds, and last but not least he has brought us together in a way that could not have been possible for centuries to come. Isn't he a darling!"[19]

A disagreement about the ownership of the Marjorie Mensah byline led to a court hearing in which the main author of the "Ladies' Corner" was finally unmasked before an expectant reading public. In 1934, the alienated former editor in chief of the *West African Times*, Kenneth MacNeill Stewart, brought a case against the newspaper in which he claimed exclusive rights to the name and output of Marjorie Mensah. The case was triggered by the 1933 publication of a slim anthology of Marjorie articles in London. Edited by Kathleen Hewitt, *Us Women* presented a selection of the most feisty and humorous articles from the "Ladies' Corner," accompanied by an introduction celebrating African women's intelligence, education, and modernity.[20] Throughout the book, a sequence of line drawings by Elise Lindsley-Sims depicted African women, equal in every way to their flapper sisters in Europe, wearing lipstick, high heels, hats, and designer dresses, clasping letters in their hands or cigarettes (see fig. 8 and fig. 9). Clearly, by 1933, the pseudonym had achieved such celebrity status and had become such a popular and profitable selling point for the *West African Times* that Stewart wished to expropriate the column. In a manner similar to that of Marjorie's detractors, he wished to demonstrate that no woman was capable of owning this intelligent feminine voice.

As with other legal cases involving disputes about pseudonymity, these proceedings and the sensational newspaper coverage of them furnish useful documentation for scholars wishing to determine the identity of authors. In court, Stewart acknowledged that the byline was invented in the pressroom by two men—the editor, J. B. Danquah, and the managing director, James Henley Coussey—but he claimed to have written all of the material for the "Ladies' Corner" since its

FIG. 8. "Up and Doing": illustration by Elise Lindsley-Sims, in *Us Women*, edited by Kathleen Hewitt (London: Elkin Mathews and Marrot, 1933), 98

FIG. 9. "We Squeeze and Squeeze Our Men": illustration by Elise Lindsley-Sims, in *Us Women*, edited by Kathleen Hewitt (London: Elkin Mathews and Marrot, 1933), 78

inception, and he demanded that the pseudonym and its royalties be handed over for his use.[21] The managers of the *Times*, meanwhile, presented evidence in court that Stewart was absent in Togoland for a large portion of 1932 and 1933 and was therefore unable to submit material to the column.[22] Devastatingly for Stewart, they also produced original manuscripts by Mabel Dove—by then Mrs. Dove-Danquah—of numerous articles for the women's page during this period.[23] The name of Mabel Dove therefore shone out as Marjorie's chief animator. The court found in favor of the *West African Times*, and Dove returned to her temporarily suspended "Ladies' Corner" with a vengeance.

Dove certainly deserves recognition for her enormous contribution to the "Ladies' Corner" and to the Ghanaian press and politics more widely, but this retrieval of authorial identity should not be made at the expense of Marjorie Mensah's pseudonymity. Dove's separation from Marjorie enabled her to perform and develop the character of a bright modern woman—a highly educated and well traveled celebrity with strong views about women's equality, fashion, literary taste, and the use of female leisure time, who was situated in a colonial cultural zone filled with English literature, elite dinner parties, social clubs, Hollywood movies, and society gossip.[24]

Dove did not mask her own femininity with experiments across gender, but she did, nevertheless, develop a particular persona in Marjorie. Rather than choosing to ventriloquize as a man, she adopted a different kind of performativity in which she drew readers' attention to the lifestyle and expectations of the modern African woman. This was not an unambiguous promotion of a Western lifestyle, though, for the modern girl in Marjorie's hands often emerged as a tragic figure. Independent of masculine control, in search of romantic love, disillusioned with local definitions of wifehood, daughterhood, and motherhood, the young Ghanaian women she depicted often turned to alcohol, cigarettes, parties, and sexual promiscuity with white men in their rebellion against the conservative values of parents and local Christian young men.[25] Marjorie Mensah thus ambivalently interrogated the image of the young, fashionable, self-confident female consumer who emerged in the 1920s and 1930s in urban locations throughout the colonial world.[26]

Thus, for all her cosmopolitan modernity—indeed, as a direct consequence of it—the popular figure of Marjorie Mensah can be regarded as the embodiment of a particular "conversation" about colonialism.[27] As Jinny Prais persuasively suggests, Marjorie was not so much a person as a *persona*, an emblem of the African professional elite's "representation of a new Africa."[28] As with the colonial discourse discussed in chapter 5, gender was the ground into which these ideological poles were planted. Marjorie was the ensign of the professional elite, a product of the colonial encounter who nevertheless offered a counter-discourse to colonialism with her insistence upon and clear demonstration of equality with white people and with men. Tempting as it is, therefore, to attribute particular articles and styles of writing to particular contributors to the "Ladies' Corner," Marjorie Mensah should be regarded first and foremost as the figure through which the established elite drew boundaries between themselves and other constituencies of Africa vying for power in the colonial period.[29]

One cannot presuppose that essential attitudinal differences separated male and female authors and correspondents from one another, but given the differences between boys and girls in colonial society—in education, upbringing, and socialization—one might reasonably assume that the literate, newspaper-reading man occupied a different subject position from the literate, newspaper-reading woman in the spectrum of gendered roles and behaviors in colonial society. Men might, as a consequence, have been more likely to share opinions with one another, and women with one another, as readers and participants in local gender debates. Even so, the provocative voice of Rosa and the emblematic voice of Marjorie Mensah challenge the clarity of any connections we might want to make between an authorial body and a narrative voice.

Rather than circling fruitlessly around this tension between authenticity and anonymity, perhaps the criteria for judging the authenticity of contributors should revolve around the competence of their gender performance. Such a combination of gender performativity and positionality provides a route out of the dilemma described previously, in which projects of feminist retrieval come into conflict with the productive destabilization of identity achieved through colonial authors' uses of pseudonyms. The questions then become, first, how successfully does an author—male or female—articulate and reperform the range of socially mobile gender positions circulating in the culture, and, second, at the most basic level, how much "masculine" bias does a "feminine" narrator convey and vice versa? Problematic as this is, from such a standpoint Rosa can be regarded as a promasculine discursive figure designed to stimulate general criticism of a particular class of women in Sierra Leone, and Marjorie Mensah can be regarded as a profeminist representative of Rosa's class of women in colonial Ghana.

Women's pages provided readers with space to develop gender-inflected social and political perspectives. These spaces in colonial West African newspapers were "largely instrumental in forming a female reading community organised around the textual representation of women as readers, as writing subjects and as textual figures."[30] Space was opened up in these pages for the first printed words of new writers, who shyly commenced letters to Marjorie with comments such as "Even as I write now I feel almost sure that some wheels shall treat [i.e., squash] this my little attempt," before praising local women for "holding up their own in spheres of Law, medicine, teaching, etc."[31] Paradoxically located within a separate sphere designed for equal expression, women were instructed by Dove, under her various pseudonyms, to "strive to be on the same plane as our men if we want to carve a niche for women in Africa."[32] This community of women readers and writers was often "situated within a reformist discourse designed to educate, empower and entertain them."[33] The women's pages furnished space for progressive political discourses about gender, including feminist commentaries on inequalities in colonial society, and also a space for women readers to take courage as writers. In addition, however, space was provided for the paternalistic styles of gender reformism of people such as Lady Clifford.

This short chapter has broken with the deference for pseudonymity displayed in several previous chapters in order to confront the methodological problems associated with attributing—or refusing to attribute—gender identities to authors. Faced with the feminist imperative to discover the gender identities of authors in order to appreciate the contents and implications of their texts, the chapter found that female pseudonyms should not simply be accepted as articulations of femininity per se, regardless of the actual gender of authors. Such an acceptance would ignore the social conditioning and positioning of male and female authors, as if these influential factors in a person's subjectivity are irrelevant to the content of texts. From a feminist standpoint, therefore, in spite of the diversity of opinion among women writing about women, the gender bias with which a pseudonymous text is loaded will indicate the operation of gender positioning and power. But in tension with this is the argument that unless one believes that women are *only* capable of writing about women, pseudonymous female contributors should be regarded as no more "natural" in their articulations of femininity than the men who adopted female pseudonyms. These pressures for an abandonment of pseudonymity in favor of biographical methods will be discussed in detail in the conclusion.

CONCLUSION
"New Visibilities"
African Print Subjects and the Birth of the (Postcolonial) Author

> Look first for the body behind the voice.
> —Ngugi wa Thiong'o, *Devil on the Cross*

IN *BLACK Skins, White Masks*, the anticolonial activist and revolutionary thinker Frantz Fanon offers a compelling account of the psychological impact of racial labeling on colonized people. When he witnesses a white child's terrified reaction to the sight of his body, Fanon too experiences a form of terror as the effects of colonial history spread across his skin and mark him permanently. Centuries of "ways of seeing" contribute to this moment of social recognition in the child.[1] In an instant, Fanon is positioned inside an archive of colonialist images, and his plural sense of self fills up with the limited scope of others' beliefs and perceptions. The whiteness of the mother-child dyad fails to mark their bodies, but the black man's color fills the entire frame: "I am being dissected under white eyes, the only real eyes," Fanon writes, appalled.[2] On realizing this, the person carrying the name "Frantz Fanon" falls apart as a complex, culturally located subject. His human specificity is replaced with a different type of specificity: a racial identity produced within a visceral imperial economy that dissects, depletes, and classifies its objects in the process of naming them.

The visual colonial economy identified by Fanon, with its "white eyes" that impose names and categories, can be regarded as an enemy of the playful, flexible, printed types of subjectivity discussed in this book. The pseudonymous writers who found publication in colonial West African newspapers—but also those named writers who played games with identity, such as Wallace-Johnson and Zik—were far more than accessible colonial subjects. The writers studied in this book engaged with the tense, antagonistic relations and representations described by Fanon, but they did so in indirect ways that escaped the colonial labels and identities that so repelled him. In the process, they questioned the stability and reliability of authorial attribution.

An ethical and methodological challenge throughout this book has been to strike a balance between respecting the slippery playfulness of pseudonymous writers in colonial West Africa and meeting the historical need to explore the motivations of the subjects who produced these types of text. Is it possible, the book has asked, to avoid analytic models that seek to differentiate between "real" and "invented" selves and yet to remain historically accurate and informative? In studying naming practices in the particular context of African-owned newspapers, this book has tried to question and debate the temptation to attach biographies and intentionality to pseudonymous authors. Pseudonymous West African writers cannot simply be regarded as hiding their "true selves"—mischievously, modestly, or otherwise—in order to voice authentic or scandalous sentiments from the other side of their masks.

In almost every chapter, however, the book has taken a biographical turn, with biographical details being inserted wherever available in order to explain writers' literary and political decisions. Yet simply to reveal authors' identities runs the risk of ignoring what the writers themselves expose in making their choices of pseudonyms: that a host of cultural and ideological assumptions about agency and identity are enacted through our desire to attach "real" names to colonial bodies and, more fundamentally, that the very act of naming in colonial contexts may stimulate imperial legal and political processes of identification and containment.

African practices of pseudonymity raise questions about the limits of biographical retrieval in the study of colonial encounters. Yet historians of empire and social anthropologists generally require named human subjects, existing in time, as the raw material and starting point for an understanding of power relations and mediations of "identity." The desires of scholars to affirm subjects' life-stories and intentions are exemplified by Vincent Carretta's controversial critique of *The Interesting Narrative of the Life of Olaudah Equiano, or Gustavas Vassa, the African* (1789), which cast suspicion on Equiano's truth-claims about his Igbo birth and questioned the authenticity of the African identity described in the two-volume slave memoir.[3] The *Life of Olaudah*

Equiano, Carretta suggested, contains considerably more "interesting narrative" than actual facts about the first-person narrator's birth. Many North American and European readers were scandalized by Carretta's assertions.[4] Nevertheless, in writing a biography of a "self-made" man such as Equiano, Carretta also illustrated the scholarly imperative for historians to discover and locate the stories of the "real" people that claim authorship of texts and to test the truth-claims of their narratives against archival sources.

Anonymity and pseudonymity manifest a different type of performativity compared to the directional, intentional behavior that is often attributed to colonial subjects—albeit heavily mediated—when they are read through identity markers such as name, race, and nation. The ways in which writers resisted imperialist representations and the ways in which they positioned themselves in relation to the webs of negative knowledge produced around colonial subjects can be regarded as "antibiographical" in orientation.[5] Resisting attribution and intentionality in a colonial economy, the writers studied in this book present researchers with something of an ethical dilemma. Can (or should) we seek to unmask pseudonymous individuals or attempt to retrieve the "body behind the voice" of writers who chose to remain anonymous in colonial societies?

Faced with politically provocative material by pseudonymous writers, colonial officials used rudimentary and questionable biographical techniques for establishing the intentions of authors. For example, in the prosecution of Wallace-Johnson for his pseudonymous article "Has the African a God?" the attorney general of the Gold Coast insisted that the seditious intentions of hidden authors could and should be established through a close reading of their publications. The "question of intention" was at the center of this case.[6] The intention of "a person who wrote a statement or made a speech . . . to cause a riot, or disturbance or something of that kind . . . [can] be inferred from the terms of the publication," the British insisted.[7] Whether or not a writer adopted a pseudonym, in the eyes of the law authorial intentionality was direct and singular in the case of African publications; furthermore and problematically, "what had to be looked at was *what the writer intended the reader to understand.*"[8] Though the defense tried to argue that contexts as well as contents had to be taken into account in interpreting the article by Effective, the prosecution insisted that close reading alone would yield truths about authorial intentionality. Wallace-Johnson lost his final appeal before the Privy Council in London on these grounds, for the court decided that "to bring into hatred" and "to bring about a [political] change" did not require "extrinsic evidence of intention" such as riots or outbreaks of anticolonial violence. "The words themselves" were sufficient to furnish evidence of seditious intention.[9]

The British thus argued for the seriousness of the article, translating Effective's excessive, satirical language into a set of unmediated and subversive political goals that would, if realized, transform the Gold Coast from a British colony to an African republic. In doing so, they refused the notion that "seeing is always shaped by a broader set of cultural assumptions and frameworks," including their own imperialist ideology.[10] As Fanon realized in his visceral encounter with white ways of seeing, images are perceived, shaped, and processed through a series of visual and ideological "cues."[11] In court, however, Effective's "words themselves" were judged for seditious intent, without any regard for the antibiographical playfulness of a writer whose pseudonym and choice of genre allowed a heightened engagement with English language, textuality, and style and gave him the freedom to satirically represent colonial government. Failing to recognize the presence of their own ideological lenses as readers or the ways in which newspaper contributors offered up their supposed "selves" for masked possession by pseudonyms, the British simply sought textual evidence of the author's sincerity and singularity of identity. As with the scholarly engagement with Equiano's narratives, they sought for sincerity above playfulness and authenticity above satire.

Pseudonymity and anonymity, however, can be regarded as forms of textuality that expose *all* names, proper or otherwise, to be masks and performances, particularly in the type of supervisory colonial society identified by Fanon. Against the British legal requirement of authorial attribution, on the one hand, and the validity of close reading, on the other hand, is the fact—made obvious in the trial of Wallace-Johnson—that when readers attribute particular intentions to authors or regard a text as the vehicle to convey what a writer wishes to communicate, a deeply deceptive cultural fiction may be produced that is complicit with the colonial regime's own naming practices.

In his famous essay on "The Death of the Author," Roland Barthes argues that the vitality of texts and readers is killed off by the attribution of authorial intentionality.[12] Once a text has been published, the author dematerializes altogether and simply becomes another reader in the crowd. When readers demand (or supply) contextual information about authors' lives in order to supplement or validate specific interpretations of a text, they perpetuate a fallacy of God-like proportions through which the physical body of the author is positioned as the origin and end point of textual truths.[13] Texts should not be treated as containers of eternally fixed meanings, however: they are productive and dynamic cultural objects that flex and sway under the pressure of a combination of their own linguistic slipperiness and readers' interpretations. With the liberation of writing from the pen-holding hand of authors comes the symbolic "death of the author."

In his critique and development of Barthes's work, Michel Foucault highlights the power relations that surround textual production and with which texts are imbued.[14] Contesting the validity of the popular need to attribute meanings, intentions, and off-page biographies to authors, Foucault gives a complex sense of the circuits of discursive power in which printed objects and their consumers circulate, and he describes authorship as a "function" produced by and within discourses of power. As he writes in a separate essay, "Politics and the Study of Discourse": "In each sentence that you pronounce—and very precisely in the one that you are busy writing at this moment, you who have been so intent, for so many pages, on answering a question in which you felt yourself personally concerned and who are going *to sign this text with your name—in every sentence there reigns the nameless law, the blank indifference: 'What matter who is speaking; someone has said: what matter who is speaking?'"*[15]

At one level, the writing practices examined in this book mesh perfectly with the arguments of these influential poststructuralist thinkers, for whom the author's identity—the matter of who is speaking—should be the last preoccupation of readers. The genre of biography stands out as particularly vulnerable to the fallacious reading practices identified by Barthes and Foucault. With its requirement for births, deaths, emotions, and intentions in its subjects, biography is more dependent than other genres upon fantasies of authorial intentionality and upon deterministic contextual explanations. By contrast, what could be more subversive of the physical presence of authors as originators of meaning than pseudonyms such as Tired and Overworked or the flesh-taunting pseudonym of Dick Carnis and the reams of "inauthentic" romantic prose he or she produced for the *Gold Coast Leader* between 1904 and 1905?

Many of the writers examined in this book are physically and historically untraceable as real people, and beyond that, many of them exist on the page simply as "author-functions" in a similar sense to that described by Foucault.[16] Except in the case of celebrity pseudonyms such as Marjorie Mensah and celebrity nicknames such as Zik and Odeziaku, pseudonyms in West African newspapers were often merely functional or untraceable to specific individuals. Although some of the writers studied here—particularly Ṣẹgilọla, Marjorie Mensah, and other authors of regular columns—played with the masking potential of pseudonyms by taunting readers with clues about their supposed identities, other writers, especially those with generic pseudonyms such as "A Traveller" and "A Banker" existed only as by-products of the content of their articles. They gestured toward no off-page presence, and they demanded no recognition or status in the eyes of others. In short, even when writing about racial discrimination and the politics of visibility in colonial society, they avoided the visual economy identified by Fanon as the source of colonial alienation and psychosis. Thus, at the commission of inquiry to which he was subpoenaed in 1938, Wallace-Johnson demonstrated the manner in which so-called proper names in colonial and postslavery cultures should be regarded as equally as slippery as pseudonyms. Authorial identity, he revealed, was considerably more complicated than the alleged intentions yielded by texts. Faced with the legal requirement that a connection be established between authorial attribution and (seditious) intentionality, Wallace-Johnson cleverly incapacitated his own proper name (see chapter 3).

So far, so Roland Barthes: the birth of the West African newspaper comes decidedly at the cost of the "death of the author." Until at least the mid-1930s, the principle of public interest displaced authorial individuality and intentionality. Here, we have a colonial version of the death of the author in which the published word is disengaged from the author's body in order to communicate unbiased political opinion—as if opinion can be unbiased—directly to the reading public. Thus, an early issue of the *Gold Coast Leader* described its staff as "'subjects who hav[e] rightly or wrongly undertaken the self-imposed task of voicing the beliefs, hopes and fears, grievances and joys of ourselves and fellow subjects."[17] Ignore the messenger, editors seemed to say: the printed message has a rationale, a public subjectivity, of its own. Similarly, in spite of the vehement gendering of colonial (and anticolonial) textual production described in previous chapters and the male domination of West African print technologies, West African newspaper readers generally ignored questions of masculinity, femininity, and gender-power dynamics within newspaper articles. Rather than questioning pseudonymous authorship, readers took up sides in the gender debates proposed by the articles, and they rarely showed an interest in the actual gender of pseudonymous correspondents.

Yet even though particular types of African pseudonymity invite a poststructuralist reading, French critical theory cannot simply be applied to diverse global cultures regardless of time and place. Barthes's and Foucault's theorizations of authorship occupy a specific moment in European cultural politics in the late 1960s, when social hierarchies, binary oppositions, and essentialist identities were challenged and transformed by political protests and strikes on the continent of Europe. There is a great deal to learn from Barthes's and Foucault's work, especially their disavowal of the fantasy that physical bodies exist within and behind texts, but not all authors should be regarded as "dead" and not all texts should be regarded as lacking in authorial intentionality by the interpreters of their writing. As Ngugi wa Thiong'o writes in his Gikuyu-language novel *Devil on the Cross*, readers in neocolonial societies should not simply trust a tale: they should "look first for the body behind the voice."[18] All stories, Ngugi insists, carry the ideological inflections of biased speakers; narratives stem from real bodies in the world, and these bodies must be identified and positioned within social and political power structures if the intentions of stories are to become clear.[19]

The intentionalist standpoint of authors such as Ngugi is essential to the debate about the ethics of "biographizing" colonial writers who have chosen to remain pseudonymous. Ngugi's insistence on authorial intentionality, on the politics of writing, and on the physical inscription of storytellers into political realities is not unique. Numerous African writers adopt a similar position, regarding literature as a form of advocacy or political protest.[20] Such a standpoint conflicts in obvious ways with the theories of the death of the author, and with the traditional concept of "art for art's sake" that prevails over formalist art criticism in Europe. Generally putting their own names to their literary outputs, postcolonial African authors often literally *face* the political consequences that a particular performance or text might bring to bear on their persons, especially when their works contain political messages that are disseminated orally in African languages. As with Azikiwe and Wallace-Johnson, who repeatedly found themselves in court in the preindependence period, many postcolonial African writers and journalists have faced trial, exile, imprisonment, and even death when regimes have identified them as enemies of the state. Famously, in Kenya in 1977 the play *Ngaahika Ndeenda* (*I Will Marry When I Want*) earned Ngugi wa Thiong'o a year in prison without trial. In Nigeria between the mid-1960s and the late 1990s, Wole Soyinka experienced numerous arrests, imprisonments, and threats to his life as a result of his persistent, outspoken critiques of successive Nigerian regimes. The dictator responsible for Soyinka's death sentence in absentia, Gen. Sani Abacha, was also responsible for the execution of the Nigerian author and activist Ken Saro-Wiwa in 1995 and for violence against other artists whose work inspired political critique, including the Afrobeat musician Fela Anikulapo-Kuti.

If African textual practices of anonymity and pseudonymity send warning signs to scholars against the temptation to "unmask" writers, again and again *The Power to Name* has employed sociological categories such as race, class, and gender in an attempt to culturally situate colonial writers, to interpret their intentions, and to understand the contents of their publications. Indeed, in cases such as Erne's Friend, where no knowledge about the author's real identity was available, numerous barriers arose against an understanding of the extent to which he or she resisted or operated within dominant discourses and power structures in colonial society.

Without the positive identification of an author—as African or European, as a man or a woman, as highly educated or newly literate—is it possible to understand the contents of a text? This question was especially pertinent in the assessment of whether a text might be parodic or serious in intention, as in I. B. A. Thomas's articulation of feminine remorse through the persona of Ṣẹgilọla. Whether the discussion revolved around gender ventriloquism, the provocative antiracist articulations of Azikiwe and Wallace-Johnson, or Marjorie Mensah's reflections on female equality, on many occasions this book has promoted conventional biographical methods and a discussion of social identities and social contexts in order to understand the articulations of pseudonymous authors.

Close reading and content analysis alone are not sufficient to develop an understanding of pseudonymity in colonial contexts. If one argument has emerged clearly from this study, it is that the contents of printed texts are influenced by our assumptions about the identity of authors. As cultural historians of the colonial encounter, we need to analyze the *effects* of the types of identity markers described by Fanon, without duplicating colonial society's oppressive ways of seeing. The prostitute Sẹgilọla's "confession" is altered by the discovery that a man is her creator, just as Rosa's declarations about the marriage prospects of well-educated ladies differ in tone if she is believed to be a man or a woman. Seen in this way, the references to gender, social position, and race in this book should be regarded as analytical rather than descriptive categories, as a means to understand the historical production of identity rather than as predetermining people's identities in the manner criticized by Fanon.

This book has examined contributors to West African newspapers at their moment of greatest resistance to externally generated labels. Nevertheless, unidentified individuals such as Erne's Friend remain suspended in a web of speculation about who they really were. Although the dangers involved in scholarly efforts to make colonial subjects visible should be emphasized, such speculation demonstrates that writers and texts cannot be studied in isolation from historical processes and social contexts.

Simplistic oppositions between pseudonymity and sociological identity are not necessary, however. The West African naming practices described in this book should instead be seen as examples of what Henry Louis Gates, in his analysis of "signifying" in African American narratives, describes as the African trickster's discursive positionality. Signifying describes the ways in which African American discourses dissemble from dominant forms through parody, obfuscation, deviation, pastiche, and repetition, all of which are used to trouble established literary genres and discourses. African tricksters embody the signifying process, for they are mediators whose "mediations are tricks."[21] Signifying is thus the means through which African American subjects, in the process of representing themselves and their stories, always "dwell at the margins . . . ever punning, ever troping, ever embodying the ambiguities of language."[22]

With this model in view, rather than remaining bound by the imperial desire to establish authorial intentionality pseudonymous articles can be seen to achieve their impact through the way they "signify upon" dominant discourses and regimes.[23] Using Gates's framework, the colonial regime's excessively literalist interpretation of "Has the

African a God?" can be seen to have occurred precisely because the article signified upon the regime in an allegorical and figurative manner.[24] The regime was forced to translate the allegory because, in order to maintain political domination, it needed to identify resistance and anticolonial intentionality. The imperialist imperative was therefore to make the native's ambiguities, puns, and insinuations transparent. A literal translation of the allegory by the very figures upon which it signified was consequently unavoidable, and in the process, the trickster-author could claim a significant psychological, if not a legal, victory.

Seen through the framework of signifying, pseudonyms do not need to be regarded in a singular way as masks that hide individuals from view. In colonial settings at least, authors' performativity and playfulness can be considered *aspects of* their authorial intentionality. Pseudonymous performativity need not be counterpoised to other types of agency; rather, pseudonymous contributors' discursive positioning and performativity provide a key to the success or failure of their articulations.

Pseudonymity continues to thrive in Africa for the realization of new identities, as a mode of managing and multiplying identity in the public sphere. In many fields of West African popular culture, including contemporary newspaper poetry, fiction, and cartooning as well as music and drama, artists work under a rich array of pseudonyms, often drawing upon folk traditions of code names, punned names, aestheticized names, metaphorical names, and masks, to increase the power of their performances.[25] In Ghanaian hiplife music, for example, performers' individual and collective pseudonyms often "creatively combine hip hop swagger, Pan-African and reggae iconographies of black pride, and traditional cultural characters," from a local vantage point in which homage is paid to iconic Akan "figures of authority, especially those valued for their wisdom and eloquent speaking," such as the "linguist" (spokesperson) of chiefly courts, the Queen Mother, and the *Nananom* (ancestors).[26]

As in the colonial period, artists' and writers' pseudonyms arise from a plurality of motivations and strategies, not only the obviously political or abusive. In Nigeria, one popular Yoruba Afrobeat singer, Bisade Ologunde, works under the name "Lagbaja," which carries the metaphorical meaning of "anonymity."[27] Lagbaja physicalizes his pseudonym through his use of the *egungun* (Yoruba masquerade in honor of the ancestors) mask on stage, incarnating his anonymity through the recognizable Yoruba presence. Tunde Awosanmi notes the difficulties experienced by the real Bisade Ologunde in managing the persona of Lagbaja. Struggling to divorce his two distinct identities, in public Bisade Ologunde is "no longer free."[28] For all its playful nonreferentiality, this pseudonym has *become* its owner, whose celebrity as Lagbaja has become inextricable from his mask.

Perhaps in parodic or competitive resistance to Lagbaja, a younger Yoruba musician recently adopted the pseudonym "Tamedu," which, as Awosanmi points out, exists above Lagbaja in the hierarchical set of Yoruba code names implying anonymity (*lagbaja, lakasegbe,* and *tamedu*).[29] Similarly, in 1920s Lagos, the Yoruba newspaperman Adeoye Deniga accused fellow editor E. M. Awobiyi of "stealing" the pseudonyms of two popular contributors.[30] One of Awobiyi's supporters protested that "sole ownership of a name" was nobody's right, for "there are more than a thousand people with the nickname Atari Ajanaku [meaning "elephant's cranium"] in Lagos alone!"[31]

These examples reveal that pseudonyms require careful management when their users attract celebrity in the public sphere. In the contemporary world of African multiple media flows, pseudonyms may be political—adopted to evade perilous official naming practices—but as in the colonial period, pseudonyms may also be satirical, designed for financial gain, or built around complex puns in which an individual embodies clever wordplay.[32] As Jesse Shipley points out in his study of Ghanaian hiplife, performers' choices of pseudonyms "call into being forms of sociality," for the act of "claiming the right to self-name and adopting new social personae based on these names is a statement about the potential of individual words and the ability of eloquence to overcome social inequalities and re-symbolize the value placed on traditional forms of speaking."[33] Public responses vividly demonstrate the success or failure of these gestures of becoming, as well as the enormous freedom gained by pseudonymous artists in their abandonment of identity markers. Political resistance and agency are not confined to the "properly" named writers invoked by Ngugi, these examples show, because pseudonymity can also provide a platform for leadership claims.

Given the detailed attention to the press in West Africa in this book, however, questions arise as to whether and how the articulations examined here can be compared with other literary genres and with readerships in other parts of the British Empire. In what ways do the print-mediated selves discussed in this book contribute to the theorization of and the broader empirical study of (post)colonial literatures? In what ways can we preserve the historical specificity of one locality's reading practices within the broad framework of a comparative study of imperial readerships?

Rather than requiring the "rebirth" of colonial writers as intentional subjects, this book has argued for a selective "resurrection" of authors, positioned in relation to power, politics, and cultural production. The primary objective of this study has been to expand the framework of theories of colonial subjectivity to accommodate the ways in which colonized subjects used pseudonyms and anonymity to deliberately alter and play with colonial power and constructions of African identity. Two types of political resistance to colonialism exist in parallel in the pseudonymous practices presented here. First, through pseudonymity, African subjects could experiment with a linguistic resistance to and evasion of interpellation by colonial authority, allowing them to experience existential freedom from the kinds of colonial signification described by Fanon. Second, and by contrast, pseudonymous newspaper articles and the use of collectively owned "anonymous" genres such as folktales enabled African subjects to articulate anticolonial views and to politically engage with colonial rule through explicit resistance to imperial power structures. Through masking, ventriloquism, and the avoidance of surveillance, colonial subjects found ways to resist others' productions of African subjectivity. In this way, West African pseudonymous writings push against linear notions of (post)colonial agency and visibility where the subject's intentions and self are linked unproblematically to the field of political action. Naming was more mobile and anonymity was more multiple than implied by the "self-versus-pseudonym" model that tends to dominate European studies of anonymity and literature, and African cultural and political networks were articulated through newspapers in ways that cannot simply be accommodated by "self-versus-other" dichotomies or by nationalist models of anticolonial agency.

APPENDIX

I. T. A. Wallace-Johnson in Court

"EXCERPT FROM COURT TRANSCRIPT," PRO CO 267/671/ 8:
LEAKAGE OF OFFICIAL INFORMATION, 1938, 10 OCTOBER 1938

24th Witness: Mr Isaac Theophilus Aqu'ma [sic] Wallace Johnson, sworn in:

Capt. Callow: You are the Organising Secretary of the West African Youth League?

Mr Johnson: I am not sure.

Capt. Callow: Will you tell the Commission what is your position in the Youth League?

Mr Johnson: I am not summoned here in connection with my position in the Youth League.

Capt. Callow: Will you be so good as to tell us what is your occupation?

Mr Johnson: I am a journalist.

Capt. Callow: I think you are aware of the nature of this Commission of Enquiry, that is to investigate the publication of two despatches?

Mr Johnson: I am not aware of anything.

Capt. Callow: May I inform you that the Commission of Enquiry is investigating the publication of two despatches.

Mr Johnson: Thank you.

Capt. Callow: I think you received a subpoena in connection with your coming here?

Mr Johnson: Of course, I did. I had to come as the subpoena said "fail at your peril".

Capt. Callow: And no doubt you read the subpoena?

Mr Johnson: I read it.

Capt. Callow: And it asked you if you would bring certain correspondence?

Mr Johnson: Yes, but I felt it was ridiculous to ask me to bring correspondence when I am summoned in my private capacity.

Capt. Callow: Well, are we to understand Mr Wallace Johnson that you decline to produce any correspondence?

Mr Johnson: Certainly, in my private capacity I decline, in fact I cannot produce any documents.

Capt. Callow: Have you anything to say to this Commission of Enquiry regarding the publication of these two despatches?

Mr Johnson: Nothing. I am not in a position to say anything in my private capacity.

Capt. Callow: Had you been invited to attend in your public capacity what would have been your view?

Mr Johnson: I do not know until that has been done.

Mr Beetham: What is your public capacity?

Mr Johnson: Well, I am the Organising Secretary of the West African Youth League.

Mr Beetham: Oh, you are?

Mr Johnson: Yes, in my public capacity.

Mr Carew: I think the name of Wallace Johnson signed articles which were subsequently published, and the subpoena I take it was addressed to him in the name of Wallace Johnson, so it would naturally compel him to say something?

Mr Johnson: I think you are only talking about what you think.

Mr Carew: My question is, did you send articles to the newspaper?

Mr Johnson: Did who send?

Mr Carew: Mr Wallace Johnson.

Mr Johnson: Who told you Wallace Johnson sent articles to the newspaper?

Capt. Callow: Mr Wallace Johnson states that he feels unable to answer that question as he feels it is only an expression of opinion.

Mr Carew: You do contribute to the press, do you not?

Mr Johnson:	I contribute to the press as a journalist.
Mr Carew:	Did you contribute these two articles to the Weekly News on August 13th and 20th and September 10th?
Mr Johnson:	(referring to the editions of August 13th and 20th) No this is not a contribution of mine at all.
Capt. Callow:	You notice your name appears?
Mr Johnson:	The name of the Organising Secretary of the Youth League.
Capt. Callow:	With your name above it?
Mr Johnson:	The name of the Organising Secretary of the Youth League appears there.
Capt. Callow:	Would you be so good as to look at that page (in Weekly News dated Sept 10th). You will agree your name appears in the second column?
Mr Johnson:	My name does not appear, only the name of the Organising Secretary of the Youth League.
Capt. Callow:	Are we to understand Mr Johnson that the Wallace Johnson whose signature that is here is identical with you?
Mr Johnson:	It may not be.
Capt. Callow:	Will you tell us Mr Wallace Johnson whether that is you or not you?
Mr Johnson:	I cannot say.
Capt. Callow:	You are not in a position to say?
Mr Johnson:	I cannot say anything about the Youth League because I am not summoned about the Youth League.
Mr Carew:	Do you admit that you send contributions to the Weekly News for publication?
Mr Johnson:	As a journalist I have been contributing to the Weekly News for 25 years.
Mr Carew:	Were these articles contributed by you in your capacity as a journalist?
Mr Johnson:	I have said these are not my contributions, I have said it here.

Capt. Callow: In fact you deny this letter is your contribution?

Mr Johnson: That is no contribution, that is not what is called a contribution to a newspaper. The word contribution is exactly another word for an article.

Mr Wright: You did address a letter to the paper, to the editor of the Weekly News which was published in the issue of August 13th?

Mr Johnson: In what capacity?

Mr Wright: It does not matter in what capacity.

Mr Johnson: In the capacity in which I am here I addressed no letter to the Weekly News.

Mr Wright: It does not matter in what capacity, it is a question did you or did you not address a letter to the editor of the Weekly News which was subsequently published?

Mr Johnson: I did not in my present capacity.

Mr Wright: Will you tell us whether or not you did send this matter to the paper?

Capt. Callow: Mr Wright is asking the question to you in any of your capacities.

Mr Johnson: I cannot answer the question because I do not know in what capacity it is put to me.

Capt. Callow: You are subpoened in any particular capacity, you are subpoened to give evidence as an individual.

Mr Johnson: Well, as an individual I did not send any article to the press.

Capt. Callow: Are we to understand Mr Wallace Johnson that you sent it in another capacity?

Mr Johnson: I do not say I sent it in another capacity. I say as an individual I did not send it.

Capt. Callow: Did you send it in another capacity?

Mr Johnson: I do not know.

Capt. Callow: Will you tell us whether, in any capacity whatsoever, you addressed this letter of the 9th of August to the editor of the Weekly News which was published in the issue of 13th of August?

Mr Johnson:	I cannot say.
Mr Callow:	What do you mean?
Mr Johnson:	I cannot tell you whether I did send it or not, I cannot discuss anything in any other capacity than the capacity in which I am here.
Capt. Callow:	Can we take it then that you decline to answer?
Mr Johnson:	I decline to answer any questions except in the capacity in which I am subpoenaed.
Mr Wright:	I do not think your subpoena summoned you in any capacity.
Mr Johnson:	It summoned Mr Wallace Johnson of 4, Bombay Lane.
Capt. Callow:	Then we may take it on record Mr Wallace Johnson that you decline to answer questions that are put to you in connection with any organisation and in connection with these articles?
Mr Johnson:	I decline to answer any question put to me in connection with any organisation at all.
Capt. Callow:	And in connection with these articles?
Mr Johnson:	Yes. Because I am not subpoenaed in that capacity.
Capt. Callow:	Have you had, Mr Wallace Johnson, any correspondence with any person in London concerning these articles that have appeared in the press on August 13th and since?
Mr Johnson:	I do not know, I refuse to answer questions that have nothing to do with me in the capacity I am here. You might as well ask me to tell something about the Governor's private affairs.
Mr Beetham:	Will you have a look at that signature and say if it is yours?
Mr Johnson:	It is the signature of the Organising Secretary of the West African Youth League.
Mr Beetham:	You do know that?
Mr Johnson:	Yes, because I am connected with the League.
Mr Beetham:	What is your connection with the Youth League?
Mr Johnson:	I am the Organising Secretary of the West African Youth League.
Mr Beetham:	Did you write that?

(Shown Exhibit No. 21 signed "Wallace Johnson")

Mr Johnson: I do not know.

Mr Beetham: You do not know?

Mr Johnson: I do not know because I am not here to say whether I know.

Mr Beetham: And yet you have just said you are the Organising Secretary of the League and that this signature is that of the Organising Secretary of the League, and yet you do not know whether you wrote it?

Mr Johnson: Because I am not here to say anything of the kind, if you wanted me to say things in connection with the Youth League you should have subpoenaed the Organising Secretary, not Mr Wallace Johnson of 4, Bombay Lane.

Mr Beetham: Mr Wallace Johnson of 4, Bombay Lane has nothing to do with the Youth League?

Mr Johnson: Certainly, in my private capacity I cannot say anything about the Youth League.

Mr Beetham: You still do not know who signed that letter?

Mr Johnson: I am not here to say anything about these letters.

Capt. Callow: Do you understand Mr Wallace Johnson that the publications in the Weekly News of Aug 13th and Sept 10th are alleged to come from you?

Mr Johnson: From who?

Capt. Callow: From you.

Mr Johnson: Me, in the capacity I am here? I do not know that.

Capt. Callow: Do you understand that the publication of these despatches caused great concern to the Civil Service of this Country?

Mr Johnson: I do not understand anything in the position I am here. I understand nothing.

Capt. Callow: Would you be surprised to learn that the publication of the despatches did cause concern in the Civil Service?

Mr Johnson: I am not concerned with them.

Capt. Callow: Then the distress of the Civil Service is no concern of yours?

Mr Johnson: How can I know whether the Civil Service is distressed or not[?] I have not any communication with the Civil Service

	telling me they are concerned with any publication, nobody has intimated to me about it.
Mr Carew:	May we take it that you refuse to give any information in connection with these articles that have appeared?
Mr Johnson:	In what capacity are you putting the question to me?
Mr Carew:	As Mr Wallace Johnson.
Mr Johnson:	As Mr Wallace Johnson pure and simple?
Capt. Callow:	As Mr Wallace Johnson[;] it may be that you are pure, but I am quite sure you are not simple.
Mr Wright:	I think you argue that you are summoned as an individual to give evidence?
Mr Johnson:	Yes, I know I am subpoened as Wallace Johnson of 4, Bombay Lane.
Mr Wright:	So you have taken it as a subpoena to an individual. You said you are the Organising Sec of the West African Youth League?
Mr Johnson:	Yes, I have said that.
Mr Wright:	I suppose the Organising Secretary of the West African Youth League is an individual?
Mr Johnson:	Yes certainly.
Mr Wright:	That is the individual who is summoned here?
Mr Johnson:	No, the individual summoned here is Mr Wallace Johnson of 4, Bombay Lane in his private capacity.
Mr Wright:	Who is the Secretary of the Youth League?
Mr Johnson:	I do not know that.
Mr Wright:	You have just said so.
Mr Johnson:	If I am summoned to come here in the capacity of Wallace Johnson of 4, Bombay Lane I come as a private individual.
Mr Wright:	If the subpoena had been addressed to your name c/o the West African Youth League's office, would that have answered?
Mr Johnson:	That is left with you, surely a Commission like this knows the correct way of doing things.

Capt. Callow: I think that you mean, and your whole attitude is, that if it had been addressed in any other way, you would have considered it on receiving it.

Mr Johnson: If it is addressed to the Youth League Office it may be, it depends how it is worded, I think the Commission ought to know better how to word a subpoena.

Capt. Callow: Then I think we can take it the situation is this, and I hope you will tell me if this is correct, that in your present position you said that you must decline to give any information concerning the publication of either of these despatches?

Mr Johnson: No that is not what I said, I said that in the capacity in which I am subpoened here I am not in a position to say anything that has anything to do with the Youth League, whether it is publication in the press of articles or having anything to do with the Youth League, in the capacity I am here I am not in a position to say anything.

Capt. Callow: Do you feel if you did it would be a betrayal of trust?

Mr Johnson: I do not feel anything, but I have not anything to say as far as that is concerned, it is not a matter of feeling.

Mr Wright: I think you answered me a little while ago that the Organising Secretary of the Youth League is an individual?

Mr Johnson: Yes.

Mr Wright: And that you are he?

Mr Johnson: That individual is Wallace Johnson.

Mr Wright: That is you is it not?

Mr Johnson: I do not know. I think if this Commission wants to know who is the Organising Secretary of the Youth League they should try and obtain the information, but not call upon me in my private capacity to say who is the Organising Secretary of the West African Youth League.

Mr Wright: Do you remember taking the oath at the beginning of the proceedings?

Mr Johnson: Yes.

Mr Wright: And your oath was that the evidence you would give would be the truth, the whole truth and nothing but the truth.

Mr Johnson:	Are you insinuating that what I am saying is not the truth?
Mr Wright:	I am only reminding you of the oath that you took.
Mr Johnson:	I object to such a reminder, that is an insult.
Mr Wright:	Did you in any capacity whatsoever write a letter dated the 9th of August 1938 to the editor of the Sierra Leone Weekly News?
Mr Johnson:	I think you are putting water on a duck's back. I am not prepared to say anything to this Commission that has reference to the West African Youth League because I am not subpoened in that capacity.
Capt. Callow:	We are much obliged for your attendance Mr Johnson, we may have to require your attendance at another day and if so you will have the proper notice.
Mr Johnson:	May I ask who is responsible for my coming here today so that I may know to whom I must apply for my expenses?
Capt. Callow:	Will you put that request in writing please[?]

Notes

INTRODUCTION

1. *Gold Coast Nation*, 28 January 1915, 814.
2. See also Osumaka Likaka, *Naming Colonialism: History and Collective Memory in the Congo, 1870–1960* (Madison: University of Wisconsin Press, 2009); Jean Comaroff and John Comaroff, "On Personhood: An Anthropological Perspective from Africa," *Social Identities* 7, no. 2 (2001): 267–83; Catherine Hall, *Civilising Subjects: Metropole and Colony in the English Imagination, 1830–1867* (Cambridge: Polity, 2002); Antoinette Burton, *At the Heart of the Empire: Indians and the Colonial Encounter in Late-Victorian Britain* (Berkeley: University of California Press, 1998).
3. Simon Gikandi, "Cultural Translation and the African Self: A (Post)colonial Case Study," *Interventions: A Journal of Postcolonial Culture* 3, no. 3 (2001): 358.
4. Ibid., 357.
5. Ibid., 356.
6. For a study of the Yoruba-language press in the 1920s, see Karin Barber, "Translation, Publics, and the Vernacular Press in 1920s Lagos," in *Christianity and Social Change in Africa: Essays in Honor of J. D. Y. Peel*, ed. Toyin Falola (Durham, NC: Carolina Academic Press, 2005), 187–208. See also Karin Barber, ed. and trans., *Print Culture and the First Yoruba Novel: I. B. Thomas's "Life Story of Me, Ṣẹgilọla" and Other Texts* (Leiden, the Netherlands: Brill, 2012).
7. Robert J. Griffin, "Anonymity and Authorship," *New Literary History* 30, no. 4 (1999): 885; see also John Mullan, *Anonymity: A Secret History of English Literature* (London: Faber and Faber, 2007).
8. Mullan, *Anonymity*, 286.
9. Griffin, "Anonymity and Authorship," 877–95; Robert J. Griffin, ed., *The Faces of Anonymity: Anonymous and Pseudonymous Publication from the Sixteenth to the Twentieth Century* (Basingstoke, UK: Palgrave Macmillan, 2003); Mullan, *Anonymity*; Marcy L. North, *The Anonymous Renaissance: Cultures of Discretion in Tudor-Stuart England* (Chicago: University of Chicago Press, 2003).
10. Barber, "Translation, Publics, and the Vernacular Press"; Barber, *Print Culture and the First Yoruba Novel*.
11. Carmela Ciuraru, *Nom de Plume: A (Secret) History of Pseudonyms* (New York: HarperCollins, 2011).
12. Mullan, *Anonymity*, 76–137.
13. Ciuraru, *Nom de Plume*, 159–77.
14. Mullan, *Anonymity*, 50.

15. Born Aphra Johnson, she wrote under the name of her husband, Behn, as well as under the pseudonyms "Aphra Amis," "Aphara," "Ayfara," "Afray," "Astrea," and "Astraea."

16. Malcolm X, "Who Are You?" available at http://www.youtube.com/watch?v=63OHMLf9wUc&feature=related (accessed 1 May 2011).

17. Malcolm X's view that all European-sounding names have their roots in the violence of slaveownership is, however, problematized by scholarship on the history of slavery, which indicates that, upon gaining freedom, many ex-slaves in the Caribbean chose European names above a "return" to African names. According to Trevor Burnard, West Africans in particular adopted a flexible and multiple approach to naming, often adopting the names of local heroes for their children or taking on overtly Christian names without undergoing Christian conversion; see Burnard, "Slave Naming Patterns: Onomastics and the Taxonomy of Race in Eighteenth-Century Jamaica," *Journal of Interdisciplinary History* 31, no. 3 (2001): 325–46.

18. See chapter 5 for a discussion of customary and ordinance marriage.

19. *Lagos Standard*, 20 September 1911, 6. The *Lagos Standard* itself was owned and edited by a Freetown-born man of Egba parentage, George Alfred Williams. For a biographical portrait of Williams, see Fred I. A. Omu, *Press and Politics in Nigeria, 1880–1960* (Atlantic Highlands, NJ: Humanities Press, 1978), 36–38. (Authors' original punctuation and grammar have been preserved throughout *The Power to Name*.)

20. K. A. B. Jones Quartey, *A Summary History of the Ghana Press, 1822–1960* (Accra-Tema: Ghana Publishing, 1974); Omu, *Press and Politics in Nigeria*; David Kimble, *A Political History of Ghana: The Rise of Gold Coast Nationalism, 1850–1928* (Oxford: Clarendon Press, 1963); Raymond Jenkins, "Gold Coast Historians and Their Pursuit of the Gold Coast Pasts—1882–1917" (PhD diss., Centre of West African Studies, University of Birmingham, 1985); Francis B. Nyamnjoh, *Africa's Media: Democracy and the Politics of Belonging* (London: Zed Books, 2005); Jennifer Hasty, *The Press and Political Culture in Ghana* (Bloomington: Indiana University Press, 2005).

21. Barber, "Translation, Publics, and the Vernacular Press," 187–208.

22. Ibid.

23. Roger Chartier, *The Order of Books: Readers, Authors, and Libraries in Europe between the Fourteenth and Eighteenth Centuries* (Cambridge: Polity Press, 1994).

24. Cameroon had the earliest newspapers in French (and German) West Africa. Published in local languages, these included *Mulee-Ngea* in 1903 from the Evangelical missionaries in Buea, *Mwendi Ma Musango* in 1906 from the Baptists in Douala, and *Elolombe Ya Cameroun* in 1908 from the Protestant missionaries. *L'Eveil du Cameroun* was started by French settlers in 1919 but was Africanized and politicized with the appearance of anticolonial francophone newspapers in the early 1940s. See Henry Muluh and Bertha Ndoh, "Evolution of the Media in Cameroon," in Festus Eribo and Enoh Tanjong, eds., *Journalism and Mass Communication in Africa: Cameroon* (Lanham, MD: Lexington

Books, 2002), 4. The African-owned press in Senegal started many years later, in the late 1940s, with *Afrique Nouvelle*, published by the Paulist Fathers in Dakar. See Victor T. Le Vine, *Politics in Francophone Africa* (Boulder, CO: Lynne Rienner, 2004), 13. For detailed analysis of francophone African journalism and its differences from anglophone newspaper production, see Thierry Perret, *Le temps des journalistes: L'invension de la presse en Afrique francophone* (Paris: Karthala, 2005).

25. See Alice L. Conklin, *A Mission to Civilize: The Republican Idea of Empire in France and West Africa, 1895–1930* (Stanford, CA: Stanford University Press, 1997).

26. For Cameroon, see Muluh and Ndoh, "Evolution of the Media in Cameroon," 4–5; Perret, *Le temps des journalistes*. For Togo, see Kate Skinner, "'You Cannot Ask Someone to Read a Newspaper for You': Quotation and Scrutiny in an Ewe-Language Newspaper, 1959–65," paper presented at the Print Cultures Workshop, Oxford University, April 2012.

27. *Gold Coast Nation*, 6 April 1916, 1299.

28. Ibid., 12 October 1916, 1507.

29. Ibid., 20–27 December 1919, 2.

30. Busi Makoni, Sinfree Makoni, and Pedzisai Mashiri, "Naming Practices and Language Planning in Zimbabwe," *Current Issues in Language Planning* 8, no. 3 (2007): 448; see also Likaka, *Naming Colonialism*.

31. *Gold Coast Nation*, 18 July 1912, 99.

32. Ibid., 20–27 December 1919, 2.

33. See, e.g., *Gold Coast Nation*, 11 March 1915, where "The Man in the Street" poses a list of questions the "amateur journalist" should ask him- or herself before submitting an article for publication in a newspaper relating to the suitability of the subject matter and whether he or she can escape the pitfalls of "atrocious English" (861).

34. As yet, it has not been possible to discover how many pseudonyms were chosen by editors rather than by contributors themselves or the extent to which contributors determined the titles of their pieces.

35. Correctly spelled, *Odoziaku* means "arranger, manager, or keeper of wealth" in Igbo.

36. For a biography of J. M. Stuart-Young, see Stephanie Newell, *The Forger's Tale: The Search for "Odeziaku"* (Athens: Ohio University Press, 2006).

37. I am indebted to Robin Law for alerting me to this memoir and the identity of its author.

38. Likaka, *Naming Colonialism*, 11–12, 16–18.

39. See the various *Reports of the Education Department* for school enrollment figures by year in British West African colonies. In colonial Ghana, for example, total school enrollment was 42,339 in 1920 and 54,151 in 1930, rising to 91,047 in 1940. See Stephanie Newell, *Literary Culture in Colonial Ghana: "How to Play the Game of Life"* (Manchester, UK: Manchester University Press, 2002), 9. For a study of literacy and education in colonial Nigeria, see Charlotte Hastings, "Metropole-Colony in Education Policy for Girls' Education in Colonial Africa,

with Particular Reference to Southern Nigeria c. 1925–40" (PhD diss., University of Edinburgh, 2011).

40. *Gold Coast Leader*, 5 July 1902, 2.

41. Ibid., 19 July 1902, 2.

42. Ibid., 11 April 1903, 2. Just as the identity of contributors is exceptionally difficult to determine, the names of the editors of West African newspapers are often impossible to retrieve at different moments in a paper's history. On this occasion, the editor and proprietor were named in court and in the columns of the *Leader* as Samuel Harrison and Fynn Egyir-Asaam, respectively. In his comprehensive study of the Gold Coast press, however, K. A. B. Jones-Quartey identifies the editors and proprietors of the *Gold Coast Leader* as J. E. Casely-Hayford, Herbert Brown, Rev. S. R. B. Attoh-Ahuma, John Buckman, and G. Acquah, but he states that their "roles and exact functions [were] undeterminable"; see Jones-Quartey, "The Gold Coast Press, 1822–c. 1930: The Chronologies," *Research Review (Institute of African Studies)* 4, no. 2 (1968): 30–46. Harrison and Egyir-Asaam are not listed by Jones-Quartey. By 1912, S. R. B. Attoh-Ahuma had become editor of the *Leader's* archrival, the *Gold Coast Nation*; see L. H. Ofusu-Appiah, ed., *The Encyclopaedia Africana Dictionary of African Biography*, vol. 1, *Ethiopia–Ghana* (New York: Reference Publications, 1977), available at http://www.dacb.org/stories/ghana/attoh_ahuma_s.html (accessed 8 July 2009).

43. PRO, CO 875/13/5, Press Censorship: Nigeria, 1942, "Minute signed S. S. Abrahams," 29 January 1942.

44. Ibid.

45. Ironically, the practice of initializing internal memos and minutes at the Colonial Office often leaves contemporary researchers with a predicament of identity like that encountered with the initialized newspaper contributions in the West African press. Though every effort has been made to fully identify the authors of Colonial Office memos and minutes, some individuals have been impossible to fully name.

46. PRO, CO 875/13/5, Press Censorship: Nigeria, 1942, "Memo signed O. G. R. W.," 2 February 1943.

47. PRO, CO 96/714/6, Bills for Newspapers, Books and Printing Presses Ordinance, Criminal Code (Amendment) Ordinance, Control of Imported Books, "Memo signed Arthur Grey Hazlerigg," 26 February 1934.

48. PRO, CO 96/716/15, Control of the Press of the Gold Coast: Newspapers, Books and Printing Presses Ordinance, 1934 (closed until 1985), "Memorandum by the Inspector General of Police [Henry W. M. Bamford] Regarding the Draft Bill (44A) cited as the Newspapers, Books and Printing Presses Ordinance, 1934," n.d.

49. Malcolm MacDonald, cited in Stanley Shaloff, "Press Controls and Sedition Proceedings in the Gold Coast, 1933–39," *African Affairs* 71, no. 284 (1972): 262.

50. Karin Barber, *The Anthropology of Texts, Persons and Publics: Oral and Written Culture in Africa and Beyond* (Cambridge: Cambridge University Press, 2007); Michael Warner, "Publics and Counterpublics," *Public Culture* 14, no. 1 (2002): 49–90.

51. *Gold Coast Leader*, 11 April 1903, 3.

52. Ibid. (italics in the original).

53. Schopenhauer cited in the *Observer* (London), 24 July 2011, 13; Daniel J. Solove, *The Future of Reputation: Gossip, Rumor, and Privacy on the Internet* (New Haven: Yale University Press, 2008), 140–41.

54. Skinner, "'You Cannot Ask Someone to Read.'"

55. *Sawyerr's Bookselling, Printing and Stationery Trade Circular*, 26 September 1885, n.p.

56. *Gold Coast Nation*, 19 October 1916, 1514. A. H. Filson wrote regularly for the *Nation*, including many solemn poems with patriotic themes.

57. For a discussion of debates about literary style in colonial Ghana, see Newell, *Literary Culture in Colonial Ghana*.

58. *Gold Coast Nation*, 21 October 1915, 1115 (italics in the original).

59. Leroy Vail and Landeg White, *Power and the Praise Poem: Southern African Voices in History* (Charlottesville: University of Virginia Press, 1991), 43.

60. Urban elites often had extensive kinship networks in rural areas, however, and should not be regarded as alienated from the villages.

61. For a comprehensive study of Ghanaian women's contribution to the press in the colonial period, see Audrey Gadzekpo, "Women's Engagement with Gold Coast Print Culture from 1857 to 1957" (PhD diss., Centre of West African Studies, University of Birmingham, 2000).

62. The extent to which women contributed items under male pseudonyms, however, is impossible to determine.

63. *Gold Coast Nation*, 27 March 1913, 263.

64. Mullan, *Anonymity*, 51.

65. On T. Payne Jackson and other early Nigerian press celebrities, see Omu, *Press and Politics in Nigeria*.

66. The politician, newspaperman, and Methodist minister Rev. Samuel Richard Brew Attoh-Ahuma (1863–1921) changed his surname from Solomon to Attoh-Ahuma in 1898; see Ofusu-Appiah, *Encyclopaedia Africana Dictionary of African Biography*.

67. Omu, *Press and Politics in Nigeria*, 44.

68. *Lagos Weekly Record*, 7 October 1893, 4.

69. *Gold Coast Leader*, 17 August 1907, 4.

70. *Sierra Leone Weekly News*, 19 June 1909, 4.

71. In his autobiography, Nnamdi Azikiwe describes how in childhood he questioned the Christian forename given to him by his parents, but he adds, "Not until I was 30 years of age did I have the courage to blast tradition and cast it away while retaining the purely African and Onitsha names, NNAMDI AZIKIWE."; see Azikiwe, *My Odyssey: An Autobiography* (London: C. Hurst, 1970), 8 (capping in the original). The catalyst for this repudiation was the refusal of the Nigerian government to enter him for the Empire Games in 1934 (ibid., 405).

72. *Sierra Leone Weekly News*, 28 April 1906, 14. For studies of the distinctive cultural positioning of the Creoles of Freetown, see Mac Dixon-Fyle and Gibril Cole, eds., *New Perspectives on the Sierra Leone Krio* (New York: Peter Lang, 2006), and Akintola Wyse, *The Krio of Sierra Leone: An Interpretive History* (London: Hurst and International African Institute, 1989).

73. *Sawyerr's Bookselling, Printing and Stationery Trade Circular*, 19 December 1885, n.p.

74. Christian missionaries often tried to provide Africans with morally uplifting leadership models, creating a genre of biographical celebrations of "great men" that influenced later cultural nationalists and pan-Africanists. See Rev. S. R. B. Attoh-Ahuma, *Memoirs of West African Celebrities* (Liverpool, UK: D. Marples, 1905); Allister Macmillan, *The Red Book of West Africa* (London: Collingridge, 1920); Magnus J. Sampson, *Gold Coast Men of Affairs: Past and Present* (London: A. H. Stockwell, 1937). Newspapers often carried written—and, from the mid-1930s onward, photographic—portraits of heroic Africans, explicitly offering them to readers as role models for emulation; see *Gold Coast Leader*, 1905. Nnamdi Azikiwe was a particularly enthusiastic producer of black role models for young West Africans: at a speech in the Glover Memorial Hall in Lagos in November 1934, for example, he "told the story of the African in world history" to emphasize "the capacity of the black peoples"; see Azikiwe, *My Odyssey*, 226–29.

75. An exception to this view of anonymity in Europe can be found in Marcy North's *Anonymous Renaissance*, which is one of the few studies to highlight the complexity of naming practices in Renaissance England and to discuss uses of pseudonyms in journals and periodicals as well as in English literature.

76. See Likaka, *Naming Colonialism*, 24–31; Makoni, Makoni, and Mashiri, "Naming Practices and Language Planning in Zimbabwe"; Newell, *Forger's Tale*.

77. Likaka, *Naming Colonialism*, 22.

78. *Gold Coast Leader*, 20 December 1902, 4 (italics in the original).

79. Ibid., 5 July 1902, 4.

80. Ibid., 13 September 1902, 4.

81. Ibid.

82. *Gold Coast Nation*, 11 July 1912, 90.

83. Ibid., 9 January 1913, 200.

84. Ibid., 202.

85. *Gold Coast Leader*, 27 June 1903, 4.

86. Ibid., 28 June 1902, 4.

87. Sawyerr edited the paper, wrote most of the articles, and owned most of the commercial outlets advertised in its columns.

88. *Sawyerr's Bookselling, Printing and Stationery Trade Circular*, 27 February 1886, front page.

89. Ibid. (italics in the original).

90. PRO, CO 96/749/5, Wallace-Johnson, Privy Council Appeal: *I. T. A. Wallace-Johnson v. The King* (closed until 1989), "Law Officers' Dept, Accra, Gold Coast: Report Entitled Wallace-Johnson versus the King: Observations of the Attorney-General of the Gold Coast upon the Appellant's Case, by H. W. B. Blackall," 13 November 1938.

CHAPTER 1 THE "FOURTH AND ONLY ESTATE"

The title of this chapter derives from an editorial published in the *Gold Coast Leader*, 1 July 1905, 2.

1. Jürgen Habermas, "The Public Sphere: An Encyclopaedia Article (1964)," *New German Critique* 1, no. 3 (1974): 49.
2. Jürgen Habermas, *The Structural Transformation of the Public Sphere: An Inquiry into a Category of Bourgeois Society* (Cambridge: Polity Press, 1989), 27–43.
3. Ibid., 142.
4. Bart Cammaerts, *Internet-Mediated Participation beyond the Nation State* (Manchester, UK: Manchester University Press, 2008), 25–27.
5. Gender-biased language has been used deliberately in this chapter to reflect ownership and readership of West African newspapers until the 1940s. For a subtle and detailed assessment of the contradictions between the imperial civilizing mission and French republican ideals in French West Africa, see Alice L. Conklin, *A Mission to Civilize: The Republican Idea of Empire in France and West Africa* (Stanford, CA: Stanford University Press, 1997).
6. Karin Barber, "Introduction: I. B. Thomas and the First Yoruba Novel," in *Print Culture and the First Yoruba Novel: I. B. Thomas's "Life Story of Me, Ṣẹgilọla" and Other Texts*, ed. and trans. Karin Barber (Leiden, the Netherlands: Brill, 2012), 41.
7. *Gold Coast Leader*, 13 February 1904, 4, and 23 July 1904, 2.
8. Ibid., 29 October 1904, 2, and 26 August 1905, 4.
9. Ibid., 26 November 1904, 6.
10. Ibid., 1 July 1905, 2.
11. Ibid.
12. Ibid., 17 June 1905, 4.
13. Ibid., 16 December 1905, 4.
14. Ibid., 24 June 1905, 3.
15. Ibid., 2.
16. Ibid.
17. Ibid., 1 July 1905, 2.
18. PRO, CO 96/714/6, 16, Bills for Newspapers, Books and Printing Presses Ordinance; Criminal Code (Amendment) Ordinance; Control of Imported Books, "Letter from James A. Busum to the Secretary of State for the Colonies," 16 February 1934. See chapter 3.
19. Ibid.
20. *Lagos Weekly Record*, 14 February 1903, 6. Governor MacGregor's Newspaper Ordinance, which remained in place until 1955 when Azikiwe finally succeeded in repealing its requirement for a bond, required "prospective newspaper proprietors to make, sign and swear an affidavit containing the address and the real and true names and addresses of its proprietors, printers and publishers" and to pay a £250 bond with sureties from which any penalties for libel and sedition would be paid; see Chris W. Ogbondah, "British Colonial Authoritarianism, African Military Dictatorship and the Nigerian Press," *Africa Media Review*, 6, no. 3 (1992): 1–18; Nnamdi Azikiwe, *My Odyssey: An Autobiography* (London: C. Hurst, 1970), 317.
21. PRO, CO 96/714/6, Bills for Newspapers, Books and Printing Presses Ordinance; Criminal Code (Amendment) Ordinance; Control of Imported Books, "Letter from James A. Busum to the Secretary of State for the Colonies," 16 February 1934.

22. *Sierra Leone Weekly News*, 11 November 1903, 6.

23. Ibid.

24. John Hartley and Alan McKee, *The Indigenous Public Sphere: The Reporting and Reception of Aboriginal Issues in the Australian Media* (Oxford: Oxford University Press, 2000), 31.

25. *Western Echo*, 18 November 1885, 4.

26. For a discussion of Lagosian elite print cultures and the numerous Yoruba-language pamphlets published by local elites between the 1880s and 1920s, see Nara Improta, "Producing Intellectuals: Books and Pamphlets in Lagos between 1880 and 1922" (PhD diss., University of Sussex, forthcoming 2014). For a study of elite and nonelite Ghanaian literary and debating clubs in the 1920s and 1930s in the context of other modes of writing, including studies of African laws, customs, and history, see Stephanie Newell, *Literary Culture in Colonial Ghana: How to Play the Game of Life* (Manchester, UK: Manchester University Press, 2002). For research into the Ewe-language press of colonial and preindependence Togoland, see Kate Skinner, "'You Cannot Ask Someone to Read a Newspaper for You': Quotation and Scrutiny in an Ewe-Language Newspaper, 1959–65," paper presented at the Print Cultures Workshop, Oxford University, April 2012.

27. *Western Echo*, 18 November 1885, front page.

28. *Gold Coast Leader*, 5 December 1925, 6.

29. Barber, "Introduction: I. B. Thomas and the First Yoruba Novel," 27–46.

30. *Western Echo*, 18 November 1885, 4.

31. *Gold Coast Leader*, 19 April 1924, 6. In practice, however, editors patrolled correspondents' contributions with a class bias, offering paternalistic advice on how to write "properly" (see chapter 2).

32. Neeladri Bhattacharya, "Notes towards a Conception of the Colonial Public," in *Civil Society, Public Sphere and Citizenship: Dialogues and Perceptions*, ed. Rajeev Bhargava and Helmut Reifeld (New Delhi: Sage, 2005), 132.

33. Barber, "Introduction: I. B. Thomas and the First Yoruba Novel," 41.

34. See Dwayne Woods, "Civil Society in Europe and Africa: Limiting State Power through a Public Sphere," *African Studies Review* 35, no. 2 (1992): 93; Kenneth Little, *West African Urbanization: A Study of Voluntary Associations in Social Change* (Cambridge: Cambridge University Press, 1965).

35. Habermas, *Structural Transformation of the Public Sphere*, xviii.

36. Bhattacharya, "Notes towards a Conception of the Colonial Public," 130.

37. Alan Lester, "British Settler Discourse and the Circuits of Empire," *History Workshop Journal* 54 (2002): 3e–32; see also Jonathan Hyslop, "On Biography: A Response to Ciraj Rasool," *South African Sociological Review* 41, no. 2 (June 2010): 104–15.

38. Lester, "British Settler Discourse and the Circuits of Empire," 26.

39. Mrinalini Sinha, "Britishness, Clubbability, and the Colonial Public Sphere: The Genealogy of an Imperial Institution in Colonial India," *Journal of British Studies* 40, no. 4 (2001): 489.

40. Ibid., 491–92.

41. Ibid., 492.

42. Ibid., 505.
43. John Hartley and Alan McKee's description of an "indigenous public sphere" in Australia segregates colonial from indigenous in a similarly restrictive way; see Hartley and McKee, *Indigenous Public Sphere*.
44. Newell, *Literary Culture in Colonial Ghana*, 27–52.
45. Nancy Fraser, "Rethinking the Public Sphere: A Contribution to the Critique of Actually Existing Democracy," in *Habermas and the Public Sphere*, ed. Craig Calhoun (Cambridge, MA: MIT Press, 1992), 108–42; Joan B. Landes, *Women and the Public Sphere in the Age of the French Revolution* (Ithaca, NY: Cornell University Press, 1988).
46. See Chantal Mouffe, *On the Political: Thinking in Action* (London: Routledge, 2005).
47. Hartley and McKee, *Indigenous Public Sphere*, 31.
48. See Improta, *Producing Intellectuals*; Newell, *Literary Culture in Colonial Ghana*.
49. See Michael Crowder, "Indirect Rule—French and British Style," *Africa* 34, no. 3 (1964): 197–205; Andrew E. Barnes, *Making Headway: The Introduction of Western Civilization in Colonial Northern Nigeria* (Rochester, NY: University of Rochester Press, 2009).
50. The ambivalent responses generated by this mind-set are discussed in chapter 4.
51. Bhattacharya, "Notes towards a Conception of the Colonial Public," 141.
52. Woods, "Civil Society in Europe and Africa," 86–87.
53. Ibid., 87.
54. Ibid. See also Jean-François Bayart, *The State in Africa: The Politics of the Belly* (London: Longman, 1994); Achille Mbembe, *On the Postcolony* (Berkeley: University of California Press, 2001).
55. Fred I. Omu, *Press and Politics in Nigeria: 1880–1960* (Atlantic Highlands, NJ: Humanities Press, 1978), 35.
56. See Philip S. Zachernuk, *Colonial Subjects: An African Intelligentsia and Atlantic Ideas* (Charlottesville: University of Virginia Press, 2000), 131–33; S. T. Kwame Boafo, "Journalism Profession and Training in Sub-Saharan Africa: A Case Study of Ghana," *Africa Media Review* 2, no. 3 (1988): 56–74.
57. Zachernuk, *Colonial Subjects*, 125–49.
58. *Gold Coast Leader*, 19 April 1924, 5.
59. Ibid.
60. *Sierra Leone Weekly News*, 11 November 1903, 6.
61. See Bhattacharya, "Notes towards a Conception of the Colonial Public," 140–42.
62. *Gold Coast Leader*, 1 July 1905, 2.
63. PRO, CO 583/265/1, Petition: Nnamdi Azikiwe (Re: Zik's Press Ltd), 1946: Secret (closed until 1977), "To The Rt Hon George Hall MP, Sec of State for the Colonies," 15 March 1946.
64. Ibid.
65. West African newspaper ordinances generally required a certain number of copies of each issue (up to five) to be placed in official depositories ranging from

the governor's residence to the Colonial Office in London. The legal requirement that the printer and proprietor sign each copy sent for deposit negatively impacted freedom of speech, but the deposit itself ensured the survival of a substantial newspaper archive.

66. There is some disagreement among media historians about the extent of official intervention in local newspapers. Francis Nyamnjoh argues that colonial regimes were intolerant of the local press and that elite West African newspapermen "met with stiff resistance by the authorities who treated them as subversives"; see Nyamnjoh, *Africa's Media, Democracy and the Politics of Belonging* (London: Zed Books, 2005), 41. Other historians, however, highlight the atmosphere of tense toleration in which African-owned presses survived; see David Kimble, *A Political History of Ghana: The Rise of Gold Coast Nationalism, 1850–1928* (Oxford: Clarendon Press, 1963); Omu, *Press and Politics in Nigeria*.

67. *Gold Coast Leader*, 5 December 1925, 6.

68. Omu, *Press and Politics in Nigeria*, 245.

69. PRO, CO 87/258/13, Gambia: Registration, Printing and Publication of Newspapers Legislation, Feb-Aug, 1944 (closed until 1972), "Minute from O. G. R. Williams," 23 March 1944.

70. Barber, "Introduction: I. B. Thomas and the First Yoruba Novel."

CHAPTER 2 ARTICULATING EMPIRE

1. See Carl Patrick Burrowes, *Power and Press Freedom in Liberia, 1830–1970* (Trenton, NJ: Africa World Press, 2004).

2. For a discussion of the ideational and ideological networks of West Africa's colonial intelligentsia, see Philip Z. Zachernuk, *Colonial Subjects: An African Intelligentsia and Atlantic Ideas* (Charlottesville: University of Virginia Press, 2000). For studies of the vernacular (Yoruba) press in this period, see Karin Barber, "Translation, Publics, and the Vernacular Press in 1920s Lagos," in *Christianity and Social Change in Africa: Essays in Honor of J. D. Y. Peel*, ed. Toyin Falola (Durham, NC: Carolina Academic Press, 2005), 187–208; Barber, "I. B. Akinyẹlẹ and Early Yoruba Print Culture," in *Recasting the Past*, ed. Derek R. Peterson and Giacomo Macola (Athens: Ohio University Press, 2009), 31–49.

3. See *Gold Coast Leader*, 12 July 1902, 4; 19 July 1902, 3; 9 August 1902, 4; 11 October 1902, 3; 28 February 1903, 3; 29 August 1903, 2

4. Padmore's letter, "Sierra Leone: The 'Undesirable Literature' Ordinance," was published in the *Manchester Guardian* on 14 June 1939; see PRO, CO 267/672/7, Deportation, Sedition, Undesirable Literature, Trade Union and Trade Disputes Legislation—Miscellaneous Representations, 1939, press cutting, "Sierra Leone: The 'Undesirable Literature' Ordinance," from the *Manchester Guardian*, 14 June 1939.

5. Section 3 of the Undesirable Literature Ordinance reads:

> Any person who imports, publishes, sells, offers for sale, distributes, or reproduces any publication the importation of which has been prohibited under section 3, or any extract therefrom, shall be guilty of an offence and liable for a first offence to imprisonment

for 2 years, or to a fine not exceeding £100, or to both such imprisonment and fine, and for a subsequent offence to imprisonment for 3 years; and such publication or extract thereof shall be forfeited to his Majesty.

Any person who without lawful excuse has in his possession any publication the importation of which has been prohibited under section 3, or any extract therefrom, shall be guilty of an offence and liable for a first offence to imprisonment for a term not exceeding one year or to a fine not exceeding £50, or to both such imprisonment and fine, and for a subsequent offence to imprisonment for a term not exceeding 2 years; and such publication or extract therefrom shall be forfeited to his Majesty.

PRO, CO 267/672/7, Deportation, Sedition, Undesirable Literature, Trade Union and Trade Disputes Legislation—Miscellaneous Representations, 1939, press cutting, "Sierra Leone: The 'Undesirable Literature' Ordinance," cutting from the *Manchester Guardian*, 14 June 1939.

6. These networks were not exclusively articulated in the English-language press. In her study of Ewe-language newspapers in the 1950s, Kate Skinner discusses the ways in which Nkrumah's speeches on the integration of Togo and Ghana circulated via the French-language press, the radio, and refugees in French Togoland. See Skinner, "'You Cannot Ask Someone to Read a Newspaper for You': Quotation and Scrutiny in an Ewe-Language Newspaper, 1959–65," paper presented at the Print Cultures Workshop, Oxford University, April 2012.

7. NNA (Ibadan), James Vivian Clinton Papers, JVC 2/1/106, "Letters to JVC," Section A., Lecture 3 (2), n.d. [c. April 1965].

8. Ibid.

9. For detailed analysis of *Drum* in Nigeria and the tensions between Ottah and Hopkinson, see Tyler Fleming and Toyin Falola, "Africa's Media Empire: *Drum*'s Expansion to Nigeria," *History in Africa* 32 (2005): 133–64.

10. *Gold Coast Leader*, 27 September 1902, 3.

11. Stuart Hall, "On Postmodernism and Articulation: An Interview with Stuart Hall edited by Lawrence Grossberg," in *Stuart Hall: Critical Dialogues in Cultural Studies*, ed. David Morley and Kuan-Hsing Chen (London: Routledge, 1996), 141 (italics in the original). See also Richard Middleton, *Studying Popular Music* (1990; Philadelphia: Open University Press, 2002), 8–9; James Procter, *Stuart Hall* (London: Routledge, 2004), 48.

12. *Western Echo*, 18 November 1885, 2.

13. *Gold Coast Leader*, 25 October 1902, 4.

14. Jennifer Hasty, *The Press and Political Culture in Ghana* (Bloomington: Indiana University Press, 2005), 8.

15. See Robert Darnton, "Literary Surveillance in the British Raj: The Contradictions of British Imperialism," *Book History* 4 (2001): 133–76; Fred I. Omu, *Press and Politics in Nigeria: 1880–1960* (Atlantic Highlands, NJ: Humanities Press, 1978); David Kimble, *A Political History of Ghana, 1850–1928* (Oxford: Clarendon Press, 1963); Raymond Jenkins, "Gold Coast Historians and Their Pursuit of the

Gold Coast Pasts, 1882–1918" (PhD diss., Centre of West African Studies, University of Birmingham, 1985).

16. See K. A. B. Jones-Quartey, *A Summary History of the Ghana Press* (Accra: Ghana Information Services Department, 1974); Francis B. Nyamnjoh, *Africa's Media, Democracy and the Politics of Belonging* (London: Zed, 2005).

17. Benedict Anderson, *Imagined Communities: Reflections on the Origins and Spread of Nationalism* (1983; London: Verso Books, 1991), 25, 70, 116.

18. Frederick Cooper, *Colonialism in Question: Theory, Knowledge, History* (Berkeley: University of California Press, 2005), 11; see also Zachernuk, *Colonial Subjects*, 1–18.

19. Cited in James M. Hagen, "'Read All about It!': The Press and the Rise of National Consciousness in Early Twentieth Century Dutch East Indies Society," *Anthropological Quarterly* 70, no. 3 (1997): 108; see also Alistair McCleary and Benjamin A. Brabon, *The Influence of Benedict Anderson* (Edinburgh: Merchiston Publishing, 2007); Kwame Appiah, *In My Father's House: Africa in the Philosophy of Culture* (Oxford: Oxford University Press, 1993).

20. *Gold Coast Leader*, 13 September 1902, front page.

21. Sir Henry Hamilton Johnston (1858–1927) was an explorer of Africa in the 1880s, a colonial administrator in numerous British African territories in the 1880s and 1890s, and a pivotal figure in British colonial policy in Africa. His publications include *The Colonization of Africa* (1899), *Liberia* (1906), and *The Backward Peoples and Our Relations with Them* (1920).

22. *Gold Coast Nation*, 11 July 1912, 90.

23. Ibid.

24. *Sierra Leone Weekly News*, 17 February 1894, 3.

25. *Gold Coast Nation*, 4 July 1912, 84. This reference to the "deportation" of editors reveals, in passing, the extent to which so-called local newspaper managers were members of the transnational migrant African communities dispersed throughout British West Africa.

26. After the publication of two overtly anticolonial articles, Davies had been fined and warned not to repeat his behavior, in February 1916. The appearance of an article wishing for Germany to win World War I finally led to his imprisonment; see Omu, *Press and Politics in Nigeria*, 190–91.

27. *Lagos Standard*, 22 November 1916, cited in *Gold Coast Nation*, 30 November–7 December 1916, 1560.

28. *Gold Coast Nation*, 30 November–7 December 1916, 1560.

29. Ibid. In his history of the Nigerian press, Omu suggests the opposite. Although the colonial governor, Lord Lugard, insisted that Davies should be prosecuted for sedition, iv Omu's version of the story the chief justice himself thought the offending article was "justifiable journalese comment"; see Omu, *Press and Politics in Nigeria*, 191.

30. *Gold Coast Nation*, 30 November–7 December 1916, 1561.

31. *Gold Coast Leader*, 5 July 1902, 4.

32. See Stephanie Newell, *Literary Culture in Colonial Ghana: "How to Play the Game of Life"* (Manchester, UK: Manchester University Press, 2002), 203–15.

33. *Gold Coast Leader*, 9 August 1902, 4.
34. *Gold Coast Nation*, 8 July 1915, 996.
35. Ibid.
36. Ibid., 11 March 1915, 861. The archconservatism of the *Nation* manifested itself on many occasions but particularly in relation to the reporting of news about women's rights in Europe. In August 1913, for example, an article on Emily Pankhurst's militant suffrage movement proposed that these women should be sent to prison on St. Helena where "they could do very little damage to other people or themselves. . . . There, perhaps, they would learn to live a quiet, contented and respectable life as all sound women ought to do"; see *Gold Coast Nation*, 28 August 1913, 391.
37. Several prominent newspapermen and intellectuals in West Africa were also ordained Christian ministers, a situation that sometimes caused tensions, as in the case of the Reverend S. R. B. Attoh-Ahuma, editor of the *Gold Coast Methodist* (later the *Gold Coast Methodist Times*) in the 1890s, who was forced to leave the Wesleyan Methodist Church as a result of his politically engaged journalism.
38. *Sawyerr's Bookselling, Printing and Stationery Trade Circular*, 29 April 1886, n.p.
39. Ibid., 19 December 1885, n.p.
40. See Newell, *Literary Culture in Colonial Ghana*, 83–97.
41. For histories of West African elites and their Janus-faced political and literary sensibilities, see Kwaku Larbi Korang, *Writing Ghana, Imagining Africa: Nation and African Modernity* (Rochester, NY: University of Rochester Press, 2004), and Roger Gocking, *Facing Two Ways: Ghana's Coastal Communities under Colonial Rule* (New York: University Press of America, 1999).
42. *Gold Coast Leader*, 28 June 1902, front page.
43. Ibid.
44. *Sawyerr's Bookselling, Printing and Stationery Trade Circular*, 26 September 1885, n.p. (italics in the original).
45. See, e.g., *Gold Coast Nation*, "Why We Complain," 27 June 1912, 80, and "Representation: Thirty-Four Years Ago," 1 March 1919, 2.
46. *Gold Coast Leader*, 27 June 1903, 4 (italics in the original). An example of this self-referential approach to the writing of history can be found in the *Gold Coast Nation* in March 1913, when the editor published a long list containing the titles and page numbers of all previous articles written by the pseudonymous contributor "Won Hu Nos"; see *Gold Coast Nation*, 27 March 1913, 3.
47. *Gold Coast Nation*, 30 April 1914, 589.
48. Ibid., 10 September 1914, 700–701.
49. *Gold Coast Leader*, 9 August 1902, 3 (italics in the original).
50. Precisely how foreign journals found their way into West African newspaper offices is a matter that deserves further investigation. One way was through subscriptions taken out by editors; another was through the donation of copies by local supporters. Thus, shortly after its inception, the *Gold Coast Leader* expressed public gratitude when "[a] certain young man in town to show his appreciation for the *Leader* so far, subscribed for a year for three of the English journals for the

use of the Editor's Office. Good. Thank you"; *Gold Coast Leader*, 6 September 1902, front page.

51. For example, in 1902 the *Gold Coast Leader* printed a letter from the *Daily News*, which "our esteemed contemporary the *West Africa* also culls"; *Gold Coast Leader*, 6 September 1902, 1–2.

52. See also Barber, "I. B. Akinyẹle and Early Yoruba Print Culture."

53. *Sawyerr's Bookselling, Printing and Stationery Trade Circular*, 26 September 1885, n.p.

54. Skinner, "'You Cannot Ask Someone to Read.'"

55. *Gold Coast Nation*, 4 July 1912, 84.

56. Ibid.

57. Ibid., 13 May 1915, 933.

58. Ibid.

59. Ibid., 8 August 1912, 112; see chapter 5.

60. Roger Chartier points out that in seventeenth- and eighteenth-century Europe, written materials played key roles in "the culture of the illiterate" and were present in workplaces, public spaces, and rituals; see Chartier, *The Order of Books: Readers, Authors, and Libraries in Europe between the Fourteenth and Eighteenth Centuries* (Cambridge: Polity Press, 1994), 19.

61. Kwame Arhin, "A Note on the Asante Akonkofo: A Non-literate Sub-elite, 1900–1930," *Africa* 56, no. 1 (1986): 28.

62. *Sawyerr's Bookselling, Printing and Stationery Trade Circular*, 29 April 1886, n.p.

63. Locally published and popular literatures in contemporary West Africa exhibit a remarkably similar attitude toward readers and reading: see Stephanie Newell, *Ghanaian Popular Literature: "Thrilling Discoveries in Conjugal Life"* (Oxford: James Currey, 2000).

64. *Nigerian Observer*, 14 November 1931, 8.

65. *Gold Coast Nation*, 9 October 1913, 424.

66. See Newell, *Ghanaian Popular Literature*.

67. *Nigerian Eastern Mail*, 18 December 1937, 8.

68. *Nigerian Observer*, 18 October 1930, 8.

69. Michael Warner, "Publics and Counterpublics," *Public Culture* 14, no. 1 (2002): 54, 75. Though Warner does not refer to Anderson's work, his definition of a public as "a relation among strangers" (35) strongly invokes the "invisible community" described by Anderson.

70. See Barber, "Translation, Publics, and the Vernacular Press."

71. Warner, "Publics and Counterpublics," 70.

72. *Gold Coast Leader*, 7–14 February 1903, 4.

73. See Karin Barber, *The Anthropology of Texts, Persons and Publics: Oral and Written Culture in Africa and Beyond* (Cambridge: Cambridge University Press, 2007), and Barber, "I. B. Akinyẹle and Early Yoruba Print Culture."

74. Barber, "Translation, Publics, and the Vernacular Press," 196.

75. Ibid., 187–91, 202.

CHAPTER 3 THE VIEW FROM AFAR

1. PRO, CO 537/4878, Control of Undesirable Publications (Eastern Sarawak), 1949, Secret, "Minute by K. G. Ashton," 16 May 1949.

2. PRO, CO 96/714/6, Bills for Newspapers, Books and Printing Presses Ordinance, Criminal Code (Amendment) Ordinance, Control of Imported Books, "Memo signed Arthur Grey Hazlerigg," 26 February 1934; see also PRO, CO 691/140/11, Control of Newspapers and Printing Presses, 1934, Tanganyika, "Minute signed 'H. B.' [H. Bushe]," 12 November 1934, and "Minute signed 'P. L. L.,'" 30 December 1934.

3. PRO, CO 96/716/15, Control of the Press of the Gold Coast: Newspapers, Books and Printing Presses Ordinance, 1934 (closed until 1985), "Memo from Arnold Hodson, Government House, Accra, to the Rt Hon Sir Philip Cunliffe-Lister, Secretary of State for the Colonies," 29 November 1934.

4. Ibid. Sir Arnold had to eat his words within two years of this statement, and his actions produced two press martyrs in precisely the sensational manner he foresaw when advocating restraint (see the first case study later in the chapter).

5. PRO, CO 96/714/6, Bills for Newspapers, Books and Printing Presses Ordinance, Criminal Code (Amendment) Ordinance, Control of Imported Books, "Memo signed Alex Fiddian," date unclear: c. 1 March 1934.

6. PRO, CO 537/6523, Security Arrangements, West Africa: Undesirable Publications—"Africa" by George Padmore (closed until 1981), "Letter from Jim Griffiths, Secretary of State for the Colonies, to Archibald Fenner Brockway MP," 13 December 1950.

7. Harry Scott Newlands, 1933, cited in Stanley Shaloff, "Press Controls and Sedition Proceedings in the Gold Coast, 1933–39," *African Affairs* 71, no. 284 (1972): 241.

8. PRO, CO 537/4878, Control of Undesirable Publications (Eastern Sarawak), 1949, Secret, "Minute signed John D. Higham," 3 June 1949.

9. Ibid.

10. PRO, CO 96/714/6, Bills for Newspapers, Books and Printing Presses Ordinance, Criminal Code (Amendment) Ordinance, Control of Imported Books, "Message from Shenton Thomas to Alex Fiddian," 27 February 1934.

11. PRO, CO 96/716/15, Control of the Press of the Gold Coast: Newspapers, Books and Printing Presses Ordinance, 1934 (closed until 1985), "Memorandum by the Inspector General of Police [Henry W. M. Bamford] Regarding the Draft Bill (44A) cited as the Newspapers, Books and Printing Presses Ordinance, 1934," n.d.

12. PRO, CO 323/977/1, Films: Replies to Confidential Circular Despatch of 8 January 1927, "Enclosure 1 in Gold Coast Confidential of 19 April 1927: Confidential Memorandum by the Governor on the Censorship of Films," signed Frederick Gordon Guggisberg, 19 April 1927.

13. Ibid., "Ceylon: from Herbert Layard Dowbiggin, Inspector-General of Police, to Leopold Charles Stennett Amery, Secretary of State for the Colonies," 30 March 1927. These concerns echo the British intelligentsia's commentaries on the morally harmful effects of popular literature on working-class readers; see Q. D. Leavis, *Fiction and the Reading Public* (Middlesex, UK: Penguin Books, 1932). Transposed into colonies, however, these moral anxieties were racialized en

route, imbued with missionary and imperialist concerns about the need to civilize Africans through literature.

14. PRO, CO 323/977/1, Films: Replies to Confidential Circular Despatch of 8 January 1927, "Confidential Circular Despatch, L. S. Amery," 8 January 1927.

15. PRO, CO 537/4878, Control of Undesirable Publications (Eastern Sarawak), 1949, Secret, "Minute signed K. G. Ashton," 16 May 1949.

16. *Sierra Leone Weekly News*, 8 July 1939, 6 (italics in the original).

17. Interestingly, although the editor of the *Sierra Leone Weekly News* did not question the sentences meted out to the young gunners (all of whom were born after 1918), civil servants at the Colonial Office expressed "horror" at the severity of the sentences, which ranged from forty-eight days to fifteen years, all accompanied by dishonorable discharge; see PRO, CO 267/671/6, Activities of West Africa Youth League, Sierra Leone Heavy Battery—Mutiny of African Gunners, May and June 1939, "Minute signed 'H. B.' [H. Bushe]," 1 July 1939.

18. PRO, CO 537/6523, Security Arrangements, West Africa: Undesirable Publications—"Africa" by George Padmore (closed until 1981), "Letter from Fenner Brockway MP to the Rt Hon James Griffiths, Sec of State for the Colonies," 29 November 1950.

19. Ibid., "Letter from Private Secretary N. D. Watson to P. L. Taylor," 8 May 1950. In addition to *Africa*, Padmore's other publications were also banned in many African colonies. For biographical material on Padmore, see George A. Padmore, *The Memoirs of a Liberian Ambassador* (Lewiston, NY: Edwin Mellen, 1966); Rupert Lewis and Baptiste Fitzroy, eds., *George Padmore: A Pan-African Revolutionary* (Kingston, Jamaica: Ian Randle, 2008).

20. PRO, CO 691/140/11, Control of Newspapers and Printing Presses, 1934, Tanganyika, "Draft letter from Secretary of State for the Colonies to the Governor of Tanganyika," 9 January 1935.

21. PRO, CO 323/685/37, Prevention of Circulation of Undesirable Publications in British Dominions, War Office, 1915, "Letter from B. B. Cutrill to the Under Secretary of State for the Colonies," 18 July 1915; PRO, CO 537/4878, Control of Undesirable Publications (Eastern Sarawak), 1949, Secret; PRO, CO 691/140/11, Control of Newspapers and Printing Presses, 1934, Tanganyika, "Minute from [signature unclear]," 3 October 1934.

22. PRO, CO 323/1749/1, Censorship—Press: Representations by Mr Noel Baker. Secret. General Defence, 1940 (closed until 1971), "Letter to Eric Cook from Private Secretary to Malcolm MacDonald, Secretary of State for the Colonies," 15 February 1940.

23. Ibid.

24. Ibid.

25. PRO, CO 96/714/6, Bills for Newspapers, Books and Printing Presses Ordinance, Criminal Code (Amendment) Ordinance, Control of Imported Books, "Memo signed Arthur Grey Hazlerigg," 26 February 1934.

26. PRO, CO 323/1073/6, Films: Institution of a Central Censorship in London of Films in Tropical Africa, 1930, "Minute signed 'G. G.' [Gordon Guggisberg]," 12 November 1930.

27. PRO, CO 96/714/6, Bills for Newspapers, Books and Printing Presses Ordinance, Criminal Code (Amendment) Ordinance, Control of Imported Books, "Memo signed Alex Fiddian," date unclear: c. 1 March 1934. Fiddian was a longstanding member of the Colonial Office. Dmitri van den Bersselaar, in "Debating Igbo Culture—The Colonial Tradition" (pcwww.liv.ac.uk/~dvdb/CH_6.pdf, 188), suggests that Fiddian joined the Colonial Office in 1912, but David Sunderland provides evidence that Fiddian joined as a clerk as early as 1905; see Sunderland, "The Departmental System of Railway Construction in British West Africa, 1895–1906," *Journal of Transport History* 23, no. 2 (2002): 97.

28. PRO, CO 537/4878, Control of Undesirable Publications (Eastern Sarawak), 1949, Secret, "Secret: Note by Colonial Office, June 1949."

29. See *Lagos Weekly Record*, 14 February 1903, 6.

30. Omu gives the sum as £500, but newspapers in the archive publish the figure as £600; see Fred I. Omu, *Press and Politics in Nigeria, 1880–1960* (Atlantic Highlands, NJ: Humanities Press, 1978), 174–82.

31. Ibid.

32. *Lagos Weekly Record*, 14 February 1903, 6.

33. Ibid. Prior to the mid-1920s, African members of the various legislative councils in British West Africa were nonelected and in a minority. Known as "unofficial" members, they were nominated by the executive committee and had to be approved by the governor prior to taking position.

34. *Lagos Weekly Record*, 14 February 1903, 6.

35. Omu, *Press and Politics in Nigeria*, 181; PRO, CO 87/258/13, Gambia: Registration, Printing and Publication of Newspaper Legislation, Feb–Aug, 1944 (closed until 1972), "Note on Registration of Newspapers Ordinance and on False Publication Ordinance," 21 March 1944.

36. Stephen Weir, *History's Worst Decisions: And the People Who Made Them* (New York: Eye Quarto, 2005), 141–42.

37. See PRO, CO 96/714/6, Bills for Newspapers, Books and Printing Presses Ordinance, Criminal Code (Amendment) Ordinance, Control of Imported Books, "Memo signed H. Duncan," 2 March 1934.

38. Ibid., "Memo signed Alex Fiddian," 1 March 1934.

39. PRO, CO 96/749/5, Wallace-Johnson, Privy Council Appeal: *I. T. A. Wallace-Johnson v. The King* (closed until 1989), "Law Officers' Dept, Accra, Gold Coast: Report entitled Wallace-Johnson versus the King: Observations of the Attorney-General of the Gold Coast upon the Appellant's Case," by H. W. B. Blackall, 13 November 1938.

40. Ibid.

41. PRO, CO 537/6523, Security Arrangements, West Africa: Undesirable Publications—"Africa" by George Padmore (closed until 1981), "Letter to P. L. Taylor from N. D. Watson," 8 May 1950.

42. Wallace-Johnson had been secretary of the African Workers' Union of West Africa in Nigeria in 1933, but he left for the Gold Coast in the wake of a police raid. See PRO, CO 583/195/4, African Workers' Union of Nigeria: Alleged Action against, 1933–34, "Report by Alex Fiddian," 5 December 1933. For biographical

material and political histories of Wallace-Johnson, see LaRay Denzer, "Wallace-Johnson and the Sierra Leone Labor Crisis of 1939," *African Studies Review* 25, no. 2–3 (1982): 159–83; Leo Spitzer and LaRay Denzer, "I. T. A. Wallace-Johnson and the West African Youth League, Part 1," *International Journal of African Historical Studies* 6, no. 3 (1973): 413–52.

43. See Shaloff, "Press Controls and Sedition Proceedings," 243.

44. PRO, CO 875/13/5, Press Censorship: Nigeria, 1942, "Secret report: Benjamin Nnamdi Azikiwe alias 'ZIK,'" Anon., 16 November 1941. See also Nnamdi Azikiwe, *My Odyssey: An Autobiography* (London: C. Hurst, 1970), in which Ocansey is described as "my great benefactor" (190).

45. Shaloff, "Press Controls and Sedition Proceedings," 243. For Azikiwe's own account of his arrival in colonial Ghana, see *My Odyssey*, 251–83.

46. RHL, MSS. Brit. Emp. s.282, Reverend C. Kingsley Williams Papers, 1927–1934.

47. Shaloff, "Press Controls and Sedition Proceedings," 242–43. Azikiwe's and Wallace-Johnson's ideological agreements and disagreements are described in Azikiwe's *My Odyssey*, 218–19.

48. RHL, MSS. Brit. Emp. s.282, Reverend C. Kingsley Williams Papers, 1927–1934.

49. Shaloff, "Press Controls and Sedition Proceedings," 242.

50. Ibid.

51. Ibid., 243.

52. K. A. B. Jones-Quartey, *A Summary History of the Ghana Press, 1822–1960* (Accra-Tema: Ghana Publishing, 1974).

53. Cited in Shaloff, "Press Controls and Sedition Proceedings," 241–42.

54. Ibid.

55. Ibid.

56. See Stanley Shaloff, "The Income Tax, Indirect Rule, and the Depression: The Gold Coast Riots of 1931," *Cahiers d'études africaines* 14, no. 54 (1974): 359–75.

57. PRO, CO 96/716/15, Control of the Press of the Gold Coast: Newspapers, Books and Printing Presses Ordinance, 1934 (closed until 1985), "Extract from a Note of a Meeting at the Colonial Office," 14 June 1934. The derogatory view of Governor Thomas in West Africa is shared elsewhere: an entry in Stephen Weir's amusing book *History's Worst Decisions* holds Shenton Thomas responsible for the fall of that "jewel of the British Empire," Singapore, between December 1941 and February 1942, when he failed to defend the colony from invasion by a weak Japanese force (141). As with the colonial Ghanaians before him, Weir characterizes Thomas as suffering from "pride and sloth, contempt for an as yet misunderstood enemy, and total lack of foresight" (141).

58. PRO, CO 96/714/6, Bills for Newspapers, Books and Printing Presses Ordinance, Criminal Code (Amendment) Ordinance, Control of Imported Books, "Draft Bill: Newspapers, Books and Printing Presses Ordinance, 1934," 20 January 1934; PRO, CO 96/716/15, Control of the Press of the Gold Coast: Newspapers, Books and Printing Presses Ordinance, 1934 (closed until 1985).

59. PRO, CO 96/714/6, Bills for Newspapers, Books and Printing Presses Ordinance, Criminal Code (Amendment) Ordinance, Control of Imported Books, "Memo signed Arthur Grey Hazelrigg," 26 February 1934.

60. PRO, CO 96/716/15, Control of the Press of the Gold Coast: Newspapers, Books and Printing Presses Ordinance, 1934 (closed until 1985), "Memorandum by the Inspector General of Police [Henry W. M. Bamford] Regarding the Draft Bill (44A) cited as the Newspapers, Books and Printing Presses Ordinance, 1934," n.d.

61. Ibid., "Memo signed Alex Fiddian," c. 1 March 1934.

62. PRO, CO 96/714/6, Bills for Newspapers, Books and Printing Presses Ordinance, Criminal Code (Amendment) Ordinance, Control of Imported Books, "Memo signed H. Duncan," 2 March 1934. The Roneo was a low-cost rotary duplicating machine that pressed ink through a stencil; Ormig duplicators, according to the Ormig Corporation's US federal trademark registration filed in 1935, were "hectographic spirit duplicating machines, which print directly from mirrorscript originals."

63. Ibid., "Memo signed Alex Fiddian," 29 March 1934.

64. Ibid., "Memo signed Kenneth Roberts Wray," 3 March 1934. See also Kenneth Roberts-Wray, *Commonwealth and Colonial Law* (London: Sage Publications, 1967).

65. RHL, MSS. Afr. s.1527, Colonial Office Correspondence and Cuttings, 1934–1939, 27 June 1934.

66. For a discussion of women's use of pseudonyms, see chapters 6 and 8.

67. *Times of West Africa*, 9 March 1934, 2.

68. PRO, CO 96/714/6, Bills for Newspapers, Books and Printing Presses Ordinance, Criminal Code (Amendment) Ordinance, Control of Imported Books, "Memo signed Kenneth Roberts Wray," 3 March 1934.

69. *Gold Coast Government Extraordinary Gazette*, "Criminal Code (Amendment) Ordinance," 21 February 1934.

70. PRO, CO 96/714/6, Bills for Newspapers, Books and Printing Presses Ordinance, Criminal Code (Amendment) Ordinance, Control of Imported Books, "Telegram from the Governor of the Gold Coast to the Secretary of State for the Colonies," 26 March 1934.

71. Shaloff, "Press Controls and Sedition Proceedings," 246. Shaloff provides extensive details about the background to the Sedition Bill, the personalities involved, and the Legislative Council debates. For details of the political confrontations between supporters of the Ratepayers' Association and supporters of the Mambii Party, see Azikiwe, *My Odyssey*, 257–59.

72. For the causes of this division and the membership of each delegation, see Shaloff, "Press Controls and Sedition Proceedings," 246.

73. Members of Parliament in Britain, especially anticolonial MPs such as James Maxton of the Independent Labour Party, frequently wrote letters to the secretary of state for the colonies and tabled questions in Parliament on behalf of colonial territories facing repressive newspaper ordinances.

74. PRO, CO 96/714/6, Bills for Newspapers, Books and Printing Presses Ordinance, Criminal Code (Amendment) Ordinance, Control of Imported Books, "Memo signed Alex Fiddian," 29 March 1934.

75. PRO, CO 96/716/15, Control of the Press of the Gold Coast: Newspapers, Books and Printing Presses Ordinance, 1934 (closed until 1985), "Memo signed I. H. Wallace," 17 May 1934. To the relief of Hodson and Colonial Office staff, the draft Newspaper Bill had not received any local publicity, as Shenton Thomas had chosen not to publish its details in the *Extraordinary Gazette*, alongside his other repressive measure.

76. See PRO, CO 96/714/6, Bills for Newspapers, Books and Printing Presses Ordinance, Criminal Code (Amendment) Ordinance, Control of Imported Books, "Memo signed Alex Fiddian," 29 March 1934.

77. Shaloff, "Press Controls and Sedition Proceedings," 262.

78. PRO, CO 96/716/15, Control of the Press of the Gold Coast: Newspapers, Books and Printing Presses Ordinance, 1934 (closed until 1985), "Memo signed Gerald Creasy," 28 December 1934.

79. Ibid., "Letter from Arnold Hodson, Government House, Accra, to Rt Hon Sir Philip Cunliffe-Lister, Secretary of State for the Colonies," 29 November 1934.

80. Ibid.

81. Azikiwe, *My Odyssey*, 261. Azikiwe was so concerned about the article that he "asked that the typescript, the galley and the chase-proofs should be sent to me. I kept possession of these for they were material evidence to prove who wrote, who edited, and who inserted this article into the newspaper" (261, 268).

82. *African Morning Post*, 15 May 1936, cited in Spitzer and Denzer, "I. T. A. Wallace-Johnson and the West African Youth League," 441–42.

83. Cited in Shaloff, "Press Controls and Sedition Proceedings," 257, 260.

84. By his own account, Azikiwe also vetoed the article, but he was persuaded to publish it by Ocansey, the managing director of the *African Morning Post*; see Azikiwe, *My Odyssey*, 261.

85. Ibid., 257.

86. Frans Dove was a prominent Sierra Leonean lawyer and long-standing member of the Gold Coast Bar, with an extensive family in Sierra Leone and Accra. He has been described as "one of West Africa's most brilliant and best known lawyers for over half a century [who] . . . became a fabulously rich man . . . [and] single-handed educated his next three brothers in law and medicine, then his sons and first two nephews for the Bar"; see K. A. B. Jones-Quartey, cited by Ian Duffield, "John Eldred Taylor and West African Opposition to Indirect Rule in Nigeria," *African Affairs* 70, no. 280 (1971): 252–68. He was the father of Mabel Dove, whose pseudonymous work for the *Times of West Africa* is discussed in chapter 8.

87. Shaloff, "Press Controls and Sedition Proceedings," 258.

88. Ibid.

89. Azikiwe, *My Odyssey*, 272.

90. *Gold Coast Spectator*, 10 February 1934, 205.

91. PRO, CO 96/759/1, Wallace-Johnson—Privy Council Appeal: *I. T. A. Wallace-Johnson v the King* (closed until 1990), "Privy Council Appeal No. 89 of 1938: Isaac Theophilus Akkunna Wallace-Johnson (Appellant) v. The King

(Respondent) from the West African Court of Appeal. Judgment of the Lords of the Judicial Committee of the Privy Council," 11 December 1939.

92. Ibid.

93. PRO, CO 96/749/5, Wallace-Johnson, Privy Council Appeal: *I. T. A. Wallace-Johnson v. The King* (closed until 1989), "Law Officers' Dept, Accra, Gold Coast: Report entitled Wallace-Johnson versus the King: Observations of the Attorney-General of the Gold Coast upon the Appellant's Case, by H. W. B. Blackall," 13 November 1938.

94. Ibid., "Extract from the *Times* (London)," 27 May 1938.

95. PRO, CO 267/671/8, Leakage of Official Information, "Excerpt from court transcript," 10 October 1938, 5.

96. Ibid., "Letter from Acting Governor of Sierra Leone to Rt Hon Malcolm MacDonald, Secretary of State for the Colonies," 14 January 1939.

97. Ibid., "Cutting from 'Sideviews: What about the Report?'—editorial by Wallace-Johnson published in the *African Standard*," 17 March 1939, n.p.

98. PRO, CO 96/749/5, Wallace-Johnson, Privy Council Appeal: *I. T. A. Wallace-Johnson v. The King* (closed until 1989), "Law Officers' Department, Accra, Gold Coast: Report entitled 'Wallace-Johnson versus the King: Observations of the Attorney-General of the Gold Coast upon the Appellant's Case,'" by H. W. B. Blackall, 13 November 1938.

99. Details of Wallace-Johnson's final arrest and imprisonment can be found in Spitzer and Denzer, "I. T. A. Wallace-Johnson and the West African Youth League, Part 2: The Sierra Leone Period, 1938–1945," *International Journal of African Historical Studies* 6, no. 4 (1973): 580–82.

100. PRO, CO 267/671/8, Leakage of Official Information, "Excerpt from court transcript," 10 October 1938, 1.

101. Ibid., 2, 4.

102. Ibid., 1–7.

103. PRO, CO 583/195/4, African Workers' Union of Nigeria: Alleged Action against, 1933–34, "Report by Alex Fiddian," 5 December 1933.

104. Ibid.

105. PRO, CO 267/671/8, Leakage of Official Information, "Excerpt from court transcript," 10 October 1938, 1–2.

106. Ibid., 2.

107. Ibid.

108. Ibid., 4.

109. Spitzer and Denzer note that "eighteen of the twenty-one lawyers in the colony [were] active in the Youth League" at this time, much to the consternation of colonial officials; see Spitzer and Denzer, "I. T. A. Wallace-Johnson and the West African Youth League, Part 2," 587.

110. At other times, Wallace-Johnson attempted to subvert the system by deliberately confounding fact with artistic creativity. A long poem entitled "The Two Friends: Being a True Story in Rhymes" is written under the pseudonym "Professor W. Daniels," but copies for the government depository are signed "Wallace-Johnson, Managing Director" according to legal requirements for the

self-identification of managers and editors of newspapers and printing presses. Perhaps with this enforced unmasking in mind, W. Daniels adds, in a three-line note at the end of this pamphlet, "These verses, as we have stated, is 'A True Story in Rhymes' but refers to no one living or dead in Sierra Leone or anywhere"; see Daniels, *Two Friends: Being a True Story in Rhymes* (Freetown: SALNEB, 1965), 7.

111. PRO, CO 267/671/8, Leakage of Official Information, "Enclosure no.1 in Sierra Leone Despatch no. 27 dated 14th January 1939: Report on the case of Rex versus I. T. A. Wallace-Johnson, by the Acting Attorney General of Sierra Leone, Charles Abbott."

112. Ann McClintock, *Imperial Leather: Race, Gender and Sexuality in the Colonial Contest* (London: Routledge, 1995); Jean Allman and Victoria Tashjian, *I Will Not Eat Stone: A Women's History of Colonial Asante* (Portsmouth, NH: Heinemann, 2000).

113. The same might be said of Wallace-Johnson's English prose style, which displays a parodic approach toward English and Englishness.

114. PRO, CO 267/671/8, Leakage of Official Information, "Excerpt from court transcript," 10 October 1938, 6.

115. John 18:33. The similarity of Wallace-Johnson's courtroom strategy to that of Jesus in this episode may be more than arbitrary: many years later, in one of his single-sheet publications under the pseudonym of Professor W. Daniels, Wallace-Johnson offered a commentary on Pilate's judicial authority. "After PILATE had adjudged Christ NOT GUILTY of the charges of TREASON AND SEDITION preferred against him, he (Pilate) took water and washed his hands to indicate that his Hands were clean. But the question still presents itself forward: Was Pilate's hands actually made clean by the act of washing them? Certainly not! The fact is, Pilate's hands were the most filthy Bible history has ever had to record because it was with the same hands that he handed Christ over to be crucified. . . . Today it seems to us that the Government of Sierra Leone is consciously or unconsciously going the PILATE'S WAY"; see J/X.0705/1 (8), "Mr Treason Comes to Town," *SALNEB Publications No. 8*, 8 May 1963, n.p. (capping in the original).

116. John 18:34.

117. John 18:36–38. I am indebted to Norman Vance for alerting me to this connection with Wallace-Johnson's court appearance.

118. African legal history scholars with useful perspectives on these issues include Martin Chanock, *The Making of South African Legal Culture,1902–1936: Fear, Favour and Prejudice* (Cambridge: Cambridge University Press, 2001); Benjamin N. Lawrance, Emily Lynn Osborn, and Richard L. Roberts, eds., *Intermediaries, Interpreters, and Clerks: African Employees in the Making of Colonial Africa* (Madison: University of Wisconsin Press, 2006).

119. PRO, CO 267/671/8, Leakage of Official Information, "Excerpt from court transcript," 10 October 1938, 1.

120. Ibid., "Rex vs. I. T. A. Wallace-Johnson: Decision by E. S. Beoku-Betts," 3 November 1938.

121. Ibid.

122. Ibid., "Cutting from editorial by Wallace-Johnson entitled 'Sideviews: What about the Report?' in the *African Standard*," 17 March 1939, n.p.

123. Ibid. See also PRO, CO 267/671/5, Sierra Leone 1939, "Activities of West Africa Youth League."

124. CO 267/671/6, Activities of West Africa Youth League, Sierra Leone: Heavy Battery—Mutiny of African Gunners, May and June 1939, "Letter from Governor Douglas Jardine to Malcolm MacDonald, Secretary of State for the Colonies," 8 May 1939. Details of Wallace-Johnson's final arrest and imprisonment can be found in Spitzer and Denzer, "I. T. A. Wallace-Johnson and the West African Youth League, Part 2," 565–601.

125. *African Standard*, 5 May 1939, 2.

126. PRO, CO 875/13/5, Press Censorship: Nigeria, 1942, "Secret report entitled Benjamin Nnamdi Azikiwe alias 'Zik,'" by S. A. S. P. [Superintendent of Police], 16 November 1941.

127. *African Standard*, 6 January 1939, 2.

128. Ibid.

129. Cited in Shaloff, "Press Controls and Sedition Proceedings," 245.

130. Nanka-Bruce's and Wallace-Johnson's loathing for one another was sealed for perpetuity when the Youth League campaigned successfully for A. W. Kojo Thompson to become municipal member for Accra, displacing Nanka-Bruce, the British government's preferred candidate, from the Legislative Council. To make matters worse, when a second election was called at Nanka-Bruce's insistence in April 1936, Kojo Thompson won again, this time with an improved result. See Wallace-Johnson, "The West African Youth League: Its Origins, Aims and Objects," *Negro Worker* 7, no. 5 (1937): 13.

131. *Sierra Leone Weekly News*, 8 July 1939, 5 (capping in the original).

132. Ibid.

133. PRO, CO 875/13/5, Press Censorship: Nigeria, 1942, "Secret report entitled Benjamin Nnamdi Azikiwe alias 'Zik,'" by S. A. S. P. [Superintendent of Police], 16 November 1941. Readership figures are always considerably larger than sales figures in African countries because each copy of a newspaper passes through the hands of many readers.

134. Ibid.

135. Ibid., "Secret letter from Governor Bernard Bourdillon to the Rt Hon Lord Moyne, Secretary of State for the Colonies," 20 November 1941.

136. Ibid., "Secret report entitled Benjamin Nnamdi Azikiwe alias 'Zik,'" by S. A. S. P. [Superintendent of Police], 16 November 1941.

137. Ibid., "Secret letter from Governor Bernard Bourdillon to the Rt Hon Lord Moyne, Secretary of State for the Colonies," 20 November 1941.

138. Ibid., "Secret report entitled Benjamin Nnamdi Azikiwe alias 'Zik,'" by S. A. S. P. [Superintendent of Police], 16 November 1941.

139. The topic of West African celebrity merits considerable further research.

140. See PRO, CO 875/13/5, Press Censorship: Nigeria, 1942, "Secret report entitled Benjamin Nnamdi Azikiwe alias 'Zik,'" by S. A. S. P. [Superintendent of

Police], 16 November 1941; PRO, CO 583/317/4, Activities of Dr Nnamdi Azikiwe, 1951 (closed until 1982), 12 January 1951.

141. Making use of newspaper articles and speeches from previous years, Azikiwe presented his political philosophy in his book *Renascent Africa* (Accra: Published by the author, 1937), providing an unambiguous statement of his anticolonial position.

142. Louis Althusser, "Ideology and Ideological State Apparatuses," in his *Lenin and Philosophy and Other Essays* (London: Verso, 1971), 162–63.

CHAPTER 4 TRICKSTER TACTICS AND THE QUESTION OF AUTHORSHIP IN NEWSPAPER FOLKTALES

1. Tokunbo A. Ayoola, "Popular Resistance Literature and the Nigerian Railway Corporation, 1955–60," in *Africans and the Politics of Popular Culture*, ed. Toyin Falola and Augustine Agwuele (Rochester, NY: University of Rochester Press, 2009), 303.

2. Ibid., 302–4.

3. Ibid., 303.

4. Ibid., 312–15.

5. Leroy Vail and Landeg White, *Power and the Praise Poem: Southern African Voices in History* (Oxford: James Currey, 1992); Osumaka Likaka, *Naming Colonialism: History and Collective Memory in the Congo, 1870–1960* (Madison: University of Wisconsin Press, 2009); Achille Mbembe, *On the Postcolony* (Berkeley: University of California Press, 2001); Graham Furniss, *Orality: The Power of the Spoken Word* (Basingstoke, UK: Palgrave Macmillan, 2004).

6. E.g., Ken Saro-Wiwa, *The Singing Anthill: Ogoni Folk Tales* (London: Saros International Publishers, 1990); Veronique Tadjo, *Chasing the Sun: Stories from Africa* (London: A and C Black, 2008); Obi Onyefulu, *Chinye: A West African Folk Tale* (London: Puffin Books, 1996).

7. Efua Sutherland, *Marriage of Anansewa: A Storytelling Drama* (1975; Harlow, UK: Longman African Classics, 1987).

8. See Evan Maina Mwangi's *Africa Writes Back to Self* (Albany, NY: SUNY Press, 2009), 107–35, for a discussion of similar processes in East African postcolonial fiction.

9. Bob W. White, "Modernity's Trickster: 'Dipping' and 'Throwing' in Congolese Popular Dance Music," *Research in African Literatures* 30, no. 4 (1999): 157.

10. Alphonse Kwawisi Tekpetey, "Kweku Ananse: A Psychoanalytical Approach," *Research in African Literatures* 37, no. 2 (2006): 74, 79.

11. See Thomas J. Lynn, "Tricksters Don't Walk the Dogma: Nkem Nwankwo's Danda," *College Literature* 32, no. 3 (2005): 1–20.

12. Edward Sackey, "Oral Tradition and the African Novel," *MFS: Modern Fiction Studies* 37, no. 3 (1991): 389.

13. F. Abiola Irele, *The African Imagination: Literature in Africa and the Black Diaspora* (New York: Oxford University Press, 2001), 58, 70.

14. Pietro Deandrea, *Fertile Crossings: Metamorphoses of Genre in Anglophone West African Literature* (Amsterdam: Rodopi, 2002); Ato Quayson, *Strategic Transformations in Nigerian Writing* (Bloomington: Indiana University Press, 2008);

Brenda Cooper, *Magical Realism in West African Fiction: Seeing with a Third Eye* (London: Routledge, 2004).

15. See, e.g., *Gold Coast Echo*, 25 September 1888, 3.

16. Likaka, *Naming Colonialism*, 5.

17. Kwesi Yankah, "African Folk and the Challenges of a Global Lore," *Africa Today* 46, no. 2 (1999): 16.

18. Since the advent of audio and visual mass communications media in West Africa, this unmediated visible relationship between performer and audience has undergone significant transformations. So-called traditional performers have often been recruited by national organizations and the media to record radio programs and television dramas. See Arinpe Adejumo, "Family Health Awareness in Popular Yoruba Arts," in *Africans and the Politics of Popular Culture*, ed. Toyin Falola and Augustine Agwuele (Rochester, NY: University of Rochester Press, 2009), 261–74; Graham Furniss and Richard Fardon, eds., *African Broadcast Cultures: Radio in Transition* (Oxford: James Currey, 2000). Audiences might recognize the oral genres deployed by these performers and might participate in performers' calls for moral commentary and response, but the medium introduces a new impersonal relationship into their contact.

19. Yankah, "African Folk and the Challenges of a Global Lore," 22.

20. Ibid.

21. Michel de Certeau, *The Practice of Everyday Life* (1984; Berkeley: University of California Press, 2002).

22. De Certeau's later work on history addresses some of these problems. See Ben Highmore, *Everyday Life and Cultural Theory: An Introduction* (London: Routledge, 2001), 145–52; Jeremy Ahearne, *Michel de Certeau: Interpretation and Its Other* (Cambridge: Polity Press, 1995), 157–62; Ian Buchanan, *Michel de Certeau: Cultural Theorist* (London: Sage, 2000).

23. De Certeau also writes about art in relation to an "aesthetics of 'tricks'"; see his *Practice of Everyday Life*, 26.

24. In Fante, *Abakuma* refers to a person who is pampered; *Sikafu* is connected with gold or money. Used to describe a person, the term *Abakuma Sikafu* means a wealthy person, but it also connotes a spoiled "brat" who is wealthy. I am grateful to Victoria Moffatt and her family for providing this translation.

25. *Gold Coast Nation*, 7–14 January 1915, 798. Ntikuma, or Ntsikuma, is the most intelligent of Ananse's sons. See Naana Jane Opoku-Agyemang, "Gender-Role Perceptions in the Akan Folktale," *Research in African Literatures* 30, no. 1 (1999): 116–39.

26. *Gold Coast Nation*, 7–14 January 1915, 799.

27. The proprietor, manager, and editor of the *Leader*, Joseph Peter Herbert Brown (1863–1919), was a key member of the Gold Coast ARPS. Casely-Hayford took over as editor of the *Leader* after Brown's death in 1919 and used it to launch the NCBWA.

28. There is a great deal more to discover about this prolific writer.

29. Many of Atu Penyin's folktales do not differ substantially from the anonymous material, however: at times, he reiterates a familiar folktale, and at other

times, he narrates a new story and produces a generalized moral from it. When he writes folktales about individual morality, Atu Penyin often makes cynical statements about the cruelty of human nature rather than issuing warnings to individuals about the type of behavior that should inspire caution. In this, he has a recognizable "voice" as a folktale author. So in one story from 1912, set "once upon a time" and featuring "a certain man," the author describes how a wealthy and kind-hearted philanthropist travels to another town and is killed, "without any provocation," in spite of his enormous charity to the citizens. "The moral of the story," Atu Penyin writes at the end, "is that in spite of his kindness, activity, and goodness a foreigner will never get on in any town or society in which he has no people of his own to back him"; see *Gold Coast Nation*, 25 April 1912, 28.

30. Ibid., 6 June 1912, 64.
31. Ibid.
32. Ibid., 27 June 1912, 81.
33. Ibid.
34. Eric Hobsbawm and Terence Ranger, *The Invention of Tradition* (Cambridge: Cambridge University Press, 1992).
35. Sackey, "Oral Tradition and the African Novel," 400.
36. *Gold Coast Nation*, 18 June 1914, 625.
37. Ibid., 4 July 1912, 87.
38. Ibid.
39. Ibid., 9 August 1930, 4. Roger Gocking notes that "Kobina Kwaansa" is "a nom de plume, and more than likely an Akan"; see Gocking, "Competing Systems of Inheritance before the British Courts of the Gold Coast Colony," *International Journal of African Historical Studies* 23, no. 4 (1990): 601.
40. *Gold Coast Echo*, 16–31 January 1888, 6–7.
41. Ibid., 7.
42. Ibid.
43. Lennard J. Davis, *Factual Fictions: The Origins of the English Novel* (1983; Philadelphia: University of Pennsylvania Press, 1997), 23.
44. Ibid., 42–70.
45. Ibid.
46. Ibid.
47. *Times of West Africa*, 16 March 1933, 2; see chapter 6.
48. Ibid. (italics in the original).
49. See Joyce Penfield, *Communicating with Quotes: The Igbo Case* (Santa Barbara, CA: Greenwood Press, 1983); Kwesi Yankah, "Proverb Speaking as a Creative Process: The Akan of Ghana," *De Proverbio* 6, no. 2 (2000): 1, available at http://www.deproverbio.com/display.php?a=3&r=119 (accessed 16 September 2011).
50. Derek R. Peterson, *Ethnic Patriotism and the East African Revival: A History of Dissent, c. 1935–1972* (Cambridge: Cambridge University Press, 2012), 23.
51. Ibid.
52. Ibid., 23–24.
53. *Gold Coast Methodist Times*, 30 September 1897, 3.

54. *Gold Coast Nation*, 22 August 1912, 122.
55. *Gold Coast Aborigines*, 25 January 1902, 3.
56. *Gold Coast Nation*, 22 August 1912, 122.
57. Ibid. The *Nation* did not publishing any winning entries, perhaps because the standard was too low or, more likely, because the one shilling entry fee was too high to attract entrants.
58. Peterson, *Ethnic Patriotism*, 24.
59. Ibid. p. 24
60. Robert Sutherland Rattray, "Some Aspects of West African Folk-Lore," *African Affairs: Journal of the African Historical Society* 28, no. 103 (1928): 2.
61. Robert Sutherland Rattray, *Akan-Ashanti Folktales* (Oxford: Clarendon Press, 1930).
62. Edward Wilmot Blyden, *African Life and Customs: Reprinted from the "Sierra Leone Weekly News"* (London: C. M. Phillips, 1908); John Mensah Sarbah, *Fanti Customary Laws* (London: William Clowes and Sons, 1897); see Joseph Ephraim Casely-Hayford, *Gold Coast Native Institutions: With Thoughts upon a Healthy Imperial Policy for the Gold Coast and Ashanti* (London: Sweet and Maxwell, 1903); see also Great Britain, Colonial Office, *Bibliography of Published Sources Relating to African Land Tenure* (London: His Majesty's Stationery Office, 1950).
63. *Western Echo*, 30 January 1886, 7.
64. Ibid.
65. Ibid.
66. Ibid.
67. Ibid., 30 December 1885, 7.
68. "A Melusine Story from the Gold Coast," *Journal of the Royal African Society* 5, no. 17 (1905): 104–7. Boneta (or Boneto) is the fish known in Fante as *Safur Nannam*. The copy of this story reprinted in the *Journal of the Royal African Society* is taken from a reprinted version in the *Gold Coast Leader*, 11 March 1905, supplement 2.
69. *Western Echo*, 24 April 1886, 7.
70. Ibid.
71. Ibid.
72. Ibid.
73. Ibid., 30 June 1886, 3.
74. Ngugi wa Thiong'o, *Devil on the Cross* (1980; London: Heinemann, 1987).
75. Amos Tutuola, *The Palm-Wine Drinkard* (London: Faber and Faber, 1952); Ben Okri, *The Famished Road* (London: Vintage, 1991).
76. Sutherland, *Marriage of Anansewa*, vi.

CHAPTER 5 PRINTING WOMEN

1. Mrs. Henry de la Pasture (1866–1945) was born Elizabeth Lydia Rosabelle Bonham and gained fame as a prolific and popular novelist during her marriage to Count Henry de la Pasture, who died in 1908. She married Sir Hugh Clifford in 1910, and her interest in literature and literacy continued unabated during their time in West Africa.

2. *Gold Coast Leader*, 29 June 1918, 8.

3. Ibid.

4. Over one hundred entries from Africans and Europeans were received in the first competition. Competitors included prominent Africans such as Nana Ofori Atta, the Omanhene of Eastern Akim; Timothy Laing, veteran newspaperman and editor of the *Eastern Star and Akwapim Chronicle*; and Ofori Kuma, the Omanhene of Akwapem. In addition, European district commissioners and other officials participated, as did European miners and African students and soldiers. A selection of these submissions, together with thirty-five essays by girls, forty-nine essays by boys, and twenty essays by boy scouts, were published in Lady Clifford's book *Our Days on the Gold Coast, in Ashanti, in the Northern Territories, and in the British Sphere of Occupation in Togoland* (Accra: Government Printing Office, 1918).

5. The prizes were also gendered: a gold brooch and certificate signed by the governor for the girls; a cricket bat and ball signed by the governor and a certificate for the boys; see Clifford, *Our Days on the Gold Coast*, 198.

6. See Sanjay Seth, *Subject Lessons: The Western Education of Colonial India* (Durham, NC: Duke University Press, 2007), 129–58; Jean M. Allman and Victoria B. Tashjian, *"I Will Not Eat Stone": A Women's History of Colonial Asante* (Oxford: James Currey, 2000).

7. Lady Clifford was keen not to create a superiority complex among educated African children, however, and in her commentary on the competition she tried to emphasize the value of "native customs" and the "wisdom of experience" possessed by parents without European schooling; see Clifford, *Our Days on the Gold Coast*, 217.

8. Ibid., 219–20.

9. The other girls' essays published in *Our Days on the Gold Coast* reiterate the sentiments of the first; see ibid., 221–41. By contrast, a large number of postcolonial popular novels by West African men problematize the theme of girls' education: the figure of the educated "modern" woman—urban, sexually liberated, a chic consumer of Western products, and often a rejecter of marriage—is represented in these novels as promiscuous and immoral, contrasted with the well-behaved nonliterate wife who has benefited from customary forms of education; see Stephanie Newell, "Representations of Women in Popular Fiction by Nigerian Men," *Journal of African Languages and Cultures* 9, no. 2 (1996): 169–88.

10. *Gold Coast Leader*, 16 May 1914, 6.

11. See Allman and Tashjian, *"I Will Not Eat Stone"*; Charlotte Hastings, "Metropole-Colony in Education Policy for Girls' Education in Colonial Africa, with Particular Reference to Southern Nigeria c. 1925–40" (PhD diss., University of Edinburgh, 2011).

12. Ann Laura Stoler, *Carnal Knowledge and Imperial Power: Race and the Intimate in Colonial Rule* (Berkeley: University of California Press, 2002); Antoinette Burton, ed., *Gender, Sexuality, and Colonial Modernities* (New York: Routledge, 1999); Angela Woollacott, *Gender and Empire* (Basingstoke, UK: Palgrave Macmillan, 2006).

13. Derek R. Peterson, *Ethnic Patriotism and the East African Revival: A History of Dissent, c. 1935–1972* (Cambridge: Cambridge University Press, 2012); Gayatri Spivak, "Can the Subaltern Speak?" in *Marxism and the Interpretation of Culture*, ed. Cary Nelson and Lawrence Grossberg (Champaign: University of Illinois Press, 1988), 271–313; Seth, *Subject Lessons*, 129–58.

14. Antoinette Burton, *Dwelling in the Archive: Women Writing House, Home, and History in Late Colonial India* (New York: Oxford University Press, 2003); Philippa Levine, ed., *Gender and Empire* (Oxford: Oxford University Press, 2004); Peterson, *Ethnic Patriotism*; Jane Guyer, ed., *Money Matters: Instability, Values and Social Payments* (Oxford: Heinemann Educational Books, 1994); Hastings, *Metropole-Colony in Educational Policy*; Woollacott, *Gender and Empire*.

15. Michel Foucault, *The History of Sexuality: The Will to Knowledge* (1976; London: Penguin, 1998).

16. See Peterson, *Ethnic Patriotism*, chapter 5.

17. Shirley Zabel, "Legislative History of the Gold Coast and Lagos Marriage Ordinance: 3," *Journal of African Law* 23, no. 1 (1979): 10–36.

18. Julius Lewin, "Some Legal Consequences of Marriage by Native Christians in British Africa," *Modern Law Review* (June 1939): 48–52; Kristin Mann, *Marrying Well: Marriage, Status and Social Change among the Educated Elite in Colonial Lagos* (Cambridge: Cambridge University Press, 1985).

19. See Anne McClintock, *Imperial Leather: Race, Gender and Sexuality in the Colonial Contest* (London: Routledge, 1995); Burton, *Dwelling in the Archive*; Timothy James Burke, *Lifebuoy Men, Lux Women: Commodification, Consumption and Cleanliness in Modern Zimbabwe* (London: Continuum, 1996); Allman and Tashjian, *"I Will Not Eat Stone."* The fact that Christian missionaries and British colonial administrators promoted these conservative gender ideals does not suggest they were operational or hegemonic in metropolitan society. The 1920s and 1930s witnessed the rise of the flapper, or sexually liberated woman, alongside the publication of erotica such as *Lady Chatterley's Lover* (1928) and the release of sensational films such as the *Gold Diggers* sequence in Hollywood. Europe and the United States were described by F. Scott Fitzgerald as living in "an age of excess" by the 1920s: for Fitzgerald, the open, "universal preoccupation with sex" in newspapers, literature, and film was nothing short of a "nuisance"; see Fitzgerald, "Echoes of the Jazz Age," in F. Scott Fitzgerald, *My Lost City: Personal Essays, 1920–1940*, vol. 4 (1931; Cambridge: Cambridge University Press, 2005), 130–38. I am indebted to Jenny Greenshields for drawing this essay to my attention.

20. An item entitled "An Editor on Tour" in the *African Morning Post* in June 1935 describes how "Mr Kobina Nortey, the Founder and Editor of the *Argus of West Africa*, left the city [of Accra] a few days ago for a tour of the Gold Coast and West Africa with a view to bringing himself into personal touch with the affairs of the people of West Africa." Nortey's plans to upgrade the printing equipment at the *Argus* are described, after which readers are informed that "this budding young literary and journalistic enthusiast is rapidly coming to the forefront. The three booklets, 'Matrimonial Tragedy,' 'The Illicit Gin Mystery' and 'The Dangerous Four,' now in circulation, are products of his pen. . . . He is compiling another

work, entitled 'Everybody's Handbook of West African Personalities' which will be printed in England." Nortey continued to write pamphlets well into the 1950s, including *Britain's Future in the Gold Coast* (Glasgow, Scotland: Civic Press, 1954), and *The Responsibility of Africans as a Race: A Talk* (Glasgow, Scotland: William MacLellan, 1957).

21. The theme of female education is also inextricable from this web of authorial preoccupations.

22. This was exemplified by the famous "Onitsha market literature" of the 1950s and 1960s in Eastern Nigeria.

23. *Lagos Weekly Record*, 12 June 1897, 4.

24. *Times of West Africa*, 16 March 1933, 2.

25. For a full edition of this narrative, see A. Native (pseud.), *Marita; or, The Folly of Love*, ed. Stephanie Newell (Leiden, the Netherlands: Brill, 2002).

26. Ibid.,103.

27. Ibid., 81. There is, of course, much more to *Marita; or, The Folly of Love* than conveyed by this précis, including a detailed critique of Gold Coast Methodism and numerous story fragments depicting a host of characters.

28. *Adelaide of Adelaide Street; or Train Up a Child in the Way She Should Go* was published as a serial in the *Sierra Leone Weekly News* between January and September 1911.

29. An exception to these negative literary representations of the mimic is the short story "Mr Courifer" by Adelaide Casely-Hayford, which uses the figure of the mimic to advocate a syncretic mixture of African and English customs in Sierra Leone; see Casely-Hayford, "Mista Courifer," in *An African Treasury*, ed. Langston Hughes (London: Victor Gollancz, 1971), 134–43.

30. *Sierra Leone Weekly News*, 18 February 1911, 6.

31. Ibid., 14 January 1911, 3 (italics in the original). The positive difference between "gay" local women and the "simple" clothing of white women is highlighted here, even in the process of commenting on the ways local women adopt white habits. For studies of clothing, mimicry, and colonial gender performances, see Alys Eve Weinbaum et al., eds., *The Modern Girl around the World: Consumption, Modernity, and Globalization* (Durham, NC: Duke University Press, 2008); Jean Allman, *Fashioning Africa: Power and the Politics of Dress* (Bloomington: Indiana University Press, 2004).

32. *Sierra Leone Weekly News*, 11 March 1911, 8.

33. Ibid.

34. See Peterson, *Ethnic Patriotism*.

35. *Sierra Leone Weekly News*, 9 September 1911, 5.

36. Joseph J. Walters, *Guanya Pau*, ed. Gareth Griffiths and John Victor Singler (Calgary, Canada: Broadview Press, 2004).

37. Oyekan Owomoyela, "Introduction," in Joseph J. Walters, *Guanya Pau: A Story of an African Princess* (Lincoln: University of Nebraska Press, 1994).

38. Kwabena N. Bame, *Come to Laugh: A Study of African Traditional Theatre in Ghana* (Accra: Baafour Educational Enterprises, 1981); Karin Barber, John Collins, and Alain Ricard, *West African Popular Theatre* (Bloomington: Indiana

University Press, 1997); Barber, *The Generation of Plays: Yoruba Popular Life in Theater* (Bloomington: Indiana University Press, 2000).

39. Allman and Tashjian, *"I Will Not Eat Stone"*; Bianca Murillo, "Commercial Space, Consumer Politics, and Establishment of Kingsway Department Stores in Accra," paper presented at the Tuning In to African Cities: Popular Culture and Urban Experience in Sub-Saharan Africa Conference, Centre of West African Studies, University of Birmingham, 6–8 May 2010.

40. Major exceptions to this rule are Marjorie Mensah of the *Times of West Africa* in the early 1930s and Ṣẹgilọla in *Akede Eko* in 1929 and 1930 (see chapters 5 and 6).

41. See Eileen Julien, *African Novels and the Question of Orality* (Bloomington: Indiana University Press, 1992); Ruth Finnegan, *Why Do We Quote? The Culture and History of Quotation* (Cambridge: Open Book Publishers, 2011).

42. *Sierra Leone Weekly News*, 17 February 1894, 3.

43. Ibid.

44. Ibid.

45. *Western Echo*, 20 January 1886, 2.

46. Femi Ojo-Ade famously sparked controversy in his article "Female Writers, Male Critics," *African Literature Today* 13 (1983): 158–79. For a feminist assessment of the critical reception of early African women writers, see Florence Stratton, *Contemporary African Literature and the Politics of Gender* (London: Routledge, 1994), 83.

47. See Edward Said, *Orientalism* (1978; London: Penguin, 2003).

48. Karin Barber's fully annotated translation of *The Life Story of Me, "Ṣẹgilọla of the Fascinating Eyes," She Who Had a Thousand Lovers in Her Life*, including an extensive introductory essay by Barber and a series of supplementary texts, was published in 2012 as *Print Culture and the First Yoruba Novel: I. B. Thomas's "Life Story of Me, Ṣẹgilọla" and Other Texts* (Leiden, the Netherlands: Brill, African Sources for African History Series).

49. Cited in ibid., 273

50. I am indebted to David Pratten for sharing his discovery of J. V. Clinton's papers.

51. NNA (Ibadan), *James Vivian Clinton Papers*, JVC 2/1/106, "Letters to JVC," Section A., Lecture 3 (2), n.d. [c. April 1965].

52. Chinua Achebe, *Things Fall Apart* (1958; London: Heinemann, 1962).

53. Flora Nwapa, *Efuru* (London: Heinemann, 1966).

54. Elechi Amadi, *The Concubine* (London: Heinemann, 1966).

55. For the opposing sides in this debate, see Graham Huggan, *The Postcolonial Exotic: Marketing the Margins* (London: Routledge, 2001), and James Currey, *Africa Writes Back: The African Writers Series and the Launch of African Literature* (Woodbridge, UK: Boydell and Brewer, 2008).

56. See Caroline Davis, "The Politics of Postcolonial Publishing: Oxford University Press's Three Crowns Series, 1962–1976," *Book History* 8 (2005): 227–44.

57. Another, better-known example of male cross-vocalization can be found in the "Ladies' Corner" (later "Women's Corner") of the *Times of West Africa* in

the early 1930s. Between 1931 and 1933, the popular but pseudonymous Marjorie Mensah was the byline of at least three different individuals, including Kenneth MacNeil Stewart (see chapter 6).

58. Ifi Amadiume, *Male Daughters, Female Husbands: Gender and Sex in an African Society* (London: Zed, 1987).

59. Ibid. See also Bolanle Awe, ed., *Nigerian Women in Historical Perspective* (Ibadan, Nigeria: Bookcraft, 1992).

60. For studies of the ambivalence of West African colonial elites, see Kwaku Larbi Korang, *Writing Ghana, Imagining Africa: Nation and African Modernity* (Rochester, NY: University of Rochester Press, 2004), and Roger S. Gocking, *Facing Two Ways: Ghana's Coastal Communities under Colonial Rule* (New York: University Press of America, 1999).

61. Barber, *Print Culture and the First Yoruba Novel*, 85.

62. Ibid.

63. Ibid., 119.

64. Ibid., 271.

65. Ibid., 85.

66. Ibid., "Introduction: I. B. Thomas and the First Yoruba Novel," 41.

67. Benedict Anderson, *Imagined Communities: Reflections on the Origins and Spread of Nationalism* (1983; London: Verso Books, 1991).

68. Barber, *Print Culture and the First Yoruba Novel*, 351.

69. Of course, Thomas himself may have composed some or all of this "paratextual" material.

70. Barber, *Print Culture and the First Yoruba Novel*, 386.

71. Ibid., 239.

72. Ibid.

73. Ibid.

74. Barber, "Introduction: I. B. Thomas and the First Yoruba Novel," 52.

75. Barber, *Print Culture and the First Yoruba Novel*, 333.

76. In 1929, Ernest S. Ikoli was replaced as editor of the *Times* by A. A. C. Titcombe, who edited the paper from 1930 to 1938; see Fred I. A. Omu, *Press and Politics in Nigeria, 1880–1960* (Atlantic Highlands, NJ: Humanities Press, 1978), 253.

77. Barber, *Print Culture and the First Yoruba Novel*, 341.

78. Karin Barber, personal communication, May 2011.

79. Barber, *Print Culture and the First Yoruba Novel*, 273.

80. See John Mullan, *Anonymity: A Secret History of English Literature* (London: Faber and Faber, 2007).

81. Marcy L. North, *The Anonymous Renaissance: Cultures of Discretion in Tudor-Stuart England* (Chicago: University of Chicago Press, 2003); Robert J. Griffin, ed., *The Faces of Anonymity: Anonymous and Pseudonymous Publication from the Sixteenth to the Twentieth Century* (Basingstoke, UK: Palgrave Macmillan, 2003); Michael Warner, *The Letters of the Republic: Publication and the Public Sphere in Eighteenth-Century America* (Cambridge, MA: Harvard University Press, 1992).

82. Barber, "Introduction: I. B. Thomas and the First Yoruba Novel," 60.

83. Barber, *Print Culture and the First Yoruba Novel*, 363.

84. Ibid., 99. Barber points out that in Thomas's English translation, this is given as Christ Church School. Similarly, other local details are altered to other actual places in the translation, maintaining verisimilitude but offering a set of cultural translations for English-speaking West African readerships.

85. Ibid., 121.

86. Ibid., 255.

87. Ibid., 89. Barber notes that "*segi* beads are a mark of high status."

88. Ibid., 279.

89. Barber, "Introduction: I. B. Thomas and the First Yoruba Novel," 35.

90. Ibid., 50.

91. Ibid., 53.

92. Barber, *Print Culture and the First Yoruba Novel*, 303.

93. Ibid., 305.

94. Patricia A. Rosenmeyer, *Ancient Epistolary Fictions: The Letter in Greek Literature* (Cambridge: Cambridge University Press, 2001).

95. Countless West African authors, from Thomas's Sẹgilọla onward, have deployed the letter for Christian puritanical ends.

96. See Stephanie Newell, *Literary Culture in Colonial Ghana* (Bloomington: Indiana University Press, 2002); Graham Furniss and Liz Gunner, *Power, Marginality and African Oral Literature* (Cambridge: Cambridge University Press, 1995); Luise White, Stephan Miescher, and David Cohen, eds., *African Words, African Voices: Critical Practices in Oral History* (Bloomington: Indiana University Press, 2002).

97. Barber, *Print Culture and the First Yoruba Novel*, 273.

98. See Newell, *Literary Culture in Colonial Ghana*.

99. *Times of West Africa*, 16 March 1933, 2.

100. Barber, *Print Culture and the First Yoruba Novel*, 103.

101. Ibid., 189.

102. Warner, *Letters of the Republic*, 38, 61, 72.

103. Clinton was born into a family of privilege, wealth, and political influence. His maternal grandfather was Chief Justice Charles McCarthy, who also served as occasional acting governor of the Gold Coast; his father was C. W. Clinton, leader of the Eastern Bar in Nigeria and proprietor of the *Nigerian Eastern Mail*. Nevertheless, Clinton's late career as a creative writer was not simply the hobby of a moneyed gentleman who wished to pass the hours of his retirement in productive activity.

104. I am indebted to David Pratten for providing these details and for sharing his archival discoveries.

105. See Ian Duffield, "The Business Activities of Duse Mohamed Ali: An Example of the Economic Dimension of Pan-Africanism," *Journal of the Historical Society of Nigeria* 4, no. 4 (1969): 571–600.

106. NNA (Ibadan), James Vivian Clinton Papers, JVC 2/1/1, "Miscellaneous Letters to and from JVC," 26 June 1963.

107. Ibid.

108. Ibid., JVC 2/1/143, "Nine Letters for J. V. Clinton," 13 September 1968.

109. Ibid., JVC 2/1/1, "Miscellaneous Letters to and from JVC," 26 June 1963.

110. J. V. Clinton, "King Eyo Honesty II of Creek Town," *Nigeria Magazine* 69 (August 1961): 182–83.

111. J. V. Clinton, "The Ibo Rebels," *Contemporary Review* 213 (August 1968): 57–61.

112. NNA (Ibadan), James Vivian Clinton Papers, JVC 2/1/193, "The Female Leg," n.d. [c. September 1970].

113. Ibid., JVC 2/1/185, "Women in Men's Jobs," n.d.

114. At several points in the 1960s, Clinton had to withdraw from the course for want of cash, and for most of the decade, he depended upon post office boxes owned by friends and family; at one point, he had insufficient cash even to buy airmail stamps to send his manuscripts to Britain; see ibid., JVC 2/1/106, "Letters to JVC," 26 August 1968.

115. Ibid., Section A., Lecture 3 (2), n.d. [c. March 1965].

116. Ibid., JVC 2/1/143 "Nine Letters for J. V. Clinton," 14 October 1964.

117. Ibid., 5 November 1964.

118. Ibid., JVC 2/1/133, "'He Followed Her There,' by Anwan Eyen Efik," n.d.

119. Ibid., JVC 2/1/106, "Letters to JVC," Section E., Lecture 10 (2), n.d. [c. March 1965].

120. Ibid., JVC 2/1/244, "'As God Made Her,' by J. V. Clinton," n.d.

121. Ibid., JVC 2/1/140, "Irvin Shaw, 'Love on a Dark Night,'" Section E., Lecture 10 (4), n.d.

122. Ibid., JVC 2/1/143, "Nine Letters for J. V. Clinton," Fragment labeled p. 29, n.d. [c. September 1968].

123. Ibid., JVC 2/1/244, "'As God Made Her' by J. V. Clinton"; JVC 2/1/105, "'The Scarlet Pimple,' by Eunice Vivian (pseud.)," n.d.

124. Ibid., JVC 2/1/143 "Nine Letters for J. V. Clinton," Section E., Lecture 10 (3), n.d. [c. September 1968].

125. Clinton's network of journalistic connections is described briefly in chapter 2.

126. NNA (Ibadan), James Vivian Clinton Papers, JVC 2/1/108, "'Popular Author,' by Eunice Vivian," n.d.

127. Ibid., JVC 2/1/152, "'Poor Deserted Bride,' by J. V. Clinton," n.d.

128. Ibid.

129. Ibid., JVC 2/1/107, "'The Burglar Next Door,' by Eunice Vivian," n.d.

130. Ibid., JVC 2/1/106, "Letters to JVC," 18 January 1965.

131. Ibid., JVC 2/1/152, "'Poor Deserted Bride,' by J. V. Clinton," n.d.

132. Ibid., JVC 2/1/106, "Letters to JVC," Section A., Lecture 3 (2), n.d. [c. March 1965].

133. Huggan, *Postcolonial Exotic*.

134. Onyile Bassey Onyile, "Abang Dance: Radiance from the River and the Efik Ideal of Femininity," *Ijele: Art eJournal of the African World* 1, no. 1 (2000), www.africaknowledgeproject.org/index.php/ijele/article/view/1293 (accessed 15 May 2011).

135. Ibid.

136. Ibid.

137. NNA (Ibadan), James Vivian Clinton Papers, JVC 2/1/209, "'How to Survive Matrimony,' by J. V. Clinton," n.d.

138. See David Pratten, *The Man-Leopard Murders: History and Society in Colonial Nigeria* (Edinburgh: Edinburgh University Press, 2007).

139. Barber, *Print Culture and the First Yoruba Novel*, 315.

140. NNA (Ibadan), James Vivian Clinton Papers, JVC 2/1/273, "'Are Those Minis Going?' by Anwan Eyen Efik," n.d. [c. March–April 1970].

141. See Wendy Griswold, *Bearing Witness: Readers, Writers, and the Novel in Nigeria* (Princeton, NJ: Princeton University Press, 2000).

CHAPTER 6 NOMINAL LADIES AND "REAL" WOMEN WRITERS

1. These methods constitute a "gynocritical" approach, defined by Elaine Showalter in her work on feminist poetics in the late 1970s and early 1980s: *A Literature of Their Own: British Women Novelists from Bronte to Lessing* (Princeton, NJ: Princeton University Press, 1977); "Toward a Feminist Poetics," in *The Critical Tradition: Classic Texts and Contemporary Trends*, ed. David H. Richter (1979; London: St. Martin's Press, 1998), 1375–86; "Feminist Criticism in the Wilderness," *Critical Inquiry* 8, no. 2 (1981): 179–205; and *The New Feminist Criticism: Essays on Women, Literature, and Theory* (New York: Pantheon Books, 1985).

2. Margaretta Jolly, *In Love and Struggle: Letters in Contemporary Feminism* (New York: Columbia University Press, 2008).

3. Audrey Sitsofe Gadzekpo, "Women's Engagement with Gold Coast Print Culture: From 1857 to 1957" (PhD diss., Centre of West African Studies, University of Birmingham, 2000).

4. Ibid., 170–72.

5. Ibid. Mabel Dove has generated considerable interest among feminist scholars. For a discussion of her short stories, see Naana Jane Opoku Agyemang, "Recovering Lost Voices: The Short Stories of Mabel Dove-Danquah," in *Writing African Women: Gender, Popular Culture and Literature in West Africa*, ed. Stephanie Newell (London: Zed Books, 1997), 67–80. For a discussion of Dove in relation to West African newspaper networks, see Jinny Prais, "Imperial Travelers: The Formation of West African Urban Culture, Identity, and Citizenship in London and Accra, 1925–1935" (PhD diss., University of Michigan, 2008). For a selection of Dove's prose fiction, drama, and articles for a variety of Ghanaian newspapers, see Mabel Dove, *Selected Writings of a Pioneer West African Feminist*, ed. Stephanie Newell and Audrey Gadzekpo (Nottingham, UK: Trend Editions, 2004).

6. Yema Lucilda Hunter, *An African Treasure: In Search of Gladys Casely-Hayford, 1904–1950* (Accra: Yema Lucilda Hunter, 2008); see also LaRay Denzer, "Yoruba Women: A Historiographical Study," *International Journal of African Historical Studies* 27, no. 1 (1994): 1–39.

7. For essays on the "modern girl" in the colonial world, see Alys Eve Weinbaum et al., eds., *The Modern Girl around the World: Consumption, Modernity, and Globalization* (Durham, NC: Duke University Press, 2008).

8. *Sierra Leone Weekly News*, 30 September 1884, 4.
9. Ibid.
10. Ibid.
11. For recent sensational examples of gender masquerading, followed by the unmasking of "fraudulent" women, see the world news coverage of the lesbian blogger "Amina Abdallah Aral al Omari" in Syria during the "Arab spring" of 2011, who was revealed in June 2011 to be a white heterosexual Scotsman, Tom MacMaster. See also the scandalous unveiling of "Yasmina Khadra," whose novel about women in Afghanistan under the reign of the Taliban, *The Swallows of Kabul*, was widely feted and nominated for women's writing prizes, only for the author to be revealed as the Algerian novelist Mohammed Moulessehoul.
12. *Sierra Leone Weekly News*, 11 October 1884, 4.
13. Ibid.
14. Ibid., 28 February 1885, 4, and 14 March 1885, 4.
15. The *Times of West Africa* was also known as the *West African Times*; the "Ladies' Corner" became the "Women's Corner" in 1933.
16. *Times of West Africa*, 21 April 1931, 2.
17. Ibid., 27 April 1931, 2.
18. Ibid., 23 April 1934, 2.
19. Ibid., 21 June 1934, 2.
20. Marjorie Mensah, *Us Women: Extracts from the Writings of Marjorie Mensah*, ed. Kathleen Hewitt (London: Mathews and Marrot, 1933).
21. *Times of West Africa*, 11 May 1934, front page.
22. Ibid.
23. Stewart certainly contributed to the polyvocal "personality" of Marjorie Mensah in the early days of the *Times of West Africa*, and so too did Ruby Quartey-Papafio of the Accra Government Girls' School; see Gadzekpo, "Women's Engagement with Gold Coast Print Culture."
24. See Dove, *Selected Writings*; Weinbaum et al., *Modern Girl around the World*.
25. See Dove, "Woman in Jade," in her *Selected Writings*, 59–90. See also Jean Allman, "Rounding Up Spinsters: Gender Chaos and Unmarried Women in Colonial Asante," *Journal of African History* 37, no. 2 (1996): 195–214.
26. Weinbaum et al., *Modern Girl around the World*.
27. Prais, "Imperial Travelers," 172–74.
28. Ibid., 172.
29. Ibid.
30. Stephanie Newell and Audrey Gadzekpo, "Introduction," in Mabel Dove, *Selected Writings of a Pioneer West African Feminist*, ed. Newell and Gadzekpo (Nottingham, UK: Trend Editions, 2004), xii. (This argument was originally formulated by Gadzekpo in her "Women's Engagement with Gold Coast Print Culture.")
31. *Times of West Africa*, 11 May 1931, 4.
32. Cited in Dove, *Selected Writings*, xiii.
33. Ibid., xii.

CONCLUSION

The chapter title derives from John B. Thompson, "The New Visibility," *Theory, Culture and Society* 22, no. 6 (2005): 31–51.

1. John Berger, *Ways of Seeing* (1972; London: Penguin, 2008).
2. Frantz Fanon, *Black Skin, White Masks* (1968; London: Pluto, 1991), 116.
3. Vincent Caretta, *Equiano the African: Biography of a Self-Made Man* (Athens: University of Georgia Press, 2005).
4. See Douglas Chambers, "'Almost an Englishman': Carretta's Equiano," *H-Atlantic* (November 2007) (accessed 15 September 2011); David Dabydeen, "Review of *Equiano the African: Biography of a Self-Made Man*," *Guardian*, 3 December 2005, available at http://www.guardian.co.uk/books/2005/dec/03/featuresreviews.guardianreview3 (accessed 15 September 2011); G. Ugo Nwokeji, "Equiano the African: Biography of a Self-Made Man," *Journal of American History* 93, no. 3 (2006): 840–41.
5. I am grateful to Brian Cummings for sharing in advance the ideas and discoveries arising from his Leverhulme Trust Major Research Fellowship project, *The Confessions of Shakespeare* (2009–12), including the notion of "anti-biography" presented in his manuscript "Shakespeare in the Underworld."
6. PRO, CO 96/749/5, Wallace-Johnson: Privy Council Appeal: *I. T. A. Wallace-Johnson v. The King* (closed until 1989), cutting from the *Times*, 27 May 1938, n.p.
7. Ibid.
8. Ibid. (italics in the original).
9. PRO, CO 96/759/1, Wallace-Johnson: Privy Council Appeal: *I. T. A. Wallace-Johnson v the King* (closed until 1990), "Privy Council Appeal No. 89 of 1938," n.d.
10. Thompson, "New Visibility," 36; see also Berger, *Ways of Seeing*.
11. Thompson, "New Visibility," 36.
12. Roland Barthes, "The Death of the Author," in *Image—Music—Text*, ed. and trans. Stephen Heath (1968; New York: Hill and Wang, 1977), 142–48.
13. Ibid.
14. Michel Foucault, "What Is an Author?" (trans. Donald F. Bouchard and Sherry Simon), in *Language, Counter-memory, Practice*, ed. Donald F. Bouchard (1969; Ithaca, NY: Cornell University Press, 1977), 124–27.
15. Michel Foucault, "Politics and the Study of Discourse," in *The Foucault Effect: Studies in Governmentality*, ed. Graham Burchell, Colin Gordon, and Peter Miller (1978; London: Harvester, 1991), 71–72 (italics in the original).
16. Foucault, "What Is an Author?"
17. *Gold Coast Leader*, 2 August 1902, 2.
18. Ngugi wa Thiong'o, *Devil on the Cross* (1980; London: Heinemann, 1987), 200.
19. See Ngugi wa Thiong'o, *Decolonising the Mind: The Politics of Language in African Literature* (Oxford: James Currey, 1986).
20. See Stephanie Newell, *West African Literatures: Ways of Reading* (Oxford: Oxford University Press, 2006).
21. Henry Louis Gates, "The 'Blackness of Blackness': A Critique of the Sign and the Signifying Monkey," *Critical Inquiry* 9, no. 4 (1983): 687.

22. Ibid., 686, 694.

23. Ibid., 691.

24. Ibid.

25. In Internet cafés throughout the continent, bloggers routinely employ pseudonyms or avatars, using them in creative and diverse ways, much as colonial newspaper contributors did. Bloggers often use multiple pseudonyms, none more "authentic" than the other, and unlike popular celebrities, they do not necessarily expect to become "known" as or by their avatars; see Andrew Heavens, "African Bloggers Find Their Voice," *BBC Focus on Africa Magazine*, 20 December 2005, available at http://news.bbc.co.uk/1/hi/world/africa/4512290.stm (accessed 9 August 2011). See also http://globalvoicesonline.org/ and http://blogafrica.allafrica.com/. For a study of gender and pseudonymous cartooning in Ghana, see Joseph Frimpong, "'Better Ghana [Agenda]'?: Akosua's Political Cartoons and Critical Public Debates in Contemporary Ghana," in *Popular Culture in Africa: The Episteme of the Everyday*, ed. S. Newell and O. Okome (New York: Routledge, forthcoming 2013).

26. Jesse Shipley, *The Entrepreneur's Aesthetic: Value, Circulation, and Celebrity in Ghanaian Hiplife Music* (Durham, NC: Duke University Press, 2013).

27. Tunde Awosanmi, personal communication, 29 May 2011.

28. Ibid.

29. Ibid.

30. Karin Barber, personal communication, 15 April 2012.

31. Ibid.

32. David Kerr (University of Birmingham), personal communication, 10 August 2011.

33. Jesse Weaver Shipley, *Living the Hiplife: Celebrity and Entrepreneurship in Ghanaian Popular Music* (Durham, NC: Duke University Press, 2013), 108–33.

Bibliography

ARCHIVAL SOURCES

Nigerian National Archives (NNA) (Ibadan)
James Vivian Clinton Papers. JVC 2/1/106. "Letters to JVC"

Public Record Office (PRO) (London, UK)
CO 87/258/13. Gambia: Registration, Printing and Publication of Newspaper Legislation, Feb–Aug, 1944 (closed until 1972). "Note on Registration of Newspapers Ordinance and on False Publication Ordinance." 21 March 1944.
———. "Minute from O. G. R. Williams." 23 March 1944.
CO 96/714/6. Bills for Newspapers, Books and Printing Presses Ordinance, Criminal Code (Amendment) Ordinance, Control of Imported Books, "Draft Bill: Newspapers, Books and Printing Presses Ordinance, 1934." 20 January 1934.
———. "Letter from James A. Busum to the Secretary of State for the Colonies." 16 February 1934.
———. "Memo signed Arthur Grey Hazlerigg." 26 February 1934.
———. "Message from Shenton Thomas to Alex Fiddian." 27 February 1934.
———. "Memo signed Alex Fiddian." Date unclear: c. 1 March 1934.
———. "Memo signed H. Duncan." 2 March 1934.
———. "Memo signed Kenneth Roberts Wray." 3 March 1934.
———. "Telegram from the Governor of the Gold Coast to the Secretary of State for the Colonies." 26 March 1934.
———. "Memo signed Alex Fiddian." 29 March 1934.
CO 96/716/15. Control of the Press of the Gold Coast: Newspapers, Books and Printing Presses Ordinance, 1934 (closed until 1985). "Memorandum by the Inspector General of Police [Henry W. M. Bamford] Regarding the Draft Bill (44A) cited as the Newspapers, Books and Printing Presses Ordinance, 1934." n.d.
———. "Memo signed I. H. Wallace." 17 May 1934.
———. "Extract from a Note of a Meeting at the Colonial Office." 14 June 1934.
———. "Memo from Arnold Hodson, Government House, Accra, to the Rt Hon Sir Philip Cunliffe-Lister, Secretary of State for the Colonies." 29 November 1934.
———. "Memo signed Gerald Creasy." 28 December 1934.

CO 96/749/5. Wallace-Johnson, Privy Council Appeal: *I. T. A. Wallace-Johnson v. The King* (closed until 1989). "Law Officers' Dept, Accra, Gold Coast: Report entitled Wallace-Johnson versus the King: Observations of the Attorney-General of the Gold Coast upon the Appellant's Case, by H. W. B. Blackall." 13 November 1938.

CO 96/759/1. Wallace-Johnson—Privy Council Appeal: *I. T. A. Wallace-Johnson v. the King* (closed until 1990). "Privy Council Appeal No. 89 of 1938: Isaac Theophilus Akkunna Wallace-Johnson (Appellant) v. The King (Respondent) from the West African Court of Appeal. Judgment of the Lords of the Judicial Committee of the Privy Council." 11 December 1939.

CO 267/671/5. Activities of West Africa Youth League.

CO 267/671/6. Activities of West Africa Youth League, Sierra Leone: Heavy Battery—Mutiny of African Gunners, May and June 1939. "Letter from Governor Douglas Jardine to Malcolm MacDonald, Secretary of State for the Colonies." 8 May 1939.

———. "Minute signed 'H. B.' [H. Bushe]." 1 July 1939.

CO 267/671/8. Leakage of Official Information. "Excerpt from court transcript." 10 October 1938.

———. "Letter from Acting Governor of Sierra Leone to Rt Hon Malcolm MacDonald, Secretary of State for the Colonies." 14 January 1939.

———. "Cutting from 'Sideviews: What about the Report?'—editorial by Wallace Johnson published in *The African Standard*." 17 March 1939, n.p.

CO 267/672/7. Deportation, Sedition, Undesirable Literature, Trade Union and Trade Disputes Legislation—Miscellaneous Representations 1939. "Resolution of the Women's Auxiliary of the West African Youth League." 3 June 1939.

———. "Sierra Leone: The 'Undesirable Literature' Ordinance." Press cutting from the *Manchester Guardian*. 14 June 1939.

———. "Memo [Anon]." 26 June 1939.

CO 267/672/9. Deputation from Sierra Leone against the Recent Ordinances. "Copy of memo." 26 July 1939.

CO 323/685/37. Prevention of Circulation of Undesirable Publications in British Dominions, War Office, 1915. "Letter from B. B. Cutrill to the Under Secretary of State for the Colonies." 18 July 1915.

CO 323/977/1. Films: Replies to Confidential Circular Despatch of 8 January 1927. "Confidential Circular Despatch, L. S. Amery." 8 January 1927.

———. "Ceylon: from Herbert Layard Dowbiggin, Inspector-General of Police, to Leopold Charles Stennett Amery, Secretary of State for the Colonies." 30 March 1927.

———. "Confidential Memorandum by the Governor on the Censorship of Films, signed Frederick Gordon Guggisberg." 19 April 1927.

CO 323/1073/6. *Films: Institution of a Central Censorship in London of Films in Tropical Africa*, 1930. "Minute signed 'G. G' [Gordon Guggisberg]." 12 November 1930.

CO 323/1518/9. "The Negro Worker": The International Trade Union Committee for Negro Workers. "Extract from minutes of the meeting of the Executive Council held at Government House, Christiansborg, Accra." 8 October 1937.

CO 323/1749/1. Censorship—Press: Representations by Mr Noel Baker. Secret. General Defence, 1940 (closed until 1971). "Letter to Eric Cook from Private Secretary to Malcolm MacDonald, Secretary of State for the Colonies." 15 February 1940.
CO 537/2622. Secret: 1948: Security: Undesirable Publications. "Telegram from the Governor of the Seychelles to the Secretary of State for the Colonies: Secret." 23 October 1948.
———. "Secret Telegram." 29 November 1948.
———. "Secret Telegram." 7 December 1948.
CO 537/4878. Control of Undesirable Publications (Eastern Sarawak), 1949, Secret. "Minute by K. G. Ashton." 16 May 1949.
———. "Secret: Note by Colonial Office." June 1949.
———. "Minute signed John D. Higham." 3 June 1949.
CO 537/6523. Security Arrangements, West Africa: Undesirable Publications—"Africa" by George Padmore (closed until 1981). "Letter from Private Secretary N. D. Watson to P. L. Taylor." 8 May 1950.
———. "Letter from Fenner Brockway MP to the Rt Hon James Griffiths, Sec of State for the Colonies." 29 November 1950.
———. "Letter from Jim Griffiths, Secretary of State for the Colonies, to Archibald Fenner Brockway MP." 13 December 1950.
CO 583/195/4. African Workers' Union of Nigeria: Alleged Action Against, 1933–34. "Report by Alex Fiddian." 5 December 1933.
CO 583/265/1. Petition: Nnamdi Azikiwe (Re: Zik's Press Ltd), 1946: Secret (closed until 1977). "To the Rt Hon George Hall MP, Sec of State for the Colonies." 15 March 1946.
———. "Memo to Mr. O. G. R. Williams, from G. Chamberlain." 15 April 1946.
———. "Letter from Nnamdi Azikiwe to the Acting Chief Secretary to the Government, Lagos." 16 July 1946.
CO 583/317/4. Activities of Dr Nnamdi Azikiwe, 1951 (closed until 1982). January–February 1951.
CO 691/140/11. Control of Newspapers and Printing Presses, 1934, Tanganyika. "Minute from [signature unclear]." 3 October 1934.
———. "Minute signed 'P. L. L.'" 30 December 1934.
———. "Draft letter from Secretary of State for the Colonies to the Governor of Tanganyika." 9 January 1935.
CO 875/12/11. Public Relations. Press Censorship: Question of Censorship on Two Articles in the "West African Pilot" (closed until 1992). "Savingram from the Governor of Nigeria enclosing two articles from *West African Pilot*, 21 and 22 March, one reviving racial feeling, the other criticizing aspects of British Policy." March 1934.
CO 875/13/5. Press Censorship: Nigeria, 1942. "Secret report entitled Benjamin Nnamdi Azikiwe alias 'Zik,'" by S. A. S. P. [Superintendent of Police]. 16 November 1941.
———. "Secret letter from Governor Bernard Bourdillon to the Rt Hon Lord Moyne, Secretary of State for the Colonies." 20 November 1941.
———. "Minute signed D. H. Mishall." 16 January 1942.

———. "Minute signed W. J. Sabine." 19 January 1942.
———. "Minute signed F. J. Pedler." 26 January 1942.
———. "Minute signed S. S. Abrahams." 29 January 1942.
———. "Press Conference Held at Government House." 30 January 1942.
———. "Minute signed J. B. Sidebotham." 31 January 1942.
———. "Draft letter from Viscount Cranborne, Secretary of State for the Colonies, to Governor Bourdillon." 30 March 1942.
———. "Memo signed O. G. R. W." 2 February 1943.
KV 2/1818. Azikiwe, Benjamin Nnamdi, 1951–2 (President of National Council of Nigeria and Cameroons).

Rhodes House Library (RHL) (Oxford)

MSS. Afr. s.1527. Colonial Office Correspondence and Cuttings, 1934–1939. 27 June 1934.
MSS. Brit. Emp. s.282. Reverend C. Kingsley Williams Papers, 1927–1934.

PUBLISHED SOURCES

Adejumo, Arinpe. "Family Health Awareness in Popular Yoruba Arts." In *Africans and the Politics of Popular Culture*, edited by Toyin Falola and Augustine Agwuele, 261–74. Rochester, NY: University of Rochester Press, 2009.
Ahearne, Jeremy. *Michel de Certeau: Interpretation and Its Other*. Cambridge: Polity Press, 1995.
Allman, Jean M. *Fashioning Africa: Power and the Politics of Dress*. Bloomington: Indiana University Press, 2004.
———. "Rounding Up Spinsters: Gender Chaos and Unmarried Women in Colonial Asante." *Journal of African History* 37, no. 2 (1996): 195–214.
Allman, Jean M., and Victoria Tashjian. *"I Will Not Eat Stone": A Women's History of Colonial Asante*. Portsmouth, NH: Heinemann, 2000.
Althusser, Louis. *Lenin and Philosophy and Other Essays*. London: Verso, 1971.
Amadi, Elechi. *The Concubine*. London: Heinemann, 1966.
Amadiume, Ifi. *Male Daughters, Female Husbands: Gender and Sex in an African Society*. London: Zed, 1987.
Anderson, Benedict. *Imagined Communities: Reflections on the Origins and Spread of Nationalism*. 1983. Reprint, London: Verso Books, 1991.
Appiah, Kwame. *In My Father's House: Africa in the Philosophy of Culture*. Oxford: Oxford University Press, 1993.
Arhin, Kwame. "A Note on the Asante *Akonkofo*: A Non-literate Sub-elite, 1900–1930." *Africa* 56, no. 1 (1986): 25–31.
———. *West African Traders in Ghana in the Nineteenth and Twentieth Centuries*. London: Longman, 1979.
Attoh-Ahuma, S. R. B. *The "Gold Coast Nation" and National Consciousness*. 1911. Reprint, London: Frank Cass, 1971.
———. *Memoirs of West African Celebrities*. Liverpool, UK: D. Marples, 1905.

Austen, Ralph A. "Interpreters Self-Interpreted: The Autobiographies of Two Colonial Clerks." In *Intermediaries, Interpreters, and Clerks: African Employees in the Making of Colonial Africa*, edited by Benjamin N. Lawrance, Emily Lynn Osborn, and Richard L. Roberts, 159–79. Madison: University of Wisconsin Press, 2006.

Austen, Ralph, and Jonathan Derrick. *Middlemen of the Cameroons River: The Duala and Their Hinterland, c. 1600–c. 1960*. Cambridge: Cambridge University Press, 1999.

Awe, Bolanle, ed. *Nigerian Women in Historical Perspective*. Ibadan, Nigeria: Bookcraft, 1992.

Ayoola, Tokunbo A. "Popular Resistance Literature and the Nigerian Railway Corporation, 1955–60." In *Africans and the Politics of Popular Culture*, edited by Toyin Falola and Augustine Agwuele, 299–320. Rochester, NY: University of Rochester Press, 2009.

Azikiwe, Benjamin Nnamdi. *My Odyssey: An Autobiography*. London: C. Hurst, 1970.

Baku, D. Kofi. "An Intellectual in Nationalist Politics: The Contribution of Kobina Sekyi to the Evolution of Ghanaian National Consciousness." PhD diss., University of Sussex, 1987.

Bame, Kwabena N. *Come to Laugh: A Study of African Traditional Theatre in Ghana*. Accra: Baafour Educational Enterprises, 1981.

Barber, Karin. *The Anthropology of Texts, Persons and Publics: Oral and Written Culture in Africa and Beyond*. Cambridge: Cambridge University Press, 2007.

——. *The Generation of Plays: Yoruba Popular Life in Theater*. Bloomington: Indiana University Press, 2000.

——. "Introduction: Hidden Innovators in Africa." In *Africa's Hidden Histories: Everyday Literacy and Making the Self*, edited by Karin Barber, 1–24. Bloomington: Indiana University Press, 2006.

——. "Introduction: I. B. Thomas and the First Yoruba Novel." In *Print Culture and the First Yoruba Novel: I. B. Thomas's "Life Story of Me, Ṣẹgilọla" and Other Texts*, edited and translated by Karin Barber, 3–75. Leiden, the Netherlands: Brill, 2012.

——, ed. and trans. *Print Culture and the First Yoruba Novel: I.B. Thomas's "Life Story of Me, Ṣẹgilọla" and Other Texts*. Leiden, The Netherlands: Brill, 2012.

——. "Translation, Publics, and the Vernacular Press in 1920s Lagos." In *Christianity and Social Change in Africa: Essays in Honor of J. D. Y. Peel*, edited by Toyin Falola, 187–208. Durham, NC: Carolina Academic Press, 2005.

Barber, Karin, John Collins, and Alain Ricard. *West African Popular Theatre*. Bloomington: Indiana University Press, 1997.

Barnes, Andrew E. *Making Headway: The Introduction of Western Civilization in Colonial Northern Nigeria*. Rochester, NY: University of Rochester Press, 2009.

Barthes, Roland. "The Death of the Author." In *Image—Music—Text*, edited and translated by Stephen Heath, 142–48. 1968. Reprint, New York: Hill and Wang, 1977.

Basso, Ellen B. "The Trickster's Scattered Self." In *Disorderly Discourse: Narrative, Conflict and Inequality*, edited by Charles L. Briggs, 53–71. New York: Oxford University Press, 1996.
Bayart, Jean-François. *The State in Africa: The Politics of the Belly*. London: Longman, 1994.
Berger, John. *Ways of Seeing*. 1972. Reprint, London: Penguin, 2008.
Bhattacharya, Neeladri. "Notes Towards a Conception of the Colonial Public." In *Civil Society, Public Sphere and Citizenship: Dialogues and Perceptions*, edited by Rajeev Bhargava and Helmut Reifeld, 130–56 . New Delhi: Sage, 2005.
Birchman, Robert L. "Class Struggles in Nigeria." *Fourth International* 6, no. 10 (1945): 308–12.
Blyden, Edward W. *African Life and Customs: Reprinted from the "Sierra Leone Weekly News."* London: C. M. Phillips, 1908.
Boafo, S. T. Kwame. "Journalism Profession and Training in Sub-Saharan Africa: A Case Study of Ghana." *Africa Media Review* 2, no. 3 (1988): 56–74.
Buchanan, Ian. *Michel de Certeau: Cultural Theorist*. London: Sage, 2000.
Buitenhuis, Peter. *The Great War of Words: British, American, and Canadian Propaganda and Fiction, 1914–1933*. Vancouver, Canada: University of British Columbia Press, 1987.
Burke, Timothy J. *Lifebuoy Men, Lux Women: Commodification, Consumption and Cleanliness in Modern Zimbabwe*. London: Continuum, 1996.
Burnard, Trevor. "Slave Naming Patterns: Onomastics and the Taxonomy of Race in Eighteenth-Century Jamaica." *Journal of Interdisciplinary History* 31, no. 3 (2001): 325–46.
Burns, Catherine. "The Letters of Louisa Mvemve." In *Africa's Hidden Histories: Everyday Literacy and Making the Self*, edited by Karin Barber, 78–112. Bloomington: Indiana University Press, 2006.
Burton, Antoinette. *At the Heart of the Empire: Indians and the Colonial Encounter in Late-Victorian Britain*. Berkeley: University of California Press, 1998.
——— . *Dwelling in the Archive: Women Writing House, Home, and History in Late Colonial India*. Oxford: Oxford University Press, 2003.
——— , ed. *Gender, Sexuality, and Colonial Modernities*. New York: Routledge, 1999.
Calvert, Albert F. *The Cameroons*. London: T. Werner Laurie, 1917.
Cammaerts, Bart. *Internet-Mediated Participation beyond the Nation State*. Manchester, UK: Manchester University Press, 2008.
——— . "Protest Logics and the Mediation Opportunity Structure." *European Journal of Communication* 27, no. 2 (2012): 117–34.
Caretta, Vincent. *Equiano the African: Biography of a Self-Made Man*. Athens: University of Georgia Press, 2005.
Casely-Hayford, Adelaide. "Mista Courifer." In *An African Treasury*, edited by Langston Hughes, 134–43. London: Victor Gollancz, 1971.
Casely-Hayford, Augustus. "A Genealogical History of Cape Coast Stool Families." PhD diss., School of Oriental and African Studies, University of London, 1992.

Casely-Hayford, Joseph E. *Ethiopia Unbound: Studies in Race Emancipation*. 1911. Reprint, London: Frank Cass, 1966.

——. *Gold Coast Native Institutions: With Thoughts upon a Healthy Imperial Policy for the Gold Coast and Ashanti*. London: Sweet and Maxwell, 1903.

Chambers, Douglas. "'Almost an Englishman': Carretta's Equiano." *H-Atlantic* (November 2007), www.h-net.org/natlantic (accessed 15 September 2011).

Chanock, Martin. *The Making of South African Legal Culture, 1902–1936: Fear, Favour and Prejudice*. Cambridge: Cambridge University Press, 2001.

Chartier, Roger. *The Order of Books: Readers, Authors, and Libraries in Europe between the Fourteenth and Eighteenth Centuries*. Cambridge: Polity Press, 1994.

Ciuraru, Carmela. *Nom de Plume: A (Secret) History of Pseudonyms*. New York: HarperCollins, 2011.

Clarence-Smith, William Gervase. "Plantation versus Smallholder Production of Cocoa: The Legacy of the German Period in Cameroon." In *Itinéraires d'accumulation au Cameroun*, edited by Peter Geschiere and Piet Konings, 187–216. Paris: Karthala, 1993.

Clifford, Lady Elizabeth Lydia Rosabelle (Elizabeth Lydia Rosabelle de la Pasture). *Our Days on the Gold Coast, in Ashanti, in the Northern Territories, and in the British Sphere of Occupation in Togoland*. Accra: Government Printing Office, in Aid of the Red Cross, 1918.

Comaroff, Jean, and John Comaroff. "On Personhood: An Anthropological Perspective from Africa." *Social Identities* 7, no. 2 (2001): 267–83.

Conklin, Alice L. *A Mission to Civilize: The Republican Idea of Empire in France and West Africa, 1895–1930*. Stanford, CA: Stanford University Press, 1997.

Cooper, Frederick. *Colonialism in Question: Theory, Knowledge, History*. Berkeley: University of California Press, 2005.

Crowder, Michael. "Indirect Rule—French and British Style." *Africa* 34, no. 3 (1964): 197–205.

Cunard, Nancy. *Negro: An Anthology*. London: Wishart, 1934.

Currey, James. *Africa Writes Back: The African Writers Series and the Launch of African Literature*. Woodbridge, UK: Boydell and Brewer, 2008.

Dabydeen, David. "Review of *Equiano the African: Biography of a Self-Made Man*." *Guardian*, 3 December 2005. Available at http://www.guardian.co.uk/books/2005/dec/03/featuresreviews.guardianreview3 (accessed 15 September 2011).

Dane, Edmund. *British Campaigns in Africa and the Pacific*. London: Hodder and Stoughton, 1919.

Darnton, Robert. "Literary Surveillance in the British Raj: The Contradictions of British Imperialism." *Book History* 4 (2001): 133–76.

Davis, Caroline. "The Politics of Postcolonial Publishing: Oxford University Press's Three Crowns Series 1962–1976." *Book History* 8 (2005): 227–44.

Davis, Lennard J. *Factual Fictions: The Origins of the English Novel*. 1983. Reprint, Philadelphia: University of Pennsylvania Press, 1997.

de Certeau, Michel. *The Practice of Everyday Life.* 1984. Reprint, Berkeley: University of California Press, 2002.

Denzer, LaRay. "Wallace-Johnson and the Sierra Leone Labor Crisis of 1939." *African Studies Review* 25, no. 2–3 (June–September 1982): 159–83.

———. "Yoruba Women: A Historiographical Study." *International Journal of African Historical Studies* 27, no. 1 (1994): 1–39.

Dixon-Fyle, Mac, and Gibril Cole, eds. *New Perspectives on the Sierra Leone Krio.* New York: Peter Lang, 2006.

Dove, Mabel. *Selected Writings of a Pioneer West African Feminist.* Edited by Stephanie Newell and Audrey Gadzekpo. Nottingham, UK: Trend Editions, 2004.

DuBois, W. E. B. *The Souls of Black Folk.* 1930. Reprint, New York: Signet Classics, 1969.

Duffield, Ian. "The Business Activities of Duse Mohamed Ali: An Example of the Economic Dimension of Pan-Africanism." *Journal of the Historical Society of Nigeria* 4, no. 4 (June 1969): 571–600.

———. "John Eldred Taylor and West African Opposition to Indirect Rule in Nigeria." *African Affairs* 70, no. 280 (1971): 255–65.

Ekpebu, L. B. *Zik of Africa: God's Special Gift to Nigeria, Africa and the World.* Ibadan, Nigeria: Sam Bookman, 1998.

Fanon, Frantz. *Black Skin, White Masks.* 1968. Reprint, London: Pluto Press, 1991.

Finnegan, Ruth. *Literacy and Orality: Studies in the Technology of Communication.* Oxford: Basil Blackwell, 1988.

———. *Why Do We Quote? The Culture and History of Quotation.* Cambridge: Open Book Publishers, 2011.

Fitzgerald, F. Scott. *My Lost City: Personal Essays, 1920–1940,* vol. 4. 1931. Reprint, Cambridge: Cambridge University Press, 2005.

Fleming, Tyler, and Toyin Falola. "Africa's Media Empire: *Drum's* Expansion to Nigeria." *History in Africa* 32 (2005): 133–64.

Foucault, Michel. "Politics and the Study of Discourse." In *The Foucault Effect: Studies in Governmentality,* edited by Graham Burchell, Colin Gordon, and Peter Miller, 53–72. London: Harvester, 1991.

———. "What Is an Author?" In *Language, Counter-Memory, Practice,* edited by Donald F. Bouchard, 124–27. 1969. Reprint, Ithaca, NY: Cornell University Press, 1977.

———. *The Will to Knowledge: The History of Sexuality,* vol. 1. 1976. Reprint, London: Penguin, 1998.

Fraser, Nancy. "Rethinking the Public Sphere: A Contribution to the Critique of Actually Existing Democracy." In *Habermas and the Public Sphere,* edited by Craig Calhoun, 108–42. Cambridge, MA: MIT Press, 1992.

Fraser, Robert. *Book History through Postcolonial Eyes.* London: Routledge, 2008.

Fraser, Robert, and Mary Hammond. *Books without Borders,* vols. 1 and 2. Houndmills, UK: Palgrave Macmillan, 2009.

Frimpong, Joseph. "'Better Ghana [Agenda]'? *Akosua's* Political Cartoons and Critical Public Debates in Contemporary Ghana." In *Popular Culture in*

Africa: The Episteme of the Everyday, edited by S. Newell and O. Okome. New York: Routledge, forthcoming 2013.
Furniss, Graham. Orality: The Power of the Spoken Word. Basingstoke, UK: Palgrave Macmillan, 2004.
Furniss, Graham, and Liz Gunner. Power, Marginality and African Oral Literature. Cambridge: Cambridge University Press, 1995.
Gadzekpo, Audrey. "Public but Private: A Transformational Reading of the Memoirs and Newspaper Writings of Mercy Ffoulkes-Crabbe." In Africa's Hidden Histories: Everyday Literacy and Making the Self, edited by Karin Barber, 314–37. Bloomington: Indiana University Press, 2006.
Gates, Henry Louis. "The 'Blackness of Blackness': A Critique of the Sign and the Signifying Monkey." Critical Inquiry 9, no. 4 (1983): 685–723.
———. The Signifying Monkey: A Theory of Afro-American Literary Criticism. New York: Oxford University Press, 1988.
Geschiere, Peter. The Modernity of Witchcraft: Politics and the Occult in Postcolonial Africa. Charlottesville: University of Virginia Press, 1997.
Gikandi, Simon. "Cultural Translation and the African Self: A (Post)colonial Case Study." Interventions: A Journal of Postcolonial Culture 3, no. 3 (2001): 355–75.
Gilson, Charles. Across the Cameroons: A Story of War and Adventure. London: Blackie and Son, 1916.
Gocking, Roger. "Competing Systems of Inheritance before the British Courts of the Gold Coast Colony." International Journal of African Historical Studies 23, no. 4 (1990): 601–18.
———. Facing Two Ways: Ghana's Coastal Communities under Colonial Rule. Lanham, MD: University Press of America, 1999.
Gold Coast Government. "Criminal Code (Amendment) Ordinance." Gold Coast Government Extraordinary Gazette, 21 February 1934.
Gorges, E. Howard. The Great War in West Africa. London: Hutchinson, 1916.
Griffin, Robert J. "Anonymity and Authorship." New Literary History 30, no. 4 (1999): 877–95.
———, ed. The Faces of Anonymity: Anonymous and Pseudonymous Publication from the Sixteenth to the Twentieth Century. Basingstoke, UK: Palgrave Macmillan, 2003.
Griffiths, Gareth, and John Victor Singler, eds. "Introduction." In Guanya Pau by Joseph J. Walters, 9–63. Ontario, Canada: Broadview Editions, 2004.
Griswold, Wendy. Bearing Witness: Readers, Writers, and the Novel in Nigeria. Princeton, NJ: Princeton University Press, 2000.
Guyer, Jane, ed. Money Matters: Instability, Values and Social Payments. Oxford: Heinemann Educational Books, 1994.
Habermas, Jürgen. "The Public Sphere: An Encyclopaedia Article (1964)." New German Critique 1, no. 3 (1974): 49–55.
Hagen, James M. "'Read All about It!': The Press and the Rise of National Consciousness in Early Twentieth Century Dutch East Indies Society." Anthropological Quarterly 70, no. 3 (1997): 107–26.

Hall, Catherine. *Civilising Subjects: Metropole and Colony in the English Imagination, 1830–1867*. Cambridge: Polity, 2002.
Hall, Stuart. "On Postmodernism and Articulation: An Interview with Stuart Hall edited by Lawrence Grossberg." In *Stuart Hall: Critical Dialogues in Cultural Studies*, edited by David Morley and Kuan-Hsing Chen, 131–50. London: Routledge, 1996.
Hartley, John, and Alan McKee. *The Indigenous Public Sphere: The Reporting and Reception of Aboriginal Issues in the Australian Media*. Oxford: Oxford University Press, 2000.
Hastings, Charlotte. "Metropole-Colony in Education Policy for Girls' Education in Colonial Africa, with Particular Reference to Southern Nigeria c. 1925–40." PhD diss., University of Edinburgh, 2011.
Hasty, Jennifer. *The Press and Political Culture in Ghana*. Bloomington: Indiana University Press, 2005.
Heavens, Andrew. "African Bloggers Find Their Voice." *BBC Focus on Africa Magazine*, 20 December 2005. Available at http://news.bbc.co.uk/1/hi/world/africa/4512290.stm, accessed 9 August 2011.
Highmore, Ben. *Everyday Life and Cultural Theory: An Introduction*. London: Routledge, 2001.
Hill, Robert A. *The Marcus Garvey and Universal Negro Improvement Association Papers: Africa for the Africans, 1923–45*. Berkeley: University of California Press, 2006.
Hobsbawm, Eric, and Terence Ranger. *The Invention of Tradition*. Cambridge: Cambridge University Press, 1992.
Hooker, James R. *Black Revolutionary: George Padmore's Path from Communism to Pan-Africanism*. New York: Frederick A. Praeger, 1967.
Huggan, Graham. *The Postcolonial Exotic: Marketing the Margins*. London: Routledge, 2001.
Hunter, Yema Lucilda. *An African Treasure: In Search of Gladys Casely-Hayford, 1904–1950*. Accra: Yema Lucilda Hunter, 2008.
Hyslop, Jonathan. "On Biography: A Response to Ciraj Rasool." *South African Sociological Review* 41, no. 2 (June 2010): 104–15.
Igwe, Agbafor. *Zik: The Philosopher of Our Time*. Enugu, Nigeria: Fourth Dimension, 1992.
Improta, Nara. "Producing Intellectuals: Books and Pamphlets in Lagos between 1880 and 1922." PhD diss., University of Sussex, forthcoming 2013.
Jenkins, Raymond. "Gold Coasters Overseas, 1880–1919, wth Specific Reference to Their Activities in Britain." *Immigrants and Minorities* 4, no. 3 (1985): 5–52.
——. "Gold Coast Historians and Their Pursuit of the Gold Coast Pasts: 1882–1917." PhD diss., Centre of West African Studies, University of Birmingham, 1985.
Jolly, Margaretta. *In Love and Struggle: Letters in Contemporary Feminism*. New York: Columbia University Press, 2008.
Jones, Jeffrey P. "A Cultural Approach to the Study of Mediated Citizenship." *Social Semiotics* 16, no. 2 (2007): 365–83.

Jones-Quartey, K. A. B. "The Gold Coast Press, 1822–c. 1930: The Chronologies." *Research Review (Institute of African Studies)* 4, no. 2 (1968): 30–46.
———. *History, Politics and Early Press in Ghana: The Fictions and the Facts.* Legon: University of Ghana, 1975.
———. "Press and Nationalism in Ghana." *United Asia* 9, no. 1 (1957): 55–60.
———. *A Summary History of the Ghana Press, 1822–1960.* Accra-Tema: Ghana Publishing, 1974.
Julien, Eileen. *African Novels and the Question of Orality.* Bloomington: Indiana University Press, 1992.
Killingray, David. *The British Military Presence in West Africa.* Oxford: Rhodes House Library, 1983.
———. "Labour Mobilisation in British Colonial Africa for the War Effort, 1939–46." In *Africa and the Second World War*, edited by David Killingray and Richard Rathbone, 68–96. Basingstoke, UK: Macmillan, 1986.
———. "Military and Labour Policies in the Gold Coast during the First World War." In *Africa and the First World War*, edited by Melvin Page, 152–70. Basingstoke, UK: Macmillan, 1987.
Kimble, David. *A Political History of Ghana: The Rise of Gold Coast Nationalism, 1850–1928.* Oxford: Clarendon Press, 1963.
Kimmel, Michael S., and Jeff Hearn, eds. *Handbook of Studies on Men and Masculinity.* London: Sage, 2005.
Kipling, Rudyard. *Kim.* 1901. Reprint, Oxford: Oxford World's Classics, 1987.
Korang, Kweku Larbi. *Writing Ghana, Imagining Africa: Nation and African Modernity.* Rochester, NY: University of Rochester Press, 2004.
Landes, Joan B. *Women and the Public Sphere in the Age of the French Revolution.* Ithaca, NY: Cornell University Press, 1988.
Lawrance, Benjamin, Emily L. Osborn, and Richard L. Roberts. *Intermediaries, Interpreters, and Clerks: African Employees in the Making of Colonial Africa.* Madison: University of Wisconsin Press, 2006.
Leavis, Q. D. *Fiction and the Reading Public.* Middlesex, UK: Penguin Books, 1932.
Lester, Alan. "British Settler Discourse and the Circuits of Empire." *History Workshop Journal* 54, no. 1 (2002): 27–50.
Levine, Philippa, ed. *Gender and Empire.* Oxford: Oxford University Press, 2004.
LeVine, Victor T. *The Cameroons: From Mandate to Independence.* Berkeley: University of California Press, 1964.
———. *Politics in Francophone Africa.* Boulder, Colo.: Lynne Rienner, 2004.
Lewin, Julius. "Some Legal Consequences of Marriage by Native Christians in British Africa." *Modern Law Review* (June 1939): 48–52.
Lewis, Rupert, and Baptiste Fitzroy, eds. *George Padmore: A Pan-African Revolutionary.* Kingston, Jamaica: Ian Randle, 2008.
Likaka, Osumaka. *Naming Colonialism: History and Collective Memory in the Congo, 1870–1960.* Madison: University of Wisconsin Press, 2009.
Little, Kenneth. *West African Urbanization: A Study of Voluntary Associations in Social Change.* Cambridge: Cambridge University Press, 1965.

Lucas, Charles. *The Empire at War*, vol. 4. Oxford: Oxford University Press, 1924.

Lunn, Joe H. "Kande Kamara Speaks: An Oral History of the West African Experience in France, 1914–1918." In *Africa and the First World War*, edited by Melvin Page, 28–53. Basingstoke, UK: Macmillan, 1987.

——. *Memoirs of the Maelstrom: A Senegalese Oral History of the First World War*. Portsmouth, NH: Heinemann, 1999.

Lynn, Thomas J. "Tricksters Don't Walk the Dogma: Nkem Nwankwo's Danda." *College Literature* 32, no. 3 (2005): 1–20.

Macmillan, Allister. *The Red Book of West Africa*. London: Collingridge, 1920.

Makoni, Busi, Sinfree Makoni, and Pedzisai Mashiri. "Naming Practices and Language Planning in Zimbabwe." *Current Issues in Language Planning* 8, no. 3 (2007): 437–67.

Mann, Kristin. *Marrying Well: Marriage, Status and Social Change among the Educated Elite in Colonial Lagos*. Cambridge: Cambridge University Press, 1985.

Mbembe, Achille. *On the Postcolony*. Berkeley: University of California Press, 2001.

McCarthy, Thomas. "Introduction." In *The Structural Transformation of the Public Sphere*, by Jurgen Habermas, xi–xiv. Cambridge: Polity Press, 1989.

McCleary, Alistair, and Benjamin A. Brabon. *The Influence of Benedict Anderson*. Edinburgh: Merchiston Publishing, 2007.

McClintock, Anne. *Imperial Leather: Race, Gender and Sexuality in the Colonial Contest*. London: Routledge, 1995.

Mensah, Marjorie. *Us Women: Extracts from the Writings of Marjorie Mensah*, edited by Kathleen Hewitt. London: Mathews and Marrot, 1933.

Middleton, Richard. *Studying Popular Music*. 1990. Reprint, Philadelphia: Open University Press, 2002.

Miescher, Stephan F. "'My Own Life': A. K. Boakye Yiadom's Autobiography—The Writing and Subjectivity of a Ghanaian Teacher-Catechist." In *Africa's Hidden Histories: Everyday Literacy and Making the Self*, edited by Karin Barber, 27–51. Bloomington: Indiana University Press, 2006.

Mouffe, Chantal. *On the Political: Thinking in Action*. London: Routledge, 2005.

Mullan, John. *Anonymity: A Secret History of English Literature*. London: Faber and Faber, 2007.

Mullen, John G. "My Experience in Cameroons during the War." *Gold Coast Leader*, 14 October 1916–8 December 1917.

——. "My Sojourn in the Cameroons during the Peaceful Days: Half Hour's Talk with Billy." *Gold Coast Leader*, 25 January–12 April 1919.

Muluh, Henry, and Bertha Ndoh. "Evolution of the Media in Cameroon." In *Journalism and Mass Communication in Africa: Cameroon*, edited by Festus Eribo and Enoh Tanjong, 4–16. Lanham, MD: Lexington Books, 2002.

Murillo, Bianca. "Commercial Space, Consumer Politics, and Establishment of Kingsway Department Stores in Accra." Paper presented at the Tuning In to African Cities: Popular Culture and Urban Experience in Sub-Saharan Africa Conference. Centre of West African Studies, University of Birmingham, 6–8 May 2010.

Mwangi, Evan Maina. *Africa Writes Back to Self.* Albany, NY: SUNY Press, 2009.
Newell, Stephanie. "Dirty Whites: 'Ruffian-Writing' in Colonial West Africa." *Research in African Literatures* 39, no. 4 (2008): 1–13.
———. *The Forger's Tale: The Search for Odeziaku.* Athens: Ohio University Press, 2006.
———. "Introduction." In *Marita; or The Folly of Love: A Novel,* by "A Native" (pseud.), 1–37. Leiden, the Netherlands: Brill, 2002.
———. *Literary Culture in Colonial Ghana: "How to Play the Game of Life."* Manchester, UK: Manchester University Press, 2002.
———, ed. *Writing African Women: Gender, Popular Culture and Literature in West Africa.* London: Zed Books, 1997.
Ngugi wa Thiong'o. *Decolonising the Mind: The Politics of Language in African Literature.* Oxford: James Currey, 1986.
———. *Devil on the Cross.* 1980. Reprint, London: Heinemann, 1987.
Nortey, Kobina. *Britain's Future in the Gold Coast.* Glasgow, Scotland: Civic Press, 1954.
———. *The Responsibility of Africans as a Race.* Glasgow, Scotland: William MacLellan, 1957.
North, Marcy L. *The Anonymous Renaissance: Cultures of Discretion in Tudor-Stuart England.* Chicago: University of Chicago Press, 2003.
Nwapa, Flora. *Efuru.* London: Heinemann, 1966.
Nwokeji, G. Ugo. "Equiano the African: Biography of a Self-Made Man." *Journal of American History* 93, no. 3 (2006): 840–41.
Nyamnjoh, Francis B. *Africa's Media: Democracy and the Politics of Belonging.* London: Zed Books, 2005.
Obeyesekere, Gananath. *Cannibal Talk: The Man-Eating Myth and Human Sacrifice in the South Seas.* Berkeley: University of California Press, 2005.
Ofusu-Appiah, L. H., ed. *The Encyclopaedia Africana Dictionary of African Biography,* vol. 1, *Ethiopia-Ghana.* New York: Reference Publications, 1977. Available at http://www.dacb.org/stories/ghana/attoh_ahuma_s.html (accessed on 1 February 2012).
Ogbondah, Chris W. "British Colonial Authoritarianism, African Military Dictatorship and the Nigerian Press." *Africa Media Review* 6, no. 3 (1992): 1–18.
Ojo-Ade, Femi. "Female Writers, Male Critics." *African Literature Today* 13 (1983): 158–79.
Okri, Ben. *The Famished Road.* London: Vintage, 1991.
Omu, Fred I. A. *Press and Politics in Nigeria, 1880–1937.* Atlantic Highlands, NJ: Humanities Press, 1978.
Opoku-Agyemang, Naana J. "Gender-Role Perceptions in the Akan Folktale." *Research in African Literatures* 30, no. 1 (1999): 116–39.
———. "Recovering Lost Voices: The Short Stories of Mabel Dove-Danquah." In *Writing African Women: Gender, Popular Culture and Literature in West Africa,* edited by Stephanie Newell, 67–80. London: Zed Books, 1997.
Owomoyela, Oyekan. "Foreword." In *Guanya Pau: A Story of an African Princess,* by Joseph J. Walters, ix–xxiv. Lincoln: University of Nebraska Press, 1994.

Padmore, George A. *The Memoirs of a Liberian Ambassador*. Lewiston, NY: Edwin Mellen, 1966.
Page, Melvin E. "Black Men in a White Men's War." In *Africa and the First World War*, edited by Melvin E. Page, 1–27. Basingstoke, UK: Macmillan, 1987.
Pelton, Robert. *The Trickster in West Africa: A Study of Mythic Irony and Sacred Delight*. Berkeley: University of California Press, 1980.
Perret, Thierry. *Le temps des journalists: L'invension de la presse en Afrique francophone*. Paris: Karthala, 2005.
Peterson, Derek R. *Ethnic Patriotism and the East African Revival: A History of Dissent, c. 1935–1972*. Cambridge: Cambridge University Press, 2012.
Prais, Jinny Kathleen. "Imperial Travelers: The Formation of West African Urban Culture, Identity, and Citizenship in London and Accra, 1925–1935." PhD diss., University of Michigan, 2008.
Priestley, Margaret. *West African Trade and Coast Society: A Family Study*. London: Oxford University Press, 1969.
Procter, James. *Stuart Hall*. London: Routledge, 2004.
Rattray, Robert S. *Akan-Ashanti Folktales*. Oxford: Clarendon Press, 1930.
———. "Some Aspects of West African Folk-Lore." *African Affairs: Journal of the African Historical Society* 28, no. 103 (1928): 1–11.
Richards, Thomas. *The Imperial Archive: Knowledge and the Fantasy of Empire*. London: Verso, 1993.
Robb, George. *British Culture and the First World War*. Basingstoke, UK: Palgrave, 2002.
Roberts-Wray, Kenneth. *Commonwealth and Colonial Law*. London: Sage Publications, 1967.
Rosenmeyer, Patricia A. *Ancient Epistolary Fictions: The Letter in Greek Literature*. Cambridge: Cambridge University Press, 2001.
Rudin, Harry R. *Germans in the Cameroons, 1884–1914: A Case Study in Modern Imperialism*. London: Jonathan Cape, 1938.
Sackey, Edward. "Oral Tradition and the African Novel." *MFS Modern Fiction Studies* 37, no. 3 (1991): 389–407.
Said, Edward. *Orientalism*. 1978. Reprint, London: Penguin, 2003.
Sampson, Magnus J. *Gold Coast Men of Affairs: Past and Present*. London: A. H. Stockwell, 1937.
Sarbah, John Mensah. *Fanti Customary Laws*. London: William Clowes and Sons, 1897.
Şaul, Mahir, and Patrick Royer. *West African Challenge to Empire: Culture and History in the Volta-Bani Anticolonial War*. Athens: Ohio University Press, 2001.
Sekyi, Kobina. *The Blinkards*. 1915. Reprint, Ibadan, Nigeria: Heinemann, 1974.
Seth, Sanjay. *Subject Lessons: The Western Education of Colonial India*. Durham, NC: Duke University Press, 2007.
Shaloff, Stanley. "The Income Tax, Indirect Rule, and the Depression: The Gold Coast Riots of 1931." *Cahiers d'études africaines* 14, no. 54 (1974): 359–75.
———. "Press Controls and Sedition Proceedings in the Gold Coast, 1933–39." *African Affairs* 71, no. 284 (1972): 241–63.

Shipley, Jesse Weaver. *Living the Hiplife: Celebrity and Entrepreneurship in Ghanaian Popular Music*. Durham, NC: Duke University Press, 2013.
Showalter, Elaine. "Feminist Criticism in the Wilderness." *Critical Inquiry* 8, no. 2 (1981): 179–205.
———. *A Literature of Their Own: British Women Novelists from Bronte to Lessing*. Princeton, NJ: Princeton University Press, 1977.
———. *The New Feminist Criticism: Essays on Women, Literature, and Theory*. New York: Pantheon Books, 1985.
———. "Toward a Feminist Poetics." In *The Critical Tradition: Classic Texts and Contemporary Trends*, edited by David H. Richter, 1375–86. 1979. Reprint, London: St. Martin's Press, 1998.
Sinha, Mrinalini. "Britishness, Clubbability, and the Colonial Public Sphere: The Genealogy of an Imperial Institution in Colonial India." *Journal of British Studies* 40, no. 4 (October 2001): 489–521.
Skinner, Kate. "'You Cannot Ask Someone to Read a Newspaper For You': Quotation and Scrutiny in an Ewe-Language Newspaper 1959–65." Paper presented at the Print Cultures Workshop. Oxford University, April 2012.
Sklar, Richard L. *Nigerian Political Parties: Power in an Emergent Nation*. Trenton, NJ: African World Press, 2004.
Spitzer, Leo, and LaRay Denzer. "I. T. A. Wallace-Johnson and the West African Youth League, [Part 1]." *International Journal of African Historical Studies* 6, no. 3 (1973): 413–52.
———. "I. T. A. Wallace-Johnson and the West African Youth League, Part 2: The Sierra Leone Period, 1938–1945." *International Journal of African Historical Studies* 6, no. 4 (1973): 565–601.
Spivak, Gayatri. "Can the Subaltern Speak?" In *Marxism and the Interpretation of Culture*, edited by Cary Nelson and Lawrence Grossberg, 271–313. Champaign: University of Illinois Press, 1988.
Stockwell, A. J. "The War and the British Empire." In *Britain and the First World War*, edited by John Turner, 36–52. London: Unwin Hyman, 1988.
Stoler, Ann Laura. *Carnal Knowledge and Imperial Power: Race and the Intimate in Colonial Rule*. Berkeley: University of California Press, 2002.
Strachan, Hew. *The First World War in Africa*. Oxford: Oxford University Press, 2004.
Stratton, Florence. *Contemporary African Literature and the Politics of Gender*. London: Routledge, 1994.
Sunderland, David. "The Departmental System of Railway Construction in British West Africa, 1895–1906." *Journal of Transport History* 23, no. 2 (2002): 87–112.
Sutherland, Efua. *Marriage of Anansewa: A Storytelling Drama*. 1975. Reprint, Harlow, UK: Longman African Classics, 1987.
Tekpetey, Alphonse Kwawisi. "Kweku Ananse: A Psychoanalytical Approach." *Research in African Literatures* 37, no. 2 (2006): 74–82.
Thomas, Lynn M. "The Modern Girl and Racial Respectability in 1930s South Africa." *Journal of African History* 47 (2006): 461–90.

Thompson, John B. "The New Visibility." *Theory, Culture and Society* 22, no. 6 (2005): 35–51.
Tijani, H. I. "Britain and the Foundation of Anti-communist Policies in Nigeria, 1945–1960." *African and Asian Studies* 8 (2009): 47–66.
———. "Britain, Leftist Nationalists and the Transfer of Power in Nigeria, 1945–1965." New York: Routledge, 2005.
———. "Communists and the Nationalist Movement." In *Nigeria in the Twentieth Century*, edited by Toyin Falola, 293–312. Durham: University of North Carolina Press, 2002.
Tutuola, Amos. *The Palm-Wine Drinkard*. London: Faber and Faber, 1952.
Tymms, T. Vincent. *The Cameroons (West Africa): A Historical Review*. London: Carey Press, 1915.
Vail, Leroy, and Landeg White. *Power and the Praise Poem: Southern African Voices in History*. Oxford: James Currey, 1992.
Van den Bersselaar, Dmitri. "Debating Igbo Culture—The Colonial Tradition." Available at pcwww.liv.ac.uk/~dvdb/CH_6.pdf, 188, accessed 3 February 2011.
Wahl-Jorgensen, Karin, ed. *Mediated Citizenship*. London: Routledge, 2007.
Wallace-Johnson, I. T. A. *A Series of Writings by Isaac T. A. Wallace Johnson*. Freetown: Sierra Leone National Service Bureau, 1963.
Walters, Joseph J. *Guanya Pau*. Edited and introduced by Gareth Griffiths and John Victor Singler. Calgary, Canada: Broadview Press, 2004.
Warner, Michael. *The Letters of the Republic: Publication and the Public Sphere in Eighteenth-Century America*. Cambridge, MA: Harvard University Press, 1992.
———. "Publics and Counterpublics." *Public Culture* 14, no. 1 (2002): 49–90.
Weinbaum, Alys Eve, Lynn M. Thomas, Priti Ramamurthy, Uta G. Poiger, Madeleine Y. Dong, and Tani E. Barlow, eds. *The Modern Girl around the World: Consumption, Modernity, and Globalization*. Durham, NC: Duke University Press, 2008.
Weir, Stephen. *History's Worst Decisions: And the People Who Made Them*. New York: Eye Quarto, 2005.
White, Bob W. "Modernity's Trickster: 'Dipping' and 'Throwing' in Congolese Popular Dance Music." *Research in African Literatures* 30, no. 4 (1999): 156–75.
White, Luise, Stephan Miescher, and David Cohen, eds. *African Words, African Voices: Critical Practices in Oral History*. Bloomington: Indiana University Press, 2002.
Woods, Dwayne. "Civil Society in Europe and Africa: Limiting State Power through a Public Sphere." *African Studies Review* 35, no. 2 (1992): 77–100.
Woollacott, Angela. *Gender and Empire*. Basingstoke, UK: Palgrave Macmillan, 2006.
Wrangham, Elizabeth. "The Gold Coast and the First World War: The Colonial Economy and Clifford's Administration." PhD diss., School of Oriental and African Studies, University of London, 1999.

Wyse, Akintola. *The Krio of Sierra Leone: An Interpretive History.* London: Hurst and International African Institute, 1989.
Yankah, Kwesi. "African Folk and the Challenges of a Global Lore." *Africa Today* 46, no. 2 (1999): 9–27.
———. *Free Speech in Traditional Society: The Cultural Foundations of Communication in Contemporary Ghana.* Accra: Ghana Universities Press, 1998.
Zabel, Shirley. "Legislative History of the Gold Coast and Lagos Marriage Ordinance: 3." *Journal of African Law* 23, no. 1 (1979): 10–36.
Zachernuk, Philip S. *Colonial Subjects: An African Intelligentsia and Atlantic Ideas.* Charlottesville: University of Virginia Press, 2000.

Index

Note: Where the identity of pseudonymous authors is known, readers are redirected to the author entry; where a pseudonym is used by multiple authors (as in the case of "Marjorie Mensah") or where an author's identity is not known, page references are given for the pseudonym.

Abacha, Gen. Sani, 177
Abang dance, 156
"A Banker" (pseud.), 7, 175
Aborigines Rights Protection Society (ARPS), 23, 81, 106–7
Abrahams, Sir Sydney S., 10, 11
"Abue" (pseud.), 110–11
Accra (Ghana), 44, 75
Accra Evening News (Accra), 160
Achebe, Chinua, 102, 103
Achimota School, 77
African Morning Post (Accra), 17, 42, 74–75, 76, 81, 82–83, 85, 120, 160
African Standard (Freetown), 93
African Workers' Union of West Africa (Nigeria), 88, 209n42
African Writers' Series (Heinemann), 138
Afrobeat, 179
Afrocentrism, 8
"A Gold Coast Native" (pseud.), 9
Ajasa, Kitoyi, 50
Akede Eko, 15, 35, 137, 139–43, 148, 149, 162
"Akosuah Dzatsui" (pseud.). See Dove-Danquah, Mabel
"Akpan James" (pseud.). See Clinton, J. V.
Ali, Duse Mohamed. See Mohamed, Duse
Althusser, Louis, 97
"A Man about Town" (pseud.), 7
Amery, Leo, 68
Ampiah, Nellie, 124
Anaman, Rev. Jacob Benjamin, 13
Ananse Spider (or Anansi), 102–3, 106–7, 109, 110, 111, 114
"A Native" (pseud.), 130, 132, 133, 137, 145
Anderson, Benedict, 44, 48, 59, 141
Anderson, Ebenezer J., 110
"A Negro" (pseud.), 7
"An Exile" (pseud.), 162
Anikulapo-Kuti, Fela, 177
anticolonialism, 8, 16, 35, 43, 49, 61, 67–69, 72–76, 79, 81–82, 85, 86, 92–94, 110, 150, 151, 170, 173, 181

"Anwan Eyen Efik" (pseud.). See Clinton, J. V.
"Aquah Laluah" (pseud.). See Casely-Hayford, G. M.
"A Reader" (pseud.), 7
Arthur Stockwell Publishers, 152
Asante, 115
Association of Indigenous Senior Officers of the Nigerian Railway Corporation, 101
associations, 36–9, 58, 95, 127, 161, 200n26
"Atari Ajanaku" (pseud.), 180
"Atoo" (pseud., also "Attoo" and "Atu"), 22, 23, 30
"A Traveller" (pseud.), 175
Attoh-Ahuma, Rev. Samuel Richard Brew, 18, 23, 128, 197n66
Awobiyi, E. M., 180
Awosanmi, Tunde, 179–80
Ayoola, Tokunbo A., 101
"A Youngman" (pseud.), 7, 114
Azikiwe, Benjamin Nnamdi, 9, 10, 11, 16, 40, 42, 43, 48, 60, 74–75, 81, 82, 84–86, 94–97, 119, 150, 170, 175, 177, 197n71
Azu, Regina, 30

Baker, Amy, 49
Bamford, Henry William, 67–68
"Banker, A" (pseud.), 7, 175
Barber, Karin, 34, 35, 60, 61, 140, 143, 146, 225n84
Barthes, Roland, 173–74, 175, 176
"Bashful" (pseud.), 7
Bates, H. C. M., 96
Behn, Aphra, 3, 194n15
Beoku-Betts, E. S., 92
Bermuda, 69
Bhabha, Homi, 106
Bhattacharya, Neeladri, 35, 36
Bible, 22, 24, 91, 111, 118–19, 214n115
biography, 5, 20, 133, 143, 159, 169, 171–72, 174, 176, 198n74
Blackall, Henry William Butler, 73, 74
Black Atlantic, 4

249

Blackie and Son Publishers, 151
Blyden, Edward Wilmot, 115
Boer, 45
Booker Prize, 120
"Bored" (pseud.), 7
Bourdillon, Sir Bernard, 11, 95–96
bourgeoisie, 29, 33, 35, 36, 37, 38, 43, 90, 112, 126, 127, 131
Brew, James Hutton, 118–19
Bridgeman, Reginald, 88
Bright, Herbert Bankole, 88
British Empire, 5, 35, 37, 40, 44, 49, 50, 73, 80–81, 86, 126, 180
British Guiana, 69
British Institute of Fiction Writing Science Ltd., 152–53, 157
Britishness, 36, 37
British West Africa, 1, 2, 12, 21, 35, 70 , 71, 77, 81, 107, 127, 129, 150
Brockway, Fenner, 69
Busum, James A., 32, 33

Callow, Capt. Graham, 88
Cameroon, 6, 194n24
Cape Coast (Ghana), 10, 33, 46, 49, 53, 58, 81, 110, 116, 124, 162
Caribbean, 21, 150
Carretta, Vincent, 171–72
Casely-Hayford, Gladys May, 160
Casely-Hayford, J. E., 40, 107, 108. 128
Catholic Girls' School (Cape Coast), 124
celebrity, 16, 17, 61, 92, 93, 94, 96, 97, 140, 150, 164, 166, 175, 180, 230n25
censorship, press, 10, 11, 12, 31, 65–66, 68–70, 74, 143
Chartier, Roger, 6
Chatterjee, Partha, 48
chieftaincy, 36, 38, 55, 103, 107, 128, 139
Christianity, 21, 36, 40, 41, 44, 48, 52, 110, 113, 114–15, 116, 119, 125–30, 132, 139, 148, 153, 157, 166, 194n17
cinema, 68, 74, 126
citizenship, 38, 40, 81
Ciuraru, Carmela, 3, 4
civil servants, 31, 41, 70, 72, 137, 151
civil society, 29, 34, 40
class, 7, 29, 33, 37, 38, 46, 47, 51, 61, 126, 131, 134, 152, 161, 162, 167–68, 177
"Cleopatra (A Local)" (pseud.), 162
Clifford, Lady Elizabeth Lydia Rosabelle, 122, 124–26, 128, 136, 139, 168, 219n1, 220n7
Clinton, Charles William, 150
Clinton, James Clark, 150
Clinton, James Vivian, 15, 45, 136, 137–38, 150–57, 158, 225n103, 226n114
clubs. *See* associations
Coker, Rev. R. A., 4
Cold War, 12, 65, 68

Colonial Office (London), 10, 11, 12, 61, 65–70, 72–73, 76–78, 80, 81, 83, 87, 88, 94, 97, 196n45, 201–2n65, 208n17
colonial officials, 30, 31, 42, 49, 51, 61, 68, 72–73, 75, 77, 81, 84, 85
Committee of Citizens on Behalf of the Inhabitants of Sierra Leone (Colony and Protectorate), 45
Communism, 48, 61, 67, 72, 74, 75, 77, 79, 82, 87, 88
Concert Party (Ghana), 133
Congo, 21, 104
Coomah, Cudjoe, 106
Cooper, Brenda, 103
Cooper, Frederick, 48
Coussey, James Henley, 164
Cripps, Sir Stafford, 85
"Cudjoe" (pseud.), 106
cultural nationalism, 18, 109, 115, 132, 198n74
Cunliffe-Lister, Sir Philip, 75, 82
Cyprus, 69, 70, 72, 73, 76
"Czar, The" (pseud.), 135

"D. A. L." (pseud.), 145
"Dama Dumas" (pseud.). *See* Dove-Danquah, Mabel
"Dan" (pseud.), 162
Danquah, J. B., 40, 43, 81, 128, 164
Davies, James Bright, 50, 204n26
Davis, Lennard, 112, 146, 147
Deandrea, Pietro, 103
de Certeau, Michel, 105–6
decolonization, 39–40
defamation, 16, 30
de la Pasture, Mrs. Henry. *See* Clifford, Lady E. L. R.
Deniga, Adeoye, 180
diaspora, 44, 140
"Dick Carnis" (pseud.), 7, 145, 174
Dodondawa, Balogun, 146, 147
Dove, Frans, 9, 84–85, 212n86
Dove-Danquah, Mabel, 79, 128, 160, 166, 168, 227n5
"Druboh" (pseud.), 35
Drum (Nigeria), 45, 152

East Africa, 1, 69, 72
Eastern Press Syndicate (Nigeria), 151
"Ebun Alakija" (pseud.). *See* Dove-Danquah, Mabel
editors. *See* newspapers: editors
education, 46, 47, 56, 61, 77, 122, 126, 129, 133, 136, 138–39, 142, 161, 167, 195n39
Edward VII (king), 53
"Effective" (pseud.). *See* Wallace Johnson, I. T. A.
Efik, 156
Egyir-Asaam, Fynn, 13, 196n42

elites, West African, 1, 2, 14–15, 34, 36, 38, 41–43, 44, 49, 56, 69, 71, 80, 95, 115–16, 127, 128–29, 132, 139, 140, 142, 150, 152, 160–62, 167, 197n60; and education, 51, 52–53, 68, 115, 129, 133, 150, 161–62, 166; and intelligentsias, 38, 39, 40, 54, 57, 67, 78; and subelites, 46–47, 114, 128, 131
Enlightenment, the, 32, 35, 38, 74
Equiano, Olaudah, 171, 173
"Erne's Friend" (pseud.), 49, 135, 177, 178
ethnicity, 17, 70, 108, 126, 134, 155, 158, 159
"Eunice Vivian" (pseud.). See Clinton, J. V.
eurocentrism, 37, 38, 53, 132
Ewe, 6, 56
"Exile, An" (pseud.), 162
experimentation, 5, 159, 166, 181
Extraordinary Gazette (Gold Coast), 80

Fanon, Frantz, 170, 171, 173, 175, 178, 181
Fante, 21, 111, 115–16, 119
femininity. *See* gender
fiction, 128–32, 134, 135, 136, 146, 147, 148, 149, 150, 153, 157, 176
Fiddian, Alex, 71, 73, 78, 81, 209n27
Filson, A. H., 14
folklore, 22, 102, 111, 115–16, 118–19, 121
folktales, 22, 57, 102–10, 111, 114, 115–16, 119, 120–21, 129, 181, 217–18n29
Foucault, Michel, 127, 174, 176
Freetown (Sierra Leone), 24, 44, 87, 88, 92, 94, 131, 161, 162

Gadzekpo, Audrey, 160, 161
Gambia, 21, 44, 69
Garvey, Marcus, 75, 94
Gates, Henry Louis, 178–79
gender, 5, 15–16, 21, 35–38, 124–26, 128–31, 133–34, 136, 138, 139, 142, 148, 149–50, 151, 155–7, 158, 159–69, 162–68, 175–76, 177, 178, 199n5, 221n19
generation, 21, 35, 55, 110, 118, 138
genre, 5, 15, 101, 112, 129, 136, 139, 146, 153, 155, 174, 178
George, Hon. C. J., 72
George V (king), 109
Ghana, 32, 33, 38, 40, 44, 65, 67, 69, 71, 72, 73, 74, 75, 76, 79, 82, 86, 102, 106–9, 124–25, 128, 150, 151, 160, 164, 166, 168, 172, 173, 179
Gikandi, Simon, 1
Gikuyu, 113, 120, 176
"Gloria" (pseud.). *See* Papafio, Mercy Quartey
Gold Coast. *See* Ghana
Gold Coast Aborigines (Cape Coast), 114
Gold Coast Echo (Cape Coast), 106, 111, 115
Gold Coast Independent (Accra), 80, 95
Gold Coast Leader (Cape Coast), 10, 13, 23, 30, 31, 32, 34, 35, 45, 49, 51, 52, 53, 55, 59–60, 76, 107, 120, 122, 160, 174, 175

Gold Coast Nation (Cape Coast), 8, 16, 23, 49, 50, 52, 54, 55, 56, 57, 58, 103, 106–7, 108, 109, 114
"Gold Coast Native, A" (pseud.), 9
Gold Coast People (Cape Coast), 54
Gold Coast Spectator (Accra), 75, 76
Gold Coast Times (Cape Coast), 111, 160
Government Girls' School (Accra), 160
Great Depression, 75, 76, 77
Griffin, Robert J., 2, 4
Griffin, W. R., 23
Guggisberg, Sir Frederick Gordon, 68, 75, 77

Habermas, Jürgen, 25, 29, 33, 35–41, 43, 48
Hall, Stuart, 46
Harrison, Samuel, 13, 196n42
Hartley, John and McKee, Alan, 33, 38
"Has the African a God?" 82–86, 88, 172, 178–79
Hasty, Jennifer, 47–48
Head, Bessie, 102
Heinemann Educational Books, 157
Herman-Hodge, H. B., 9
Hewitt, Kathleen, 164, 165
Higham, John D., 67
hiplife, 179, 180
Hobsbawm, Eric, 109
Hodson, Sir Arnold Weinholt, 65, 74, 81–84
Hollywood, 68, 166, 221n19
Hong Kong, 69, 72, 76
House of Commons, 71, 87
Howard University (USA), 74
Huggan, Graham, 155

Ikoli, Ernest, 43
illiteracy, 12, 56, 57, 67, 206n60
imperialism, 36, 66, 76, 133, 172, 173, 179, 181
Independent Labour Party, 45
India, 37, 69, 73, 75
Indirect Rule, 38
International African Service Bureau (London), 45
International League against Imperialism, 76
International Trade Union Committee of Negro Workers, 76
Irele, Abiola, 103

"Jack Never Fear" (pseud.), 58
Jackson, John Payne, 40
Jackson, Thomas, 50
"J. A. G. of Saltpond" (pseud.), 9
Jardine, Sir Douglas, 45, 54, 87
"J. C." (pseud.), 9, 130–32, 133
Jefferson, Thomas, 33, 41
"Jim Crow" (pseud.), 7, 8
Johnson, Hon. Dr. O., 72
Johnson, Scott, 152–55
Johnston, Sir Henry Hamilton (Harry), 49, 204n21
"Jumôkê" (pseud.), 141

"K. A." (pseud.), 14
"K. A. S." (pseud), 9
Kenya, 69, 72, 120, 177
Kenyatta, Jomo, 1
"K. S." (pseud.), 24, 54
Ku Klux Klan, 45
Kumasi, 30, 57–58
Kwaansa, Kobina, 111

"Lagbaja" (pseud.). See Ologunde, Bisade
Lagos (Nigeria), 34, 44, 46, 60, 137, 140, 142, 144, 145, 148, 149, 180
Lagos Standard, 50
Lagos Weekly Record, 40
"Langa Langa" (pseud.). See Herman-Hodge, H. B.
League Against Imperialism, 81, 84, 88
League of Coloured Peoples, 45
legislation, 30, 31, 45, 61, 65–66, 70–73, 78, 83, 93, 97, 109, 126–28, 129, 134, 142, 148–49, 150; Book and Newspaper Registration Ordinance, Gold Coast (1897), 77; Criminal Code, Gold Coast (1902), 49; Criminal Code, Nigeria (World War I), 50; Criminal Code (Amendment) Ordinance, Gold Coast (1934), 32, 76–77, 80–84, 163–64; Forestry Bill, Gold Coast (1911), 109; Marriage Ordinance, Gold Coast (1884), 127–28; Marriage Ordinance, Lagos (1884), 127–28; Ordinance for Regulating the Printing and Publishing of Newspapers, or Newspaper Ordinance (no. 10), Lagos (1903), 32, 71–72, 199n20; Newspaper Registration Ordinance, Gold Coast (1894), 77; Newspapers, Books and Printing Presses Ordinance, Gold Coast (1934), 76, 77, 81; Sedition Bill, Gold Coast (1934) (*see* Criminal Code [Amendment] Ordinance, Gold Coast); Sedition Ordinance, Nigeria (1927), 81; Sedition Ordinance, Sierra Leone (1939), 45; Slander of Women Ordinance (no. 10), Lagos (1900), 126–7; Undesirable Literature Ordinance, Sierra Leone (1939), 45, 202–3n15
legislative councils (British West Africa), 35, 80, 81, 107, 209n33, 215n130
Lester, Alan, 36, 37
libel, 13, 16, 30–31, 49, 50, 68, 71, 74, 88, 105, 107, 142, 199n29
liberalism, 32, 33, 42, 54, 66, 67, 69, 74, 82, 86
Liberia, 44, 49, 115, 132
Liberia Recorder (Monrovia), 132
Likaka, Osumaka, 9, 21, 104
Lincoln University (USA), 74
Lindsley-Simms, Elise, 164, 165
literacy, 7, 46–47, 56, 58, 67, 125, 131, 136, 152; and gender, 124, 126, 136

literary style, 14, 51, 53, 86, 195n33
London, 10, 11, 12, 21, 35, 45, 55, 61, 65–66, 68, 69, 70–75, 78, 81, 82, 84, 85, 86, 87, 88, 97, 150, 164, 173

MacDonald, Malcolm, 70
Malawi, 72
Malaya, 69
Malcolm X, 3, 4, 92
"Man about Town, A" (pseud.), 7
"Man in the Moon, The" (pseud.), 7
"Man in the Street, The" (pseud.), 9, 52
"Marjorie Mensah" (pseud.) 79, 112–13, 129, 147–48, 160, 162–67, 168, 175, 177. *See also* Dove-Danquah, Mabel
marriage, 102, 126–32, 133–35, 149, 156, 157, 161–62, 166, 220n9
masculinity. *See* gender
masking, 36, 144, 146, 149–50, 158, 171, 172, 173, 175, 177, 179, 181, 228n11
Mauritius, 46
McCarthy, Muriel Eunice, 150
Methodist Church, 130
metropolitan, 12, 35, 37, 46, 53, 67, 69, 139
Mfantsipim School (Cape Coast), 110
Mia Denyigba, 13
Middleton, Richard, 46
mimicry, 18, 130–31, 133, 222n31
missionary presses, 6, 30, 33, 53, 115
modernity, 1, 30, 38, 56, 103, 131, 132, 133, 148, 161, 164, 166
Mohamed, Duse, 43, 120, 150
Moi, Daniel Arap, 120
Moscow, 74
Mouree (Moree), Ghana, 116
Mullan, John, 2, 3, 4
mythology, 101–2, 115–16, 118, 119

Nanka-Bruce, Frederick Victor, 80, 95, 215n130
National Congress of British West Africa (NCBWA), 107
National Council for Civil Liberties (UK), 85
nationalism, 39, 40, 43, 47–48, 181
"Native, A" (pseud.), 130, 132, 133, 137, 145
"Negro, A" (pseud.), 7
Negro Welfare Association, 45, 76, 84
Negro Worker, 74, 79, 88
Negro World, 75
Nelsons Publishers, 126
networks, 37, 39, 44–46, 69, 71, 72, 150, 203n6, 204n25
Newlands, Harry Scott, 77
News from Nigeria, 151
New South Wales, 36
newspapers: African-language, 2, 34, 56, 60, 137, 147; Anglophone, 10, 13, 30, 32, 34, 40, 42, 44, 45, 46, 103, 106, 128–30; as archive, 54–55, 160; editors, 15, 32, 34,

39–43, 46–47, 49, 50–51, 53, 55, 59–60, 71, 72, 77, 80, 93, 95, 114, 128, 140, 142, 150, 196n42; and freedom of the press, 11, 12, 32–33, 38, 41, 42, 45, 65–66, 69, 71, 72, 74, 79, 81, 86, 97, 129; and historical discourse, 54–56, 57, 110, 115–16, 120; letters pages, 15, 140, 143, 146, 149, 161–62, 163, 168; and newsprint, 10, 30, 33, 34, 38, 39, 43, 46, 58, 90, 105–6, 109, 121, 129, 134, 175; ordinances (*see* legislation); and popular press, 42, 60, 96, 133, 137, 147, 164; proprietors, 13, 24, 30, 32, 40, 42, 52, 71, 72, 74, 75, 77, 78, 139, 196n42; and readers, 34, 39, 46–48, 49, 51–52, 56, 59–60, 105, 109, 110, 134, 135, 140, 142, 143; women's pages, 79, 112, 136, 147, 151, 160–61, 166, 168
New Zealand, 36
Ngugi wa Thiong'o, 102, 103, 120, 176, 177, 180
Nigeria, 21, 33, 40, 44, 69, 71, 72, 74, 101, 138, 139, 149, 155, 157, 177
Nigerian Daily Record (Enugu), 151
Nigerian Daily Times (Lagos) 96, 143, 160
Nigerian Eastern Mail (Calabar), 15, 58, 137, 150, 151
Nigerian Information Division, 151
Nigerian Observer (Port Harcourt), 58
Nkrumah, Kwame, 43, 203n6
Nortey, Kobina, 221–2n20
Northcote, Ag Governor Geoffrey, 81
Nyasaland. *See* Malawi

obituaries, 20, 88
Ocansey, Alfred John, 74–75, 76
"Odeziaku," also "O. Dazi Aku" (pseuds.). *See* Stuart-Young, J. M.
Ofori Atta, Nana Sir, 80
Olaore Green, Sarah E., 4
"Old Black Joe" (pseud.), 7
Ologunde, Bisade, 179, 180
Omu, Fred, 17
Onitsha, 9, 222n22
Onyile, Onyile Bassey, 156
orality, 57, 104–6, 110, 134, 147; and folktales, 101, 102, 104, 113–14, 120; and history, 57, 118–19; and naming, 21–22, 96; and performance, 103, 104, 147, 217n18; and print, 38, 55–57, 102, 103–5, 112–15, 120–21; and protest, 14, 101–2, 177
Order of the British Empire (OBE), 150, 151
Ottah, Nelson, 45
"Overworked" (pseud.), 7, 10, 174

Padmore, George, 45, 69, 74, 75, 94
Palestine, 69
pan-Africanism, 8, 18, 48, 49, 75, 76
Papafio, Mercy Quartey, 160
Papafio, Ruby Quartey, 160
parables, 9, 22, 57, 110, 135

"Parasite de Sycophant" (pseud.), 7
parody, 7, 8, 79, 90–91, 92, 145, 158, 161, 177, 178, 180
patriarchy, 102, 124, 135
Penyin, Atu, 108–9, 110, 217–18n29
periodicals, 29, 30, 198n75
Peterson, Derek, 113–14
petitions, 32, 42, 45, 58, 71, 81, 129
poetry, 2, 9, 14, 20, 101, 102, 111, 120, 140, 150, 160, 179, 197n56, 213n110
political leadership, 40, 81, 94, 107–8, 119, 132, 180, 198n74
polygyny, 111, 127–30, 132, 134, 148
popular arts, 42, 49, 102, 113, 120, 126, 128, 132, 133, 137, 138, 141, 143, 147–54, 157, 158, 179–80, 207n13, 220n9
Poyser, Sir Kenneth, 10
Prais, Jinny, 166
Pratten, David, 152
press laws. *See* newspapers; legislation
private sphere, 23, 52, 88, 90–91, 93, 105, 126–27, 128, 139, 146
Privy Council (London), 73, 85–86, 88, 173
pro-colonialism, 48, 50, 74
"Professor W. Daniels" (pseud.). *See* Wallace-Johnson, I. T. A.
propaganda, 69, 77, 96
prostitution, 7, 133, 136, 137, 140, 141, 146, 148, 158, 162, 178
"Proud of Name" (pseud.), 7
proverbs, 104, 105, 111, 113, 114, 129
public interest, 24, 40, 51–52, 59, 135, 175
public opinion, 12, 29, 30, 31, 34, 35, 39, 40, 41, 43, 61, 65, 66, 71, 72, 81, 109, 121, 132
public relations, 12, 66, 72, 74, 80, 81
publics, 7, 36, 37, 39, 40, 56, 59–61, 92, 104, 113, 115, 122; and readerships, 2, 7, 10, 12, 34, 44, 59–60, 74, 120–21, 150, 175
public sphere, 14, 17, 23, 25, 29–43, 48, 60, 66, 74, 85, 94, 97, 104, 105, 109, 113, 126, 127, 135, 139, 140, 150, 179, 180, 201n43

Quartey, Asuana, 163
Quayson, Ato, 103
Quist, Isaac Emmanuel, 30, 31

race, 3, 4, 7, 8, 34, 37, 42, 45, 49, 52, 68, 70, 75, 77, 96, 118, 137, 150, 170, 172, 177, 178; and racial stereotypes, 29–30, 38, 170
"Rambler" (pseud.), 8, 9
Ranger, Terence, 109
Ratepayers Association (Gold Coast), 80
Rattray, Robert Sutherland, 115
"Reader, A" (pseud.), 7
readers, 52–53, 72, 74, 106, 107, 110, 111, 126, 133, 137, 141, 145–47, 149, 150, 155, 162, 168, 175, 176. *See also* newspapers: readers
realism, 6, 57, 103, 111–13, 118, 128, 144, 146, 147, 153

Index ⌒ 253

Red Cross, 122
Red International of Labour Unions (Profintern), 76
Reuters, 44
Rex versus I. T. A. Wallace-Johnson, 87–91
Richards, Sir Arthur, 42
riddles, 113, 114
Roberts-Wray, Sir Kenneth, 78
"Robertus" (pseud.), 14
"Rosa" (pseud.), 161–62, 167–68, 178

Sackey, Edward, 103, 110
Sacoom, S., 106–7
Sapara, Oguntola O., 4
Sapara Williams, Hon. C. A., 32, 72
Sarawak, 69
Sarbah, John Mensah, 115
Saro-Wiwa, Ken, 102, 177
satire, 79, 83, 88, 101, 131, 143–44, 162, 173, 180
Sawyerr, Akilagpa, 80
Sawyerr, T. J., 52–53, 54, 58, 198n87
Sawyerr's Bookselling, Printing and Stationery Trade Circular (Freetown), 20, 24, 56
Schopenhauer, Arthur, 13
"Scrutineer" (pseud.), 30
sedition, 11, 16, 30, 50, 71, 72–78, 82–86, 97, 105, 164, 175, 199n20; and literature, 32, 49, 78–79, 140
"Segilola of the Fascinating Eyes" (pseud.). *See* Thomas, I. B.
Sekyi, William Esuman Gwira (Kobina), 75, 76, 81, 128
self-government, 35, 54
Senegal, 195n24
sexuality, 115, 126–29, 136, 149, 157, 166, 220n9, 221n19, 228n11
Seychelles, 69
"S. H." (pseud.), 14
Shaloff, Stanley, 76
Shipley, Jesse, 180
Sierra Leone, 33, 44, 45, 53, 71, 82, 84, 85, 87, 92–93, 115, 135, 168
Sierra Leone Daily Mail (Freetown), 151
Sierra Leone Weekly News (Freetown), 9, 33, 41, 69, 87, 89, 93, 95, 120, 131, 135, 161–62, 208n17
Singapore, 210n57
Sinha, Mrinalini, 37
Skinner, Kate, 56
slavery, 4, 17, 44, 175, 194n17
Solove, Daniel J., 13
South Asia, 37, 72
Soviet Union, 74
Soyinka, Wole, 102, 177
"S. S." (pseud.), 106–7, 110
Spear, 152
Stewart, Kenneth MacNeill, 164, 166, 228n23
Stoler, Ann Laura, 126
Straits Settlements, 69, 164

Stuart-Young, J. M., 9, 175
Subaltern Studies Group, 37
subjectivity, 1, 5, 91, 157, 168, 178, 181; and print, 3, 6, 7, 9, 23, 46, 56, 58–59, 90, 104, 137, 142, 148, 149, 170, 175, 181
surveillance, 13, 34, 39, 42, 51, 67, 75, 84–85, 96, 97, 126, 181
Sutherland, Efua, 102, 103, 120
Swift, Jonathan, 144

"Tamedu" (pseud.), 180
Tanganyika. *See* Tanzania
Tanzania, 69, 72
"The Czar" (pseud.), 135
"The Man in the Moon" (pseud.), 7
"The Man in the Street" (pseud.), 9, 52
Thomas, Isaac Babalola, 15, 35, 136, 137–38, 139–49, 146–47, 153, 155, 156, 157–58, 175, 177, 178
Thomas, Sir Thomas Shenton Whitelegge, 67, 72, 74, 76–80, 81, 84, 85, 163, 210n57
Thompson, A. W. Kojo, 215n130
Times of Nigeria (Lagos), 50
Times of West Africa (Accra), 76, 79, 81, 147, 160, 162–66
"Tired" (pseud.), 7, 10, 137, 174
Togo, 6, 13, 56, 166
Trade Unions, 101
"Traveller, A" (pseud.), 175
trickster, 5, 89, 93, 101, 102–4, 106, 109–10, 178–79. *See also* Ananse
Trinidad, 46, 69, 71
Tsekpo, G. K., 13
Tutuola, Amos, 102, 120
"Tyrtaeus" (pseud.), 162

Uganda, 69, 72
United States of America, 21, 49, 68, 75, 79, 150
urbanization, 39, 46, 61, 133, 136, 138, 155, 161, 166, 220n9

Vail, Leroy and White, Landeg, 14
"Veritas" (pseud.), 30
"Vivian James" (pseud.). *See* Clinton, J. V.
"Vivian Warner" (pseud.). *See* Clinton, J. V.

Wallace-Johnson, Isaac Theophilis Akunna, 10, 16, 17, 43, 69, 74–77, 80, 82–86, 87–97, 108, 170, 172–73, 175, 177, 213–14n110, 214n115
Walters, Joseph J., 132–33, 136
Warner, Michael, 59, 61, 149, 206n69
Wesleyan Church, 13
West African Court of Appeal, 84, 85
West African Pilot (Lagos), 42, 95, 96
West African Students Union (WASU), 81
West African Times. See Times of West Africa
West African Youth League, 69, 87–91, 95, 213n109; Women's Auxiliary, 45

Western Echo (Cape Coast), 33, 34, 40, 54, 115, 116, 118, 130, 136
West Indies, 72
White, Bob W., 103
Wilberforce Hall (Freetown), 94
Williams, Rev. Charles Kingsley, 75
Woman's Weekly (London), 137, 152, 154
women's magazines, 137, 151–53, 155, 157
women's rights, 15–16, 39, 205n36
"Won Hu Nos" (pseud.), 16
Woods, Dwayne, 39, 40

World War I, 54, 61, 107, 110
World War II, 6, 25, 30, 65
writing competitions, 60, 122–25, 220n4

Yankah, Kwesi, 104, 105
Yoruba print culture, 7, 21, 34, 60, 138, 140, 142, 143, 147, 149, 158, 162, 200n26
"Youngman, A" (pseud.), 7, 114

Zik. *See* Azikiwe, Nnamdi
Zik Press Ltd., 42, 61, 96

www.ingramcontent.com/pod-product-compliance
Lightning Source LLC
Chambersburg PA
CBHW031239290426

44109CB00012B/367